From Jewish Prophet to Gentile God

The Origins and Development of New Testament Christology

The Edward Cadbury Lectures
at the University of Birmingham,
1985-86

P.M.Casey

James Clarke & Co.
Cambridge, England

Westminster/John Knox Press
Louisville, Kentucky

Published in Great Britain by
James Clarke & Co. Ltd
P.O. Box 60
Cambridge CB1 2NT

Published in the United States by
Westminster/John Knox Press
100 Witherspoon Street
Louisville, Kentucky 40202-1396

British Library Cataloguing in Publication Data:
Casey, Maurice
  From Jewish prophet to Gentile God.
  1. Christology
  I. Title
  232.01

  ISBN 0 227 67920 2

Library of Congress Catalogue Card Number:
91-50391

ISBN 21960-8

PRINTED IN GREAT BRITAIN
2 4 6 8 9 7 5 3 1

Printed by
Billing & Sons Ltd, Worcester

To
Steph and Alli
who restore my soul

Table of Contents

Preface

This book is a revised version of the Cadbury Lectures delivered at the University of Birmingham in the autumn term of 1985. I am grateful to all those who made these lectures possible. First of all, I thank Edward Cadbury, who endowed the Cadbury lectures. I would particularly like to thank also the Department of Theology, and Dr M.D. Goulder in the Department of Adult Education, for their invitation, their warm hospitality, and their enthusiasm for scholarship. This was very refreshing and I enjoyed myself no end. The questions from those who heard the lectures were always of interest. It was especially helpful to have my New Testament colleagues Prof. J.N. Birdsall and Dr M.D. Goulder always in the audience, together with Prof. D.W. Hardy and Dr D.F. Ford at the final lecture. Their comments have prompted a number of alterations, for which I alone am however responsible.

I would also like to thank Prof. J.D.G. Dunn and other members of the erstwhile postgraduate seminar at Nottingham, who discussed an early form of some of the hypotheses proposed in this book. I am also grateful to my Nottingham colleague Dr D.J.Davies for helpful discussions of identity and other problems, seen from an anthropological perspective. Many students have been helpful in discussing the most difficult aspects of the theoretical analysis of ancient Judaism and early Christianity. I would particularly like to thank Allison Anthony (née Birch), Stephanie Exell (née Hawkins) and Jonathan Stock-Hesketh for the combination of criticism and creativity which marks out the outstanding scholars which in other times all of them might have become.

I am also grateful to James Clarke for taking on the publication of this work, after some trials and tribulations with others. The terms of the Cadbury lectures allow for considerable revision. The main one has been to move the analysis of ancient Judaism, in terms derived from the study of modern Judaism, into chapter 2. It was originally scattered throughout the lectures, and was not easy to understand. I hope it is clear in its present place. The very beginning of lecture 1 is now the introduction: otherwise chapter 3 is lecture 1, chapter 4 is lecture 2 and so on, with chapter 10 the eighth and final lecture. I have added many references to primary sources which could not be included in orally delivered lectures. I have also been prevailed upon to add documentation from secondary sources. Critical discussion of the massive secondary literature would however have made too large a book, and there is so much new argument that clarity is more important. It should go without saying that I have learnt massively from the work of other scholars, both within this field and outside it. The General Bibliography lists recent work on New Testament Christology: more detailed bibliography is supplied in the footnotes. Works translated into English are given their English titles: where two dates are given, the first is that of the original publication in another language. Commentaries and tools of study are not listed. The bibliography of Hultgren is invaluable for further information.

There are also a few additions to the text of the original lectures. The only notable one is the expansion of chapter 7 part 2, The Vindication of Jesus. This is based on a paper, "Did Jesus Rise from the Dead?", read at Sheffield University in December, 1986, and to the Jesus Seminar at a meeting of British New Testament scholars at Durham in 1987. I am grateful for many critical comments, which have enabled me to say more clearly what I meant. Like so many parts of this book, the subject deserves a monograph to itself. Otherwise, small additions have been made at various points, with a view to clarifying the argument.

Finally, this book is dedicated to Allison Anthony and Stephanie Exell. Since working through much of the material with me as students, they have become very dear friends, and their contribution to my life has been a constant delight for many years.

Nottingham, 4th May, 1990

Abbreviations

Most abbreviations are standard. Those for biblical books follow the RSV: those for periodicals and series of monographs follow S.Schwertner, *International glossary of abbreviations for theology and related subjects* (1974). Others are as follows:

AJBI	*Annual of the Japanese Biblical Institute*
ANRW	*Aufstieg und Niedergang der Römischen Welt*, ed H.Temporini and W.Haase (1972-).
BAR	*Biblical Archaeology Review*
BJRLM	*Bulletin of the John Rylands Library of Manchester*
Casey, *Son of Man*	P.M.Casey, *Son of Man. The Interpretation and Influence of Daniel 7* (1980)
CBQMS	Catholic Biblical Quarterly Monograph Series
Dunn, *Making*	See general bibliography
EJ	*Encyclopaedia Judaica*
ERS	*Ethnic and Racial Studies*
ForB	*Forschung zur Bibel*
GTA	*Göttinger Theologische Arbeiten*
HBT	*Horizons in Biblical Theology*
JJSoc	*The Jewish Journal of Sociology*
JSNT	*Journal for the Study of the New Testament*
JSNT.SS	*Journal for the Study of the New Testament*, Supplement Series
Moule, *Origin*	See general bibliography
SBL.DS	Society of Biblical Literature, Dissertation Series
SBL.MS	Society of Biblical Literature, Monograph Series
Schürer-Vermes-Millar	E.Schürer, (rev.) G.Vermes and F.Millar, *The History of the Jewish People in the Age of Jesus Christ*, 3 vols (1973-87)
ScRel/StRel	*Sciences religieuses/Studies in religion*
Sem	*Semeia*
SF	*Social Forces*
SJLA	*Studies in Judaism in Late Antiquity*
StPh	*Studia Philonica*
TDNT	*The Theological Dictionary of the New Testament* (1933-73. ET 10 vols, 1964-76).

Chapter 1
Introduction

The deity and incarnation of Jesus have been part of orthodox Christian belief for centuries, and any challenge to orthodox christology provokes vigorous debate, at both a popular and a scholarly level. The Bishop of Durham had only to suggest that the doctrines of the virgin birth and bodily resurrection of Jesus are not *literally* true to provoke a public outcry. The most recent phase of scholarly debate came to public attention with the publication in 1977 of *The Myth of God Incarnate*. The subsequent discussion has not, however, produced a coherent and convincing account of the origins and development of New Testament christology. Nor has this been achieved in the more learned monographs produced in recent years.[1]

The purpose of this book is to put forward a new way of analysing the evidence, and to use this in elaborating a new theory to explain why New Testament christology developed as it did. The new mode of analysis is presented in chapter 2. It is largely based on the work which Jewish scholars have done in analysing modern Judaism, the major concept being that of identity. I then remove the secondary christology of John's Gospel (ch 3) and the synoptics (ch 4). This leaves the way clear to argue that the Jesus of history recreated Jewish identity from a prophetic perspective, thereby making christological development essential (ch 5). This development moved in accordance with the development of purely Jewish figures (ch 6). It began when the Christian community was still wholly Jewish, but it proceeded more vigorously because of the needs of the Gentile mission (chs 7-9). This development was limited by the nature of Jewish monotheism. Only when the Johannine community, removed from the synagogue by "the Jews", had Gentile self-identification, could they develop the deity and incarnation of Jesus (chs 3, 9).

Throughout this book, I pay particular attention to the culture of Jesus and the earliest Christians. This is at the heart of the pattern of christological development itself, and it enables us to explain such important points as Jesus' predictions of the imminent coming of the kingdom of God, and the development of Christian belief in his deity and incarnation. The final chapter assesses the significance of the new theory for the truth or falsity of Christian belief. I hope that I have thereby fulfilled the intentions of Edward Cadbury, that the lectures which he endowed should be concerned with the relations, past, present and future, of Christianity to civilisation and culture.

1. J.Hick (ed), *The Myth of God Incarnate* (1977). For subsequent debate, cf M.Green (ed), *The Truth of God Incarnate* (1977); A.Heron, "Article Review: Doing Without the Incarnation?", *SJTh* 31, 1978, 51-71; M.D.Goulder (ed), *Incarnation and Myth: The Debate Continued* (1979); A.E.Harvey (ed), *God Incarnate. Story and Belief* (1981); R.G.Crawford, *The Saga of God Incarnate* (1985); T.V.Morris, *The Logic of God Incarnate* (1986); J.Hick, "The Logic of God Incarnate", *RelSt* 25, 1989, 409-23. For the most important monographs, see bibliography; s.v. Dunn, Hurtado, Moule, Pokorny: also Jewett. A critical assessment of this work cannot be offered in this book.

Chapter 2
Modes of analysis

1. Modern Judaism

Judaism today is a remarkable phenomenon which has given rise to a vigorous field of study. During the Second World War, a long tradition of anti-semitism reached its climax in the holocaust. This was a major factor in the foundation of the modern state of Israel, a state with a colossal immigration rate of Jews from many countries. These immigrants are sometimes described as American, Ethiopian, German, Russian or with reference to any other country of origin. Differing perceptions of identity were highlighted in the case of Oswald Rufeisen, or Brother Daniel. He was an ethnically Jewish person with a distinguished record of Jewish activity. When he applied for entry to Israel, he was not allowed to register as a person of Jewish nationality. A majority of the Supreme Court of Israel, but by no means all Israeli Jews, argued that he was not a Jew for the purpose of the Law of Return and for the purpose of registration, because of his conversion to Christianity.

Identity problems of this kind are not confined to Israel. If you regard yourself as a black American Jew, other people's perceptions of your identity will not be uniform. Jews do not form the only definable religion, nor the only definable ethnic group, in the United States. You can be an American Catholic, an Afro-American, an Italian American or an Irish American. Thus the main centres for serious academic study of modern Judaism have been Israel and the United States, both highly educated societies which contain the problems for study. These studies have made powerful analytical use of three concepts which will be employed in this analysis of Second Temple Judaism and early Christianity: identity, ethnicity and orthodoxy.[1]

There are, however, significant differences between Second Temple Judaism and modern Judaism, and the rise of Christianity has itself been a major feature in the changing relationships between Jews and Gentiles. I shall not therefore try to use these concepts in exactly the same way as they are used by investigators of modern Judaism; and we must begin with an examination of them.

2. Identity

I define identity as follows: by the identity of a group I mean everything which is perceived to make it that group and not another group. By an identity factor I mean any single feature of that group which is perceived to make it that group and not another group. For example, sabbath observance may reasonably be

11

treated as an identity factor of Judaism, because most Jews observe the sabbath (Shabbat) on Friday evening and Saturday, while most Gentiles do not, and Jews and Gentiles generally perceive sabbath observance as a feature of Judaism. From an individual's point of view, the identity factors of a group are the features which make the individual a member of the group or an outsider. Thus on the whole anyone who observes Shabbat is Jewish, and those of us who do not are Gentiles. Ethnically Jewish people who do not observe Shabbat are liable to assimilate further into the Gentile world. Correspondingly, Gentiles who observe Shabbat are seriously assimilating into the Jewish community.

The self-identification of an individual or a group denotes their own view of themselves. Self-identification is normally in harmony with other people's views of oneself, because if we do not basically see ourselves as others see us we experience severe dissonance. It is, however, fundamental both to the study of identity in general and to the theories proposed in this book that there are cases where the identity of individuals and of groups may be differently perceived. Falashas may be perceived as Jewish, more or less Jewish or not really Jewish. Brother Daniel perceived himself to be Jewish because he was ethnically and culturally Jewish, and he had been generally treated as Jewish. People who do not perceive him as Jewish have an overriding conviction that Christians are not Jews. British Jews may perceive themselves as both British and Jewish: some people do not perceive them as British.[2] For analytical purposes it is important that we do not react to these cases by declaring our own perceptions right and other people's wrong, or by arguing that we ought to accept people's self-identification, so that we define Falashas and Brother Daniel alike as *really* Jewish simply because they so perceive themselves. Both conflicts about identity and perceived changes in identity will be inaccurately described if we do not isolate the different perceptions that are possible and the kind of people who hold them. Alien and bigoted people should not be defined out of existence, a particular danger in dealing with ancient people who cannot answer back.

To measure identity, an identity scale is necessary. The most important insight to have emerged from recent methodological work is that an identity scale must be drawn up in such a way as to perform the functions that are needed.[3] For the study of early Christianity and contemporary Judaism, we need to be able to measure cases where people's identity is so clearly Jewish that everyone would perceive them as Jewish, and where it is so clearly Gentile that everyone would perceive them as Gentile. We also need to be able to measure assimilation so that we can see when people are moving into or out of Judaism, and how differing perceptions of them would be held by different people.

For the purposes of this study I specify eight identity factors of Second Temple Judaism: ethnicity, scripture, monotheism, circumcision, sabbath observance, dietary laws, purity laws and major festivals. I have selected these eight factors because they are analytically fruitful and generally in harmony with the perceptions of our primary sources. Anyone who scores 0/8 is clearly Gentile, and would be universally perceived as Gentile in the ancient world. It would make no difference to this if such a person wrote a *midrash* or contributed to a collection for the poor in Jerusalem. Secondly, anyone who scores 8/8 is clearly Jewish, and would be perceived as Jewish by everyone in the ancient world. It would not matter if he healed on the sabbath, or refused to attend the Temple on the grounds that the priesthood was illegitimate and corrupt. Some Jews might disapprove of him with great vigour, but he would certainly be Jewish in their eyes. Thirdly, if anyone gets an intermediate score, assimilation one way or the other is usefully measured. For example, 1 Maccabees 1.11ff tells us about apostate Jews who removed the marks of circumcision and intermarried with Gentiles, a process which produces children of mixed ethnicity. The perception that the removal of two identity factors amounts to serious assimilation is universal in our primary sources, and it is not difficult to understand.

3. Ethnicity

One of these identity factors should be examined in greater detail. Ethnicity is fundamental to Jewish people. Ancient Judaism is, however, generally treated as a religion, and this restriction has often been unfruitful. Jews today are generally perceived to form an ethnic group, and this approach is so fruitful that I shall adopt it. A standard dictionary definition of "ethnic group" will be useful:

> The term denotes a social group, which, within a larger cultural and social system, claims or is accorded a special status in terms of a complex of traits *(ethnic traits)* which it exhibits or is believed to exhibit. Such traits are diverse, and there is much variety in the complexes that they form. Prominent among them are those drawn from the religious and linguistic characteristics of the social group, the distinctive skin-pigmentation of its members, their national or geographic origins or those of their forbears. ... *Ethnic* as an adjective is often used interchangeably with *religious, racial, national, cultural* and *sub-cultural*. Thus, in the U.S. ... the Jewish population is sometimes treated as an ethnic group, sometimes, erroneously, as a racial group, sometimes as a sub-cultural group within the total American culture.
>
> ... in the last thirty years [i.e. before 1964] ... *ethnic group* has come to be more closely associated with *ethos* or *custom* as the latter is now analysed and understood in terms of laws of social learning and social inheritance as against former conceptions of biological and genetic determination of culture patterns.... Modern social science literature recognises that where religion, culture and common biological origin are shared by a group, the bonds are mutually reinforcing...[4]

In the light of definitions of this kind, Jews may reasonably be regarded as forming an ethnic group. The vast majority of them are physically descended from Jews. They have their own language, Hebrew. Hebrew is the *lingua franca* of Israel. It is kept alive in many diaspora communities by its use in terms and expressions such as 'Shabbat', by the known fact that Hebrew is the language of the ancestors in which the Torah is written, and by the possession, study and liturgical use of the bible and of other traditional Hebrew texts. Jews have a common geographic origin in the land of Israel. They do have their own religion, Judaism, though irreligious Jews are generally perceived to be Jewish, so that Jewish religion is only a part of distinctively Jewish culture. This contains many customs, such as circumcising male children on the eighth day after birth, which are observed very widely, to the extent that they are perceived as serious indications as to whether a person is Jewish or not. Other customs, such as keeping separate crockery for meat and cheese dishes, are not widely observed, but are none the less distinctively Jewish and perceived as such. The fact of Jewish ethnicity is consequently not generally in doubt.

When Jewish ethnicity is taken for granted as part of our theoretical apparatus, we can discuss more fruitfully how religious Jewish people really are. Surveys can be conducted only among Jews of our own time, but some of the results are applicable to ancient Judaism. For example, one survey showed that 7% of Conservative American immigrants to Israel did not remove leavened bread from the house at Passover: that is, they did not observe a biblical regulation at a major festival. Further, 11% of those questioned had not fasted on the previous Yom Kippur, while no more than 48% reported that they "attend Synagogue at least weekly". When results like this are replicated, as they regularly are, we should not be surprised or puzzled at allegations that committed ancient Jews did not always observe the Law. Much smaller percentages are recorded for some observances, including dietary laws. In a survey of a generally conservative Jewish community at Providence, U.S.A., no more than 32% said that they used separate dishes in the home for milk and meat, including no more than 16% of the third generation, and in so far as these figures are subject to error, the true figure is presumably lower.[5] When we find or must conjecture variations in the observance of dietary and other laws in ancient Judaism, we should view this in the same light as we would obtain from a dynamic analysis of modern Judaism.

Given that ethnicity is clear, it is not surprising that it may be perceived as an overriding factor. People may be perceived as Jewish if it is the only one of the eight identity factors that they have, and they may be perceived as Gentile if they have all the other seven identity factors, but not ethnicity. It is important for our purposes both that such perceptions are possible and that they are neither necessary nor universal. Israeli secularists are normally perceived to be Jewish, as are assimilating Jews everywhere. Similarly, proselytes who are circumcised, and whose strict observance includes all the other seven identity factors, are not necessarily perceived as fully Jewish. Falashas may also be perceived as not fully Jewish, even if they are strictly observant, for their black skins may be perceived to disprove their Jewish ethnicity. On the other hand, completely assimilated Jews may be perceived as Gentiles, especially if they marry Gentiles and do not circumcise their male children. They may also have Gentile self-identification. This may be implicit in that they behave like Gentiles and are content to pass for Gentiles, though they remain aware of being different because of their Jewish birth: or it may be more explicit in that they call themselves "Greek", "Roman", "British" or whatever their perceived identity may be, and do not regard their Jewish parents as relevant to their identity.

Evidence that some ethnically Jewish people had Gentile self-identification is clear enough in our primary sources. 1 Maccabees 1.11ff tells us that some Jews removed the marks of circumcision. This action must be perceived as undermining Jewish identity, and it may or may not be accompanied by explicit statements to the effect that they were becoming Greek. Thus 1 Maccabees makes comments such as "Lawless men went out from Israel" (1.11), and its use of terms such as "lawless" (1.34) and "impious" (6.21) evidently refers to the same kind of people. Josephus goes further, saying that they "concealed the circumcision of their genitals so that they might be Greeks even when undressed" (A.J.XII,241). An attempt to enforce a similar perception is recorded at 2 Maccabees 6.6, where banning of the sabbath and the festivals is said to have been accompanied by a prohibition of confessing to being a Jew. Sources which continue to perceive assimilated Jews as Jewish produce some paradoxical expressions. At A.J.XII, 362, Josephus records that "renegades of the Jews did much harm to the Jews": at A.J. XIII,4, Bacchides gathered together "those of the Jews who had abandoned the customs of their fatherland", and the trouble caused was so severe that it led to Jonathan's appointment as "general of the Jews" (A.J.XIII, 6). Expressions of this kind result from the universal perception of faithful Jews as a social group whom we call "the Jews". Assimilating Jews effectively leave this group, and we and they continue to call this group "the Jews" even when we are all perfectly well aware of the Jewish ethnicity of those who assimilate.

A similar variety of perception is found concerning people who assimilate into Judaism from the Gentile world. In our period, men who took on some identity factors, but who were not circumcised, were generally perceived as judaizers rather than as Jews.[6] Some people went further. Izates was perceived by Ananias to have done enough for salvation without being circumcised, but the stricter view of Eleazar reinforced his natural feeling that "he would not certainly be a Jew, unless he were circumcised". He therefore undertook circumcision, despite the concern expressed especially by his mother that the people of Adiabene "would not put up with a Jew ruling over them" (A.J.XX, 38-48). The Talmudic regulations for the admission of proselytes declare that the circumcised, immersed and duly admitted proselyte "is as Israel in all respects" (bT Yeb 47b). Reservations are none the less perceptible, as for example in the ruling that a proselyte may not be a judge in cases involving the death penalty (bT San 36b), and the view that when praying in the synagogue a proselyte should say "the God of *your* Fathers" (M.Bik.I,4). A similar variety is found in perceptions of people who were compelled to be circumcised. Herod the Great was accused by Antigonus of being "half-Jewish", and Josephus attributes this perception to his being of Idumaean descent (A.J.XIV, 403). Josephus himself, however, in dealing with the incident when the Idumaeans accepted Jewish customs including circumcision, comments that they began from then onwards "to be Jews" (A.J.XIII, 258).

Intermarriage necessarily produces people who are ethnically partly Jewish and partly Gentile. Such people are more obviously in a position where their ultimate self-identification may depend on subsequent experience, and a conscious decision to belong to one community or the other.[7] Timothy is perhaps our most famous ancient example. We know from Acts 16.1ff that he had a Jewish mother and a Greek father. His mother was clearly assimilating, for she married a Gentile and did not ensure that her son was circumcised on the eighth day. Despite his attempts to shift the concept of Jewish identity for the sake of converting Gentiles (Rom 2.28-9: Phil 3.3), Paul did circumcise him. This must have increased the number of people who would perceive him as Jewish, a perception evidently held by Paul and by Timothy himself. Timothy could then engage in the Gentile mission, generally perceived by Christians as a Jew who, like Peter and Paul, was not observant when observance of the Law would have been dysfunctional in the Christian community.[8]

4. Religion, Ethnicity and Social Function

A fundamental question is raised by the isolation of eight identity factors of Second Temple Judaism. To what extent are these identity factors religious? Only three, scripture, monotheism and the major festivals, are *obviously* religious. One of them, ethnicity, is a social rather than a religious factor, and this leads us into observations which concern the nature of being Jewish. No less than five of these eight identity factors may reasonably be perceived as social factors which have received religious legitimation. This is perhaps most obvious in the development of new customs. For example, Erub allowed Jews who lived very near each other to interact more freely on the sabbath, and it allowed them to double the sabbath limit. In both cases, it was a condition that specified and uniquely Jewish customs be followed, such as putting food in an appropriate place. These uniquely Jewish customs have the clearly Jewish social function of enabling Jews to interact with other Jews more freely than a simple interpretation of other sabbath laws would allow. At one level, this should be regarded as the opposite of assimilation, since freedom to enjoy the sabbath was gained by doing more Jewish activities rather than less. Another example of the development of religiously legitimated laws with a social function may be seen in the massive development of purity law during our period. A function of the attempt to remain pure in daily life was to reinforce Jewish identity and separate Jews from Gentiles.

Once the social function of some identity factors is observed so clearly, we can perceive the social nature of others. Circumcision is not only the habit of a defined social group, surrounded by evidently social ceremonies, it is found in other parts of the world too, and there, as here, it functions as a boundary marker of a social group. Dietary laws, like purity laws, separate Jews from Gentiles, since the refusal to eat pork or any other food which is not kosher means that observant Jews will not eat most Gentile meals. But once we have perceived that ethnicity, circumcision, sabbath observance, dietary and purity laws are social factors, we cannot help noticing also the social function of the more obviously religious factors. The strict form of monotheism not only marked Jews off from Gentiles, it also prevented observant Jews from taking a full part in the social and political life of a Greek city. Scripture was venerated by Jews, and contained the complete legitimation of their position as the people chosen out from among all others, with laws interpreted to demand the other identity factors and prevent intermarriage. It was read at Jewish meetings every week. Only Jews could take a full part in their major religious festivals.

The social nature of these identity factors does not mean that they are not religious: it means that when a religion is coterminous with an ethnic group, its identity factors are both social and religious. It should be noted that they are for the most part concerned with activity rather than belief. This is functional for an ethnic group, because it would be dysfunctional to remove members on the ground that they did not hold enough belief or were not intense enough in their piety, whereas a religion may flourish more religiously if only religious people are allowed to be members. The nature of these identity factors involving activity has a further consequence; it opens up the possibility that some people may assert and reinforce their Jewish identity by acting in accordance with the Law for social rather than religious reasons. I shall argue that the Maccabean crisis made this of visible practical importance, and that it is essential for understanding Jewish opposition to Jesus and to St Paul.

5. Orthodoxy
For this purpose a concept of orthodoxy is necessary. Gentile Christians usually define orthodoxy in terms of right belief, and consequently it is generally felt that there was no orthodoxy in the Judaism of our period.[9] Orthodox Judaism today, however, is a movement centred on careful observation of detailed *halakhah*. I suggest that there were similar Jews in the ancient period, and that current analysis suffers from the lack of a similar term for them. Our primary sources have no term of this kind, because such people did not form a sufficiently defined movement. We therefore have no choice but to use an existing term in a new sense. This should not be misleading, provided that a reasonably careful definition is kept in mind. I therefore propose the following definition of orthodox Jews in the Second Temple period:

Orthodox Jews accepted as divinely inspired the accounts of the history and halakhah of the Jewish people recorded in the written and oral Laws, and codified in sacred books such as the Pentateuch. In the face of threats of assimilation, they stood firm as guardians of the Law, seeking to ensure that it was observed and applied to the whole of life. This led them to discuss and codify additional enactments, both orally and in written collections such as the Zadokite document and the book of Jubilees. This was a central concern of their lives, and in this way they embodied and defended Jewish identity. Orthodox Jews thus included both Pharisees and Essenes. A significant proportion of Jews did not observe the additional enactments of the orthodox, and some Jews did not obey the halakhah at all. The difficulties which this caused for the orthodox world-view are evident in works such as Daniel 9 and 4 Ezra.

For the origins of this orthodox Jewish mind-set, we must go back at least to the time of the destruction of the First Temple, when Judaea was conquered, Jerusalem sacked, and many of the people exiled to Babylon. In Babylon many Jews maintained their own separate identity, partly by gathering together their traditions, their history, their stories, their law, their prophecies and their psalms. When Cyrus sacked Babylon, some exiles were able to return to Jerusalem, and by the end of the sixth century, the Second Temple had been built, with the restoration of the cult under the high priest at the urging of prophets. In the fifth century, another wave of returning exiles under Ezra brought back "the Law" from Babylon. We do not know its exact contents, but it is clear that it corresponded approximately to the traditions now found in our Pentateuch.[10] Its acceptance by the community is to be explained by its collection of Jewish traditions. When it was read, the people heard an authoritative version of the stories of Abraham, Isaac and Jacob, of the Exodus from Egypt, of the revelation of the Law itself to Moses and of the conquest of the land under Joshua.

This outburst of Jewish identity enabled them to accept some new items, such as living in booths at the feast of Tabernacles, which was now assumed to have been celebrated in this way *until* the time of Joshua (Neh 8.17). This also enabled Ezra to carry through what should be the most notorious reform in biblical history, the compulsory divorce of "foreign" wives. This was carried through, and is recorded in the sacred book of Jews and Christians, with no concern for the wives and children who were thrown out. It was not necessitated by the written Law alone, for this merely recorded that at the time of the conquest of the land under Joshua, the people had been forbidden to intermarry with Hittites, Girgashites and people of that ilk (Deut 7.1ff). At Ezra 9-10, however, this is evidently the law said to legitimate the compulsory divorces from "foreigners", and at Neh 13.28 Nehemiah apparently used this to justify the removal of a priest who was married to a daughter of Sanballat. This application and expansion of the halakhah is the central mode of orthodox Judaism.

Orthodoxy was vigorously reinforced in the Maccabean period. By 170 B.C., Greek culture had become so influential in Jerusalem itself that it threatened Jewish identity.[11] Intermarriage was again a threat to Jewish ethnicity, and the highpriesthood was bought by successive hellenized Jews, Jason and Menelaus. The permission to run Jerusalem by Jewish law was revoked at Jason's request, a gymnasium was built, and some Jews removed the marks of circumcision, a drastic and deliberate undermining of Jewish identity (1 Macc 1.11ff; 2 Macc 4). In 167 B.C., the hellenistic king Antiochus Epiphanes, with help from ethnically Jewish people who had hellenized, began a persecution in which people were put to death for obeying the Jewish Law (1 Macc 1.41ff; 2 Macc 6ff). We know, for example, of 1,000 Jews who had escaped and who were slaughtered when they refused to defend themselves on the sabbath (1 Macc 2.32ff, cf 2 Macc 6.11). Children who were circumcised were hung from their mothers' necks when their parents were killed (1 Macc 1.60-61). In these circumstances, only two reactions are possible. You can't sit on the fence. Either you give in to hellenization, or you uphold the Jewish Law. Given that Jewish Law embodied Jewish identity, and had done so with such vigour already in the time of Ezra and Nehemiah, it was inevitable that some people stood firm.

The internalization of the Law in the orthodox wing of Judaism is clearly shown by those who died rather than abandon their strict interpretation of sabbath law as meaning that they could not fight on the sabbath. This is not a biblical regulation: it was an expansion of the halakhah which only the most orthodox could have produced, and which the community as a whole would never take on. But what were orthodox Jews committed to? In these circumstances they could not fail to be committed to the *external* observances of the Law, for this is what showed which side you were on. The situation is well illustrated by the story of Eleazar in 2 Maccabees 6. Eleazar was tortured and killed because he refused to disobey the purely external ordinance not to eat pork. Given the opportunity to bring and eat kosher food and pretend it was pork, he refused, commenting, "It is not worthy of our time of life to make pretence, so that many of the young should suppose that Eleazar in his ninetieth year has gone over to foreign customs, and because of my pretending and for the sake of a short life free from harm, they too should go astray because of me"(2 Macc 6.24-5). Eleazar could not have had a more external commitment than is shown in his refusal to pretend to disobey a purely external ordinance for the sake of the impression this would make on others. He could not have been more sincere than to die for this reason.

As a result of the Maccabean crisis, two known sects, the Qumran community and the Pharisees, separated themselves from the rest of Israel in order to observe the Law more accurately. The Pharisees stood out among the people by their commitment to the traditions of the elders, which they gradually expanded by the central mode of applying existing halakhah to the whole of daily life. The Maccabean victory made this more possible, and no subsequent events in our period undermined it. Hellenism continued to be a constant threat in the cities of Palestine, and the Pharisees are recorded to have been especially respected in the cities (Jos. A.J.XVIII, 15), for there the threat was tangible. Further, identity does not need external threat for its maintenance. Once there were Pharisees who had the observance of the Law at the centre of their lives, they did not need anything more than their own associates to keep it there, and to keep it expanding to cover all possible situations. Moreover, both the Pharisees and the Qumran sect were a product of a situation affecting the whole of Judaism, and since the careful keeping and expansion of the Law was a reinforcement of some aspects of Jewish identity, other Jews might respect and follow some parts of this stricter halakhah without necessarily joining either sect.

We must now consider a fundamental question. How religious do you have to be to keep the Law strictly? I suggest that the observance and expansion of detailed halakhah is on a different trajectory from religious experience, as that is understood both in the Jewish prophetic tradition, and in Gentile Christianity which owes so much to it. It is also on a different trajectory from love of one's neighbour. People could be very religious and delight in the Law of the Lord with *all* its statutes and ordinances: the Qumran hymns carry on the tradition of some of the psalms at this level, and the authors of Daniel are among the religious Jews of our period who should be placed in this category. Here too we should no doubt place scribes and Pharisees such as Hillel, Johanan son of Zakkai and the Gamaliels, together with Jacob the brother of Jesus, the lawyer of Mark 12.28-34 and perhaps the Pharisees of Luke 7.36ff, 13.31 and Acts 15.5. It was however also possible to be affected by the massively attested concern for external observances, without being inwardly religious or loving one's neighbour. Our Jewish sources do not say this explicitly because it is severely dysfunctional for them all (cf however 1QH II, 14ff: 1QS II, 11-18; II,25-III,6). It is, however, an inevitable deduction from their massive stress on external observances, seen in the light of the evident social need for this stress.

6. Conclusions

We now have a fruitful analytical structure with which to approach the origins and development of New Testament christology. As we analyse the Jesus movement and the major stages of christological development, we can relate views of Jesus to Jewish/Gentile identity, and consider the relationship between christological development and identity change. We must begin by uncovering the origins of christology. In chapter 5, I shall argue that the ministry of Jesus himself made further development inevitable. Before we can see him clearly, however, we must go back through our primary sources to recover him from the combination of authentic material and later developments which they offer us. We shall not be content to slough off top layers to discover a pristine layer beneath. Secondary developments will be placed where they belong in the developmental process, and related to the identity of the communities in which they are found. This will ensure that when we have seen what the origins of christology were, and have uncovered the generative process which led to subsequent growth, we can put all "secondary" material in its proper place as the product of the communities which needed to produce it. We must turn first to the most deceptive development, the Gospel attributed to St John. It purports to give us a picture of the Jesus of history. In chapter 3, we must separate its developments from the authentic core, and explain why the Johannine community needed its secondary developments, and why they presented them as history.

1. The bibliography to this field of study is vast. EJ, "Jewish Identity", has a basic introduction: M.Sklare, *America's Jews* (1971), is an excellent textbook. I have found the following studies particularly helpful or stimulating: R.Loewe, "Defining Judaism: Some Ground-Clearing", *JJSoc* 7, 1965, 153-75; L.Herz, "A Note on Identificational Assimilation among Forty Jews in Malmo", *JJSoc* 11, 1969, 165-73; A.Memmi, W.Ackermann, N.Zobermann and S.Zobermann, "Differences and Perception of Differences among Jews in France", *JJSoc* 12, 1970, 7-19; M.Roshwald, "Who is

a Jew in Israel?", *JJSoc* 12, 1970, 233-66; B.Lazerwitz, "Intermarriage and Conversion: A Guide for Future Research", *JJSoc* 13, 1971, 41-63; Z.Strelitz, "Jewish Identity in Cape Town, with special Reference to Out-Marriage", *JJSoc* 13, 1971, 73-93; B.Lazerwitz, "Religious Identification and its Ethnic Correlation: a Multivariate Model", *SF* 52, 1973, 204-20; H.S.Himmelfarb, "Measuring religious involvement", *SF* 53, 1975, 606-18; A.D.Lavender, "Jewish intermarriage and marriage to converts: the religious factor and the ethnic factor", *Jewish Sociology and Social Research* 2, 1976, 17-22; S.N.Herman, *Jewish Identity: A Social Psychological Perspective* (1977); E.Krausz, "The Religious Factor in Jewish Identification", *International Social Science Journal* 29, 1977, 250-60; B.Lazerwitz, "The community variable in Jewish identification, *JSSR* 16, 1977, 361-9; D.Glanz and M.I. Harrison, "Varieties of Identity Transformation: The Case of Newly Orthodox Jews", *JJSoc* 20, 1978, 129-41; H.S.Himmelfarb, "Patterns of assimilation-identification among American Jews", *Ethnicity* 6, 1979, 249-67; B.Lazerwitz and M.Harrison, "American Jewish Denominations: A Social and Religious Profile", *American Sociological Review* 44, 1979, 656-66; H.S.Himmelfarb, "The Study of American Jewish Identification: How it is Defined, Measured, Obtained, Sustained and Lost", *JSSR* 19, 1980, 48-60; T.Benski, "Identification, group survival and inter-group relations: the case of a middle-class Jewish community in Scotland", *ERS* 4, 1981, 307-19; E.Tabory and B.Lazerwitz, "Americans in the Israeli Reform and Conservative Denominations: Religiosity under an Ethnic Shield?", *RRelRes* 24, 1982-3, 177-87; L.Weissbrod, "Religion as National Identity in a Secular Society", *RRelRes* 24, 1982-3, 188-205; A.Dashevsky and B.Lazerwitz, "The Role of Religious Identification in North American Migration to Israel", *JSSR* 22, 1983, 263-75; N.Kokosalakis, *Ethnic Identity and Religion: Tradition and Change in Liverpool Jewry* (1983); C.S.Liebman, "Extremism as a Religious Norm", *JSSR* 22, 1983, 75-86; H.S.Himmelfarb, "Natural Trends in Jewish Ethnicity: A Test of the Polarization Hypothesis", *JSSR* 23, 1984, 140-54; H.Ayalon, E.Ben-Rafael and S.Sharot, "Variations in ethnic identification among Israeli Jews", *ERS* 8, 1985, 389-407; R.J.Simon (ed), *New Lives*. The Adjustment of Soviet Jewish Immigrants in the United States and Israel (1985); J.R.Wyman, "Linguistic methods in cultural analysis: A reconsideration", *Semiotica* 57, 1985, 51-71; W.P.Zenner, "Jewishness in America: Ascription and Choice", *ERS* 8, 1985, 177-83; H.Ayalon, E.Ben-Rafael and S.Sharot, "Secularization and the Diminishing Decline of Religion", *RRelRes* 27, 1986, 193-207; S.L.Gilman, *Jewish Self-Hatred* (1986); R.Karklins, "Determinants of ethnic identification in the USSR: the Soviet Jewish case", *ERS* 10, 1987, 27-47; U.Santamaria, "Black Jews: the religious challenge or politics versus religion", *Archives Européennes de Sociologie* 28, 1987, 217-40; W.Shaffir and R.Rockaway, "Leaving the Ultra-Orthodox Fold: Haredi Jews who Defected", *JJSoc* 29, 1987, 97-114. More generally, H.Mol, *Identity and the Sacred* (1976); A.L.Epstein, *Ethos and Identity* (1978); M.Gordon, *Human Nature, Class and Ethnicity* (1978); H.Mol (ed), *Identity and religion: international cross-cultural approaches* (1978); R.F.Baumeister, *Identity. Cultural Change and the Struggle for Self* (1986).

2. Cf *EJ* "Apostasy", "Falashas", "Jew", "Jewish Identity"; G.J.Abbink, *The Falashas in Ethiopia and Israel: the Problem of Ethnic Assimilation* (1984); M.Ashkenazi and A.Weingrod (ed), *Ethiopian Jews and Israel* (1987); S.Kaplan, "The Beta Israel and the Rabbinate: law, ritual and politics", *Social Science Information* 27, 1988, 357-70; Roshwald, op.cit.; C.Holmes, *Anti-Semitism in British Society 1876-1939* (1979); G.C.Lebselter, *Political Anti-Semitism in England 1918-1939* (1978); N.Nugent and R.King, "Ethnic minorities, scapegoating and the extreme right", in R.Miles and

A.Phizacklea, *Racism and political action in Britain* (1979), 28-49.

3. Cf especially Ayalon et al., Himmelfarb, Lazerwitz, Simon, op.cit.

4. *A D' 'tionary of the Social Sciences,* ed. J.Gould and W.J.Kolb (1964), "Ethnic Group" (M.M.Turmin). For secondary literature, cf n.1 supra.

5. For these American immigrants to Israel, E.Tabory and B.Lazerwitz, op. cit., esp Table 2, p.182. For dietary observance in the Providence community, M.Sklare, op. cit., 113-4, 152 n.7, reporting from S.Goldstein and C.Goldschneider, *Jewish Americans: Three Generations in a Jewish Community* (1968), 201.

6. There was no fixed terminology, and "Godfearers" could be used with reference to full Jews. Cf Y.Amir, "The Term Ioudaismos: A study in Jewish-Hellenistic Self-Identification", *Immanuel* 12, 1982, 34-41; T.M.Finn, "The God-Fearers reconsidered", *CBQ* 47, 1985, 75-84; L.H.Feldman, "The Omnipresence of the God-Fearers", *BAR* 12, 1986, 59-69; R.S.Maclennan and A.T.Kraabel, "The God-Fearers - A Literary and Theological Invention", *BAR* 12, 1986, 46-53, 64; F.Millar, "Gentiles and Judaism: God-Fearers and Proselytes", Schürer-Vermes-Millar III.1 (1986), 150-76; S.J.D.Cohen, "Respect for Judaism by Gentiles according to Josephus", *HThR* 80, 1987, 409-30; M.H.Williams, "*Theosebes gar en* - The Jewish Tendencies of Poppaea Sabina", *JThS NS* 39, 1988, 97-111.

7. Recent research has shown that Jews who marry Gentiles do not necessarily assimilate, and has begun to explore the complex variety of experience and perception surrounding intermarriage. Cf especially Lazerwitz, op.cit., *JJSoc* 13, 1971, 41-63; Strelitz, op. cit.; G.Cromer, "Intermarriage and Communal Survival in a London Suburb", *JJSoc* 16, 1974, 155-69; Lavender, op.cit.; E.Mayer, *Love and Tradition. Marriage between Jews and Christians* (1985); Y.Ellmann, "Intermarriage in the United States: A Comparative Study of Jews and Other Ethnic and Religious Groups", *Jewish Social Studies* 49, 1987, 1-26.

8. I cannot enter here into detailed debate with the secondary literature on Timothy's identity. It is regrettable that we do not know how observant Timothy and his mother were, nor whether Timothy's father judaized in more ways than by marrying a Jewish woman. Cf recently S.J.D.Cohen, "Was Timothy Jewish (Acts 16:1-3)? Patristic Exegesis, Rabbinic Law and Matrilineal Descent", *JBL* 105, 1986, 251-68, relying partly on D.Daube, *Ancient Jewish Law* (1981), 22-32: C.Bryan, "A Further Look at Acts 16: 1-3", *JBL* 107, 1988, 292-4.

9. For a debate about orthodoxy in Second Temple Judaism seen largely in terms of belief rather than activity, N.J.McEleney, "Orthodoxy in Judaism of the First Christian Century", *JSJ* IV, 1973, 19-42: D.E.Aune, "Orthodoxy in First Century Judaism?", *JSJ* 7, 1976, 1-10: L.S.Grabbe, "Orthodoxy in First Century Judaism?", *JSJ* 8, 1977, 149-53: N.J.McEleney, "Orthodoxy in Judaism of the First Christian Century", *JSJ* IX, 1978, 83-8. Cf M.Smith, "Palestinian Judaism in the First Century", in *Israel, its Role in Civilisation,* ed M.Davis (1956), 67-81.

10. For details Cf especially D.J.Clines, *Ezra, Nehemiah, Esther,* New Century Bible (1984); H.G.M.Williamson, *Ezra, Nehemiah,* Word Biblical Commentary 16 (1985).

11. Detailed discussion of hellenization in Israel cannot be attempted here. For major issues, cf M.Hengel, *Judaism and Hellenism* (2 vols. 1968. ET from 2nd ed., 1974); M.Hengel, *Jews, Greeks and Barbarians* (1976. ET 1980); L.H.Feldman, "Hengel's Judaism and Hellenism in Retrospect", *JBL* 96, 1977, 371-82; F.Millar, "The Background to the Maccabean Revolution: Reflections on Martin Hengel's Judaism and Hellenism", *JJS* 29, 1978, 1-21; L.H.Feldman, "How Much Hellenism in Jewish Palestine?" *HUCA* 57, 1986, 83-111; G.Delling, "Die Begegnung zwischen Hellenismus und Judentum", *ANRW* II.20.1 (1987), 3-39.

Chapter 3
God Incarnate - Jesus in the Johannine Community

1. Deity and Incarnation
The Gospel attributed to St John is the only New Testament document in which the deity and incarnation of Jesus are unequivocally proclaimed.[1] In the prologue, Jesus' deity is made explicit: "In the beginning was the Word, and the Word was with God, and the Word was God" (Jn 1.1). At the prologue's climax, "the Word was made flesh and dwelt among us", and his name and title are given as "Jesus Christ" (Jn 1.14,17). This is an explicit declaration of the incarnation in the strong sense in which I use that term, that is, of the process by means of which a fully divine being is born as a person.[2] John's prologue ends with a brief summary of Jesus' nature and mission on earth: "No-one has seen God. Only-begotten God,[3] who is in the bosom of the Father, he has revealed him" (Jn 1.18). As the Gospel approaches its original end, Thomas declares on behalf of those who had not seen Jesus but who had faith in him, "My Lord and my God" (Jn 20.28). Throughout the Gospel, Jesus is portrayed as conscious of his position as the incarnate Son of God who is co-equal with the Father. The classic declaration is "I and the Father are one" (Jn 10.30), a declaration so provocative that "the Jews" immediately took up stones to throw at Jesus. At John 10.33, they give their reasons - "for blasphemy, and because, although you're a man, you make yourself God." Throughout this Gospel, Jesus refers to himself as "the Son" and to God as his Father. God is the Father of others as well, but John calls other people God's children, never his "sons", reserving the term "son" for Jesus alone. This is another indication that John saw an ontological rather than merely functional difference between Jesus and other people, and its significance is brought out particularly well at John 5.17ff.

Chapter 5 begins with a healing performed on the sabbath, at which Jesus ordered a man to carry his pallet. In the debate with "the Jews" which follows, Jesus justifies his apparent breach of sabbath law by identifying himself closely with God his Father: "My Father works until now, and I work" (John 5.17). Many Jews believed that God was continuously active, on the seventh day as on others. Jesus associates himself so closely with the divine activity that he effectively lays claim to divinity, claiming God as his own Father as well. John tells us that "the Jews" understood his words in this way: "For this reason, therefore, the Jews sought all the more to kill Jesus, because he not only abrogated the Sabbath, but also called God his own Father, making himself equal with God" (Jn 5.18). It is striking that, whereas Jesus justifies his action in appearing to break the sabbath, he does not attempt to answer any charge that he called God his own Father, or made himself equal with God. Similarly at John 10.33ff, when "the Jews" threaten to stone Jesus for blasphemy, and on the ground that he makes himself God, Jesus does not deny the charge but justifies his position, asserting as he does so "I am the Son of God", and "the Father is in me and I am in the Father." Thus the deity of Jesus, and more specifically his position as the unique Son of God, was known to him and set forth by him in public debate with hostile contemporaries.

Jesus' exalted position is filled out with massive discussion throughout this Gospel. At 8.58 he declares his pre-existence in open debate with "the Jews": "before Abraham was, I am." The Jewish reaction of taking up stones to throw at him shows that they have interpreted his words as a claim to divinity. There are passing references to his pre-existence elsewhere in the Gospel, and lengthy exposition of him as the bread which came down from heaven in chapter 6, which is also delivered in open debate with the Jews. "For the bread of God is he who comes down from heaven and gives life to the world.... I am the bread of life.... I have come down from heaven not to do my own will but the will of him who sent me ... what then if you see the Son of man going up where he was before?" (Jn 6.33,35,38,62). His unity with the Father, and his position as the revealer of the Godhead, are expounded in his reply to Philip's request, "Show us the Father" (Jn 14.8): "Have I been with you for such a long time and yet you do not know me, Philip? He who has seen me has seen the Father. What do you mean, 'show us the Father'? Do you not believe that I am in the Father, and the Father is in me? The words which I say to you I do not speak of my own accord, but the Father remains in me and does his works. Believe me that I am in the Father and the Father in me." Given the exposition of Jesus' divinity already noted, we must interpret passages like this of the mutual indwelling of two persons of the Godhead. Jesus' divine position is further indicated by a passage in the same discourse where he can answer prayer, in a context which evidently refers to the period after his return to the Father (Jn 14.13-14). Another function which Jesus claims after his resurrection is that of sending the Paraclete, the distinctive Johannine description of the Holy Spirit (Jn 16.7).

All this material is coherent, and quite unlike anything else in the New Testament. The measured and open declaration of the deity of the Word in the first verse of the Gospel demonstrates clearly that the author was in no way embarrassed by the full divinity of Christ. It sets up the interpretation of Jesus' pre-existence as evidence of deity, an interpretation attributed both to "the Jews" and to Jesus himself, yet absent from other literature of this period. This evidence also shows that, in this document, the description of Jesus as "the Son" is an expression of his deity.

2. Historicity

It is well known that the presentation of Jesus in the fourth Gospel is historically inaccurate. None the less, there has been a reaction against the conventional critical view, a "new look" on the fourth Gospel, which sees a greater degree of unique and accurate historical information in it, while conservative evangelical scholars have continued to maintain the literal truth of its every word.[4] This question is crucial for plotting out the development of New Testament christology. I therefore argue next that the unique aspects of John's christology are the product of the Johannine community, and that these developments can be located in changes which took place in the community.

It is simplest to begin with the title "the Son" or "the Son of God", because it is easiest to measure. In John, Jesus uses terms of this kind no less than 23 times, in public debate as well as in private teaching. Mark however attributes such a term to Jesus no more than once (Mk 13.32), and Q contains just one such saying, in which "the Son" occurs three times (Mt 11.27/Lk 10.22). If the historical Jesus had used this key term extensively as John says he did, the faithful Christians who transmitted the synoptic tradition would have transmitted it extensively. In that case, the Gospel writers would not have failed to record Jesus' extensive use of this term, for all of them have further examples of it in their own editorial work, as well as in comments attributed to other beings. The synoptic evidence is confirmed by the absence of such terms from the early speeches of Acts.[5] If "the Son" had been the main term which the historical Jesus used to express his divinity, the earliest apostles were bound to have used it too, and it would have been transmitted to Luke who would not have had reason to leave it out.

With this terminology goes a great deal of profound material, which is equally important but not so easy to count. As an example, we may consider John's exposition of the mutual indwelling of the Father and the Son. In this case too, the absence of such material from the synoptics is fundamental, because the mutual indwelling of Father and Son would hardly have been omitted by the faithful Christians who transmitted and recorded the synoptic material, if it had been expounded by the historical Jesus. Again, Jesus' pre-existence, and his post-resurrection functions of answering prayer and sending the Paraclete, are absent from his teaching in the synoptics: faithful Christians would not have left them all out if he had really expounded them.

This argument is not confined to those aspects of Johannine christology which explicitly involve Jesus' deity and incarnation. There is a massive amount of supporting christological development which is equally striking because of its absence from the synoptic Gospels. I have noted the discourse of John 6, with Jesus' pre-existence and return to the Father. The central declaration "I am the bread of life" (Jn 6.35,48) is filled out with the necessity of the eucharist for salvation: "Amen, amen, I tell you, unless you eat the flesh of the Son of Man and drink his blood, you do not have life in you. He who eats my flesh and drinks my blood has eternal life, and I will raise him up at the last day, for my flesh is true meat and my blood is true drink. He who eats my flesh and drinks my blood remains in me and I in him" (Jn 6.53-56). The necessity of the eucharist for salvation, Jesus' pre-existence and the mutual indwelling of Jesus and the believer are obvious and dramatic features of a public discourse which goes far beyond the words of institution of 1 Corinthians 11.24-5 and Lk 22.19-

20 (cf Mk 14.22-4, Mt 26.26-8), and could hardly have been so ignored if its teaching were genuinely that of the historical Jesus. Other writers would, however, have been more likely to place it at the Last Supper, or to offer a mundane as well as a theological explanation of what Jesus meant. The Johannine discourse, expounding the eucharist without mentioning it, would have been unintelligible if it had been delivered like that.

The "I am" statement at John 6.35,48 is only one of a group of such statements, including "I am the light of the world", "I am the Resurrection and the Life", and "I am the Way, the Truth and the Life" (Jn 8.12, 11.25, 14.6). The synoptic Jesus does not make statements of this kind. If the Jesus of history did in fact make them, the omission of every one of them from the synoptics is simply incomprehensible.

The same applies to the witness of John the Baptist. He took up the current expectation of a redemptive figure (Mk 1.7-8/Mt 3.11-12/Lk 3.16-17), and when he was imprisoned he sent messengers to ask Jesus, "Are you the one who is coming, or are we to look for someone else?" (Mt 11.3/Lk 7.19). John the evangelist develops this into an unambiguous positive witness to Jesus, putting in the mouth of John the Baptist the ringing declaration, "Behold the Lamb of God who takes away the sin of the world" (Jn 1.29, cf 1.36). The Baptist ascribes pre-existence to Jesus, explicitly declares that he is the one whom he had previously foretold, claims to have done so by a special revelation, and identifies him as the Messiah (Jn 1.16,29-34, 3.27ff). If John the Baptist had borne witness to Jesus like this, the faithful Christians who transmitted the synoptic tradition would have found his clear witness divinely inspired and unforgettable, and we would read it in Matthew, Mark and Luke.

John the Baptist's witness was not merely past history. The community's perspective appears clearly in the prologue, where the Baptist bears witness to the Word made flesh: "John bears witness concerning him and has cried, saying, 'This was him of whom I said, "The one who comes after me has become before me, because he was before me"'" (Jn 1.15). This *was*, not this *is*, him of whom I spoke, for the perspective is that of the community after the death and resurrection of Jesus. The same perspective appears from time to time in the discourses, disconcerting the modern reader as it did some of the ancient copyists. In chapter 3, Jesus teaches Nicodemus alone about rebirth by baptism and the Spirit, rebirth being a Greek concept which would hardly have been known in Jesus' environment. At John 3.11 Jesus suddenly begins to address Nicodemus in the plural, criticising the lack of insight into his teaching, and proceeding, "If I tell you (plural again!) earthly matters and you do not believe, how will you believe if I tell you heavenly matters? And no-one has gone up into heaven except the one who came down from heaven, the Son of man who is in heaven" (3.12-13). The ascension of the Son of man and his presence in heaven clearly have their *Sitz im Leben* at the time of the community.

All these points enable us to locate the source of Johannine christology in the beliefs of the Johannine community, a fact for which we have independent attestation in the Johannine epistles. For example, the term "the Son", the fourth Gospel's characteristic term for Jesus, is used no less than 22 times in 1 John. The more profound theological material, and the uniquely Johannine concepts, are found there too.[6]

In attributing all his christology to Jesus, John followed a practice which is alien to our culture, but typical of the culture to which he belonged.[7] In the Jewish world in which the Johannine traditions began their process of development, it was normal to attribute developing traditions to the perceived fountain-heads of those traditions. All we know of "Deutero-Isaiah" is that he belonged to the tradition of repeating, interpreting, reapplying and bringing to life a stream of prophetic tradition which descended ultimately from Isaiah of Jerusalem, and that it was out of this tradition that he preached to the exiles in Babylon. Similarly, Law might be attributed to the revelation to Moses on Mt Sinai. An outstanding example is the book of Jubilees. This is an expanded version of part of the Pentateuch, including additional orthodox *halakhah* such as the prohibition of sexual intercourse on the sabbath (Jub 50.8). Again, the psalms were attributed to David, all 3,600 of them, together with 450 songs, according to 11QPsa XXVII. Wisdom likewise might be attributed to Solomon, and apocalyptic revelations were ascribed to a variety of ancient patriarchs, of whom Enoch was only the most widespread and distinguished. A similar custom was found in the Greco-Roman world, as for example in the works of Plato, who attributed most of his opinions to Socrates.

It must be deduced that John followed the same cultural habit, attributing the community's beliefs to the fountainhead of their traditions, Jesus himself. In the same way, John the Baptist's witness was interpreted in terms of the community's beliefs. Consequently, the fourth Gospel, like the books of Isaiah, Jubilees and 1 Enoch, provides us with information about the development of the community which produced it, starting from the authentic traditions which it contains. It is quite clear that the material in the Gospel has been edited, and that more than one person may have done this. When I refer to the author, therefore, I simply mean the person or people who wrote or dictated John 1-20 in its present form. I propose to argue that this "author", whom we may alternatively call the final redactor, wrote as a member of a group who had Gentile self-identification.[8]

3. Gentile Self-identification

The most striking evidence of the Gentile self-identification of the author and his community is the repeated description of the people with whom Jesus disagrees as "the Jews". John uses the term more than 60 times, and in the majority of cases it denotes opponents of Jesus, despite the fact that all Jesus' disciples at this stage were Jewish.[9] John's version of the event known to us as the cleansing of the Temple begins, "now the Passover of the Jews was near" (Jn 2.13). This itself indicates Gentile self-identification, and it typifies many uses of the term in narrative. Then immediately after the story of the cleansing, "The disciples remembered that it was written, 'Zeal for your house will consume me'. The Jews therefore answered and said to him, 'What sign do you show us, that you do this?'" (Jn 2.17-18). The contrast is reinforced with further mention of these two groups, "the Jews" and "his disciples", in the immediate sequel. This use of the term "the Jews" is not found in the synoptic accounts of this incident (Mk 11.15ff/Mt 21.12ff/Lk 19.45ff). At John 13.33, Jesus himself speaks of "the Jews" as if they were an outside group. On two occasions, he refers to the Law as *"your* Law" (8.17, 10.34), and at 15.25 he explains to the disciples the hatred of the world by quoting scripture: "But so that the word may be fulfilled which is written in their Law, 'they hated me without cause'." The description *"their* Law" again betrays the self-identification of an essentially Gentile group for whom the Law belonged to an alien group, "the Jews". This description is intelligible only from a Gentile perspective. With this also goes the perception of the Jews as a group rejecting the Gospel. At the time of Jesus, some Jews did indeed reject him, but other people who were quite obviously Jewish became his disciples, accepted his message and formed the nucleus of the early church after the resurrection.

In addition to this direct evidence of Gentile self-identification, there is indirect evidence of the presence of Gentiles in the Johannine community. In chapter 10, Jesus expounds and interprets the parable of the good shepherd, commenting, "And I have other sheep who are not of this fold: these too I must lead, and they will hear my voice, and they shall be one flock with one shepherd. Because of this, the Father loves me because I lay down my life to take it up again" (Jn 10.16-17). The "other sheep" are surely Gentiles, and this is a prediction of the entry of Gentiles into the community, a process which did not begin until after Jesus' death.[10]

Again, the high priest's declaration that one man should die for the people is interpreted at John 11.51-2: "He did not say this of his own accord, but since he was high priest that year he prophesied that Jesus would die for the nation, and not for the nation only, but so that he might gather together the scattered children of God into one group." Here the reference to Gentiles is especially clear, since diaspora Jews belonged to "the nation" or "the people" just as much as Judaean Jews. The reference to "the scattered children of God" cannot be confined to diaspora Jews because the power to become children of God has been given to "as many as received him", "those who believe in his name" (Jn 1.12), and after a successful Gentile mission these necessarily included Gentiles. Thus when "some Greeks" came to see Jesus (Jn 12.20), they did not succeed in doing so, for the Gentile mission could not begin until after his death: "now the ruler of this world will be cast out and I, when I am lifted up from the earth, will draw *everyone* to myself" (Jn 12.31-2).

This kind of evidence is further supported by the Greek background to the theology of this Gospel. The hellenistic concept of rebirth employed in chapter 3 is outstanding because it is purely hellenistic. It is, however, difficult to understand items such as the choice of the Greek term *logos* in the prologue, if the author was not deliberately seeking to appeal to Gentiles as well as to Jews. Further evidence of Gentiles in the community is provided by the author's habit of explaining Jewish terms and customs. At 1.38, for example, he interprets "rabbi" as "teacher", and at 2.6 he explains that the six stone water-pots were "for the purification ceremonies of the Jews", an accurate description of a Jewish custom from a Gentile perspective, necessary only if the prospective audience included a significant proportion of Gentiles.

This can be described more incisively with the eight-point identity scale proposed in chapter 2. From an ethnic perspective, the community contained both Jews and Gentiles: we cannot measure the proportions accurately, so I shall symbolise mixture with a half. Scripture gets another half: the community accepted the authority of scripture as a witness to Jesus, but did not accept its commands to follow its *halakhah*. Monotheism gets another half: the deity of Jesus means that the community remained monotheistic from a Gentile perspective, but it was not monotheistic from a Jewish perspective. This does not give us a symbolic 1.5 out of 3, where the halves might be thought too symbolic to be accurate: it is 1.5 out of 7 or 8, a difference which is big enough to be real and decisive.

Circumcision is presented as an alien custom: "Moses gave *you* circumcision ... and on the Sabbath *you* circumcise a man" (7.22). The sabbath is explicitly removed: Jesus "abrogated the Sabbath" (Jn 5.18). Dietary laws are never mentioned: it might be argued that we should not count them (so 1.5 out of 7, not 8), but we should note the implication that we are well clear of an orthodox Jewish environment. Purity is identified as belonging to an alien group: stone water-pots were "for the purification of the Jews" (Jn 2.6, cf 11.55). Purity is not however mentioned very often, another indication that we are not in an orthodox environment. The figurative use of purity as resulting from washing by Jesus (Jn 13.10, implying baptism), and from the words of Jesus (Jn 15.3), should be interpreted as the replacement of Jewish purity laws by Christian purity. Major festivals are repeatedly identified as belonging to an alien group: for example, "Now the feast of the Jews, Tabernacles, was near" (Jn 7.2), and again, "Now the Passover of the Jews was near" (Jn 11.55). In this instance, the measurement of 1.5 out of 7 or 8 is not precise in numerical terms, but the message is clear. The author's view of the basic identity factors of Judaism provides further evidence of his Gentile self-identification.

This is also a fruitful context in which to see the implication of John's symbolism, that Jesus embodied and replaced significant aspects of Jewish religion and culture. Jesus went up to Jerusalem for "the Passover of the Jews" (Jn 2.13, cf 6.4, 11.55), but he was the lamb of God (Jn 1.29,34), and when he was slaughtered at the same time as the Jewish Passover lambs (cf Jn 19.14), he fulfilled the scripture that "a bone of it shall not be broken" (Jn 19.36, cf Ex 12.46, Num 9.12). As the lamb of God, he took away the sin, not of "the Jews", but of "the world" (Jn 1.29), a term which clearly includes Gentiles. Just before the second Passover, "the feast of the Jews" (Jn 6.4), he fed some 5,000 people miraculously (Jn 6.4ff), and surpassed the manna in the wilderness: "Amen, amen I say to you, Moses has not given you the bread from heaven, but my Father gives you the true bread from heaven.... I am the bread of life" (6.32,35).

In a debate which results in many of "the Jews" rejecting Jesus, the criteria for the new covenant community are faith in Jesus and participation in the Christian eucharist. At the first Passover at the beginning of the public ministry, Jesus not only cleansed but also effectively replaced the Temple, a fact understood by the disciples after the resurrection when they remembered the words which he had spoken in debate with "the Jews" (Jn 2.13-22, esp 19-22).

Jesus also replaced "the feast of the Jews, Tabernacles". A significant aspect of the ceremonies was the water libation. "But on the last great day of the feast Jesus stood and cried, saying, 'If anyone is thirsty, let him come to me and let him who believes in me drink. As the Scripture says, rivers of living water shall flow from his stomach'" (7.37-8). Light was another major aspect of the feast. When the golden candlesticks were lit in the court of the women, it is said that there was not a courtyard in Jerusalem that was not lit up by the light of the place of the water drawing (M.Sukk. V,3). This is the cultural context of Jesus' declaration, "I am the light of the world" (Jn 8.12).

The shepherd is another significant symbol. The Old Testament portrays both God and accepted leaders of Israel as shepherds, contrasting them with existing shepherds who do not look after the people (cf e.g. Ezek 34; Zech 11.4-17; Ps 78.70-72). Jesus declares, "I am the good shepherd" (Jn 10.11). This is part of a complex allegory setting off a discourse at the feast of Hannukah, when Jews celebrated their deliverance from the persecution of Antiochus IV Epiphanes. Antiochus' full title was "Antiochus God Manifest" *(Theos Epiphanes),* and statues of him were set up in the Temple during the persecution. For Jews, his claim to deity was blasphemous, and some people thought Antiochus mad, calling him Antiochus *Epimanes*. Some Jews also believed that the death of the righteous martyrs had enabled God to deliver Israel (cf Dan 11.35; 2 Macc 7.37-38; 4 Macc 17.20-22). John reapplies all these basic aspects of Hannukah to Jesus and the Jews. Jesus does not reject the accusation of "the Jews" that he makes himself God (Jn 10.33), for in John's view he was indeed God manifest. "The Jews" declare "he is mad" (10.20), and make to stone him for blasphemy (10.31ff). Jesus achieves more than the Maccabean martyrs, for it is not only Israel whom he delivers (Jn 10.15-17). "The Jews" ask him in a horrid pun, "How long will you frustrate us?", literally, "How long do you take our life?" (Jn 10.24). In his reply, Jesus tells them bluntly, "But you do not believe, because you do not belong to my sheep" (Jn 10.26). This is another clear exclusion of "the Jews" from salvation.

The vine is another example of John's replacement symbolism. It was a traditional symbol of Israel (cf e.g. Ezek 19.10-14; Ps 80.9-20). At Jn 15.1ff we find that Jesus is "the true vine", and anyone who does not remain in him is cast out (Jn 15.6). I have noted also the implication that Jewish purity laws are replaced by Christian purity, which results from baptism and from the words of Jesus (cf Jn 13.10; 15.3).

All this material forms a coherent whole. The Johannine community perceived "the Jews" as an alien group. The community had admitted Gentile converts, and thus its theology has some specifically Greek aspects. The community rejected most of the major identity factors of Judaism. The Gospel's symbolism transfers major Jewish symbols to Jesus himself and it does so in a context of rejection of "the Jews" and a ministry directed at "the world", resulting in the salvation of those who believe. It must therefore be concluded that the Johannine community had Gentile self-identification.

4. Cast out of the Synagogue

The evidence for the crucial break with "the Jews" is found in two passages which do not belong to the environment of the Jesus of history. At John 9.22, the parents of a man healed by Jesus were afraid because the Jews had already agreed that if anyone confessed Jesus as Christ, he should be put out of the synagogue. At 12.42-3, we are given the even more surprising information, "however many even of the rulers believed in him, but they did not confess him because of the Pharisees, to avoid being put out of the synagogue, for they loved the glory of men rather than the glory of God." The seriousness of these measures is intensified by the prediction of 16.2.

There are three obvious difficulties with the historicity of the threats of 9.22 and 12.42-3. In the first place, confession of a person, whether as Messiah (Jn 9.22) or more vaguely (Jn 12.42-3), is not a feasible cause of expulsion from the synagogue. Secondly, "many of the rulers" would form too powerful a group for expulsion to be possible. Any attempt to throw them out of the synagogue would result in their use of force, with consequent splits in Judaism, not victory for the Pharisees. Thirdly, if confessing Jesus had resulted in expulsion from the synagogue, the disciples would have been expelled from the synagogue. Of this, however, there is no trace, not even in John, let alone in the synoptics.

The agreement, therefore, belongs to a later period. The terms of 9.22 enable us to analyse it further. Here the confession is explicitly that of Jesus as Christ: already by the time of Paul and Acts that was a central identity factor of the Christian community. Further, the agreement is that of "the Jews". We have reached the point of a split between Christianity and Judaism. Our Jewish sources give us a rough date of A.D.85 for the formulation of the Benediction against the heretics, done by Samuel the Small at the behest of Gamaliel II.[11] Gamaliel II was son of Simeon, son of Gamaliel I. Since both Gamaliel I and Simeon his son are two of the only five people from our period identified by our sources as Pharisees (Acts 5.34; Jos. *Life* 190-1), we may reasonably infer that Gamaliel II was a Pharisee. This benediction gives us evidence that, at about the time when the fourth Gospel was written, central Jewish authorities were taking the kind of measures that might result in Christian Jews and judaizers being cast out of the synagogue. It is entirely coherent that "the Jews", in the place where the fourth Gospel was written, agreed to cast Christians out of the synagogue, and that doubtful Jews who held high office were fearful of the most rigorous Jews, the Pharisees.

By this time social conditions were such that many Jews might well perceive a sufficient threat to their identity for them to act on the instructions of leading Pharisees. Gentiles had sacked the cultic centre of Jerusalem with much slaughter, defiling and destroying the holy places. Many Gentiles had entered the Christian churches, and in doing so had remained Gentiles rather than becoming Jews. If we measure average Pauline Christians on our eight-point identity scale, they get only monotheism and part of scripture, with some sensitivity to dietary laws for the sake of "weaker brethren".[12] About 1.5 out of 8, without ethnicity or circumcision, means that Jewish people perceived them as Gentiles. Jews who joined the Christian community were thus liable to assimilate into the Gentile world, believing that salvation meant membership of the largely Gentile Christian community which did not observe the Law, rather than membership of the Jewish community which did. This became the more important after A.D.70, when many Jews had been killed and the cultic centre destroyed. If it was to survive, Judaism had to reconstitute itself round its own identity. It did so, with Pharisees like Gamaliel II at the centre because they encapsulated visible and measurable Jewish identity, ensuring the maintenance of all Judaism's identity factors by expanding the regulations governing their observance.[13] This is the situation in which local rulers of the Jews might well fear the Pharisees, and decide that membership of the covenant community was more important than continued adherence to Jesus.

The plain implications of our primary sources should, therefore, be accepted. The Johannine community contained people who were thrown out of the synagogue after A.D.70, when Jewish identity was recreated under Pharisees like Gamaliel II.

5. Assimilating Jews

What kind of Judaism had they belonged to? The answer is nothing exotic, though it is a form of Judaism which has no name in the primary sources or in the secondary literature. We might call it "assimilating Judaism". I have noted that some Jews assimilated during our period, as many do now.[14] Many Jews lived in Greek cities, and although there was a Jewish area in some Greek cities, there was no advanced ghetto system to form a complete bar to social interaction. Some direct information has also been noted from specific situations. The most dramatic comes from Judaea and Jerusalem, in the run-up to the Maccabean revolt. Many Jews were so hellenized that they dropped several of the identity factors of Judaism. Some even removed the marks of circumcision, a drastic repudiation of Jewish identity, while intermarriage is also clearly attested (cf e.g. 1 Macc 1.11-15). We also have evidence from Philo that there were people who adhered to an allegorical interpretation of the Law, but who did not observe it literally (*De Mig* 89-93). Since Philo's illustrations of the need to observe the law are the sabbath, festivals and circumcision, these people must have been moving out of the Jewish sphere. Philo makes this point more directly in saying that, by being observant, these people would avoid the complaints and accusations of the majority. I have noted Timothy, whose Jewish mother married a Greek man, and did not have him circumcised on the eighth day (cf Acts 16.1-3).[15] A more dramatic example is Tiberius Iulius Alexander, son of Alexander the Alabarch and nephew of Philo. After serving as the Roman commander in Alexandria, he was the senior general of the Roman legions under the future emperor Titus when they sacked Jerusalem.[16]

All such evidence must be borne in mind when we consider the kind of Judaism adhered to by those members of the Johannine community who transmitted and produced its Jewish traditions, and who had to decide what to do when "the Jews", led by "the Pharisees", agreed to cast people out of the synagogue if they confessed Jesus as Messiah. It was clearly hellenized Judaism, because of the purely Greek language and evident influence of Greek culture in the Gospel. It must also have been at the less observant and more easily assimilable end of the Jewish spectrum, for the following reasons. Firstly, despite controversies over the observance of the Law, there is no dispute over minor details of Law observance. The nearest we get to debate over a minor detail is the question of healing on the sabbath, and this is instructive. It comes from authentic tradition, and on both occasions it transmutes immediately into the question of the abrogation of the sabbath, that is, into debate about one of the identity factors of Judaism (Jn 5.9ff, 9.14ff). Further, there is no mention of minor details of the Law, except when they have some other function. Thus, large stone pots for purification (Jn 2.6) may be a minor detail, but this is an explanation of the presence of pots which are being used to provide water that can be changed into wine, and the explanation is necessary precisely because some of John's audience would not otherwise understand why they were there.

Thirdly, the disputes with "the Jews" in this Gospel involve the identity of Judaism. Both healing narratives immediately transmute into disputes about breaking the sabbath: John 5.18 also involves the deity of Jesus, and the sabbath dispute of chapter 9 is followed by a second debate in which the same allegation is clear. As a result of the dispute with the Jewish community, both the pre-existence and the sonship of Jesus are treated in this Gospel as indications of deity. This is especially clear in chapters 5 and 10, and found also in chapter 8, where the Jews take up stones to throw at Jesus, following his declaration that he was pre-existent and greater than Abraham.[17] I have noted messiahship at 9.22, an identity characteristic of Christianity over against Judaism. Some Jews also leave after the discourse of chapter 6, which has participation in the Christian eucharist (rather than membership of the chosen people) as a criterion for salvation, in a context of dispute with the Jews. "The Jews", however, claim to be disciples of Moses (Jn 9.28-9, cf 9.18,22), and "the chief priests" sought to kill not only Jesus but also Lazarus, for "many of the Jews were leaving because of him" (Jn 12.11), so that "the Pharisees" declared that "the world" had gone after him (Jn 12.19). These last two comments come from the wholly implausible run-up to the passion, in which the Pharisees ironically see faith in Jesus as a cause of the Roman destruction of Jerusalem (Jn 11.47-8). The *Sitz im Leben* of this view is among the orthodox Jews who were soon to write 4 Ezra, and who believed that the destruction of Jerusalem was divine judgment on the Jewish people because they had not observed the law. At 7.49, the Pharisees duly accuse "this crowd", that is, most of the Jewish people, of not knowing the Law.

All these points form a coherent whole. The Judaism which the former Jews of the Johannine community left behind was on the assimilating end of the spectrum, as Jewish Christianity had been throughout the Gentile mission in the diaspora. Jews whose Jewish identity was strongest remained in the Jewish community, where the Pharisees publicly displayed the visible identity factors of Judaism. It was the more assimilated who left. They took much Jewish religion and culture with them, but they were ready to abandon the visible identity factors of Judaism in the wake of their conflict with "the Jews".

6. The Johannine Community

Major aspects of the history of the Johannine community as it affects the rise of christology can now be reconstructed.[18] It was descended from the Jesus movement, which was purely Jewish, and which became a mixed community of Jews and Gentiles as a result of a successful mission to the Gentiles. The Johannine community remembered the entrance of Gentiles as an event which took place relatively soon after the death and resurrection of Jesus. As the community developed, its Jewish members continued to attend the synagogue, probably being joined there sometimes by some Gentile members of the community. The community knew authentic traditions about the Jesus of history, as we know from their presence in the Gospel as it stands. The development of these traditions was important in holding together a mixed community of Jews and Gentiles, not least because Jews could always return to membership of the synagogue alone. In the synagogue, where Jesus was necessarily famous at least as a Jewish prophet, he was also a subject of debate. We must infer that the stories of his miracles were especially effective in impressing Jews who were not sure how important he was (cf Jn 2.11; 7.31; 10.19-21; 14.11). Those Jews who belonged to the Christian community were necessarily of an assimilating kind, since they regarded faith in Jesus rather than obedience to the Law as essential for salvation.

Jewish and Gentile members alike searched the Old Testament scriptures as a resource in which they saw Jesus and his significance foretold. Their adherence was further reinforced by their common experiences. The common experiences which we must infer from the Gospel are prayer, preaching, discussion, baptism, common meals including the eucharist, reading and inter-pretation of the Old Testament scriptures. Chapters 3 and 6 give us some insight into the kind of beliefs which were eventually reinforced by the repeated experience of baptism and the eucharist. In other words, the community developed in a generally typical manner, but it was sufficiently distinct from other Christian communities to have specific secondary traditions. These included Jewish arguments such as that from circumcision at John 7.22-3, as well as culturally Jewish material like the midrashic use of traditions in chapter 6: both of these are generally derived from the extensive Jewish influence in the community, though either might have been actually written by a person whose birth and self-identification were Gentile. The final redactor of John 6 evidently did have Gentile self-identification, since at 6.41 the sceptical crowd are described as "the Jews", and at 6.49 Jesus refers to the Exodus generation as *"your* fathers" (cf 6.32).

This mixed community of Jews and Gentiles was drastically affected by the events surrounding the revolt against Rome, which began in A.D.66 and led to the destruction of Jerusalem in A.D.70. After this destruction, Judaism reconstituted itself without its cultic centre. It did this round the Pharisaic form of Judaism, because Pharisaic adherence to the Law embodied and protected visible Jewish identity. At about this time, some Jews agreed to exclude Jewish Christians from the synagogue, some of them probably by means of the blessing against the heretics. In the area where the Johannine community lived, perhaps because of a more specific local agreement among the Jewish authorities, this was a specific measure against Christians. We have seen that it had been preceded by arguments within the Jewish community about Jesus, and it is not probable that these arguments ceased when Christian Jews were compelled to leave the synagogue. This gives us the correct context for most of the arguments about Jesus now found in historical form in the fourth Gospel. Many of the rulers of the local community had great respect for Jesus, but they followed the lead of Pharisees in holding Judaism together, rather than let it dissipate by means of Christianity into the Gentile world. In this they were joined by many other Jews, whose rejection of the Christian community must be inferred from passages such as 6.66 (cf 8.31ff; 12.42-43).

None of these people should be called "crypto-Christians", for this is an anachronistic description which misrepresents the centre of their life-stance. Nor is there any evidence that the community was divided into separate groups, of whom they were one.[19] These people were Jews, as they always had been. We must infer that they perceived Jesus as God's agent, whose teaching represented a true form of Judaism: that in varying degrees they had accepted the rising christology of the Johannine community: and that to some extent they had joined in the specific practices of the Christian community. They will not, however, have ceased to obey the Law. When the split between Christianity and Judaism came, they opted to retain the Jewish identity which had always made them what they were, certain in the knowledge that neither the will of the Father nor the teaching of Jesus could possibly require them to leave the covenant community, the community to which Jesus and his first disciples had uniformly belonged. The message which embodied Judaism could not require them to leave Judaism. The split was at one level a simple one: Christians could at this point of crisis be *in* the Jewish community or *out* of it, and the Christian community was defined by a single identity marker, its attitude to Jesus of Nazareth. This explains why the actual criterion for throwing people out can be put so simply as "confessing him" or "confessing him as Christ" (Jn 9.22; 12.42).

Jews who were thrown out of the synagogue are likely to have suffered a severe shock. Their choice had not however been inevitable. It was possible for people to remain in the synagogue, provided that they rejected Christianity. It follows that those Jews who left it were those for whom Christian belief and fellowship were more important than Jewish ethnicity, Law and life. They will naturally have found a warm welcome in the Christian community to which they already belonged. This is the social context of the Gentile self-identification of the Johannine commnity. The community had for a long time included people who were born Gentile, and who had remained identifiably Gentile. Some of them are likely to have attended the synagogue, observing the sabbath and major festivals, but not undertaking circumcision and becoming proselytes whose self-identification was Jewish. Others will not have gone even as far as this, and the community will for a long time have had a Gentile wing. The increasing number of Gentiles in the community and the rise of its christology now combined with the aftermath of the revolt against Rome to produce a major identity crisis. At this moment, the community lost all those Jews whose Jewish identity was strong enough for them to remain inside the Jewish community when the moment of decision came. It kept some people who had to be put out of the synagogue because they would not have voluntarily left it. When there was a crisis, however, they were prepared to abandon their membership of the Jewish community in order to remain inside the Christian community. These people had been assimilating already, and their choice meant that in the long term they had effectively opted for Gentile identity. They would drop sabbath, purity, major festivals, and mostly the dietary laws: they would not be motivated to press for the circumcision of their grandchildren.

The community which had thrown these people out was universally known as "the Jews", and the people responsible for the fourth Gospel continued with this terminology, much as Josephus refers to "the Jews" in contexts where some ethnically Jewish people have clearly left that community.[20] The Johannine community was not however motivated in any way to drop its Jewish traditions, because these were a vital part of its own identity. For example, being thrown out of the synagogue by "the Jews" would not make Johannine Christians want to drop the tradition that John the Baptist predicted the coming of one mightier than himself (Jn 1.26-7): it would rather reinforce the natural process of interpreting his witness in the light of later beliefs so that it became an explicit guarantee of the divine legitimation of Christianity, including christological beliefs which "the Jews" had rejected.[21] Again, there was no reason to drop the purely Jewish argument of John 7.22-3. On the contrary, this was perceived to justify the abrogation of the sabbath, and it demonstrated that "the Jews", who observed the sabbath and rejected the Johannine community, were wrong.

John's condemnation of faithful Jews who remained in the Jewish community is severe: "Your accuser is Moses, on whom you set your hope. For if you believed in Moses, you would have believed me, for he wrote about me" (5.45-6); "If God were your father ... you belong to your father the devil and you want to carry out your father's desires" (8.42,44). In a sense Christianity was what Judaism should have been, but the conflict with "the Jews" was too great for the author to put it like that. The community perceived their beliefs as true rather than as truly Jewish, and their option for religion rather than ethnicity is well expressed in the condemnation of Jews who had been sympathetic to Christianity, but who remained in the Jewish community when the crisis came: "They loved the glory of men rather than the glory of God" (12.43).

Thus, thrown out by the ethnic group "the Jews", the religious Johannine community took on the Gentile self-identification which some of their members had always had, and to which all their members were already sympathetic. This left them without an obvious term for themselves. Since they were not Jews, they were Gentiles, but "Greeks" and "nations" were the normal terms for that, and most Greeks and most of the nations were idolators, "the world" which rejected the community as much as did "the Jews". "Disciples" could be clung to while the Gospel traditions were transmitted, expanded and written down, but the removal of the literary context leaves the term "disciple" very vague, for many non-Christian teachers had disciples. Thus "Christian" at length became the normal term, but it was not yet generally available. Hence the terminological peculiarity of "disciple" being the positive term for the community's identity in the Gospel, yet absent from 1 John. None the less, the fact of Gentile self-identification is clear. Whoever the Johannine community were, they knew they were not "the Jews", and this change in identity was the factor which opened the way for the development of the deity and incarnation of Jesus.

For a full understanding of this process, we must look in detail at the earlier development of christology (chs 6-9). We shall see that the continuous rise in the status and functions of Jesus was limited only by monotheism. This limitation was due to the fact that monotheism was an identity factor of the Jewish community. This is the restraint which was removed when Jews in the Johannine community had to make their identity decision. Jesus was already rising towards deity, as other Jewish messianic and intermediary figures might be perceived to do, because God was the highest form of being that could be contemplated, in both Judaism and in the Greco-Roman world. The removal of the Jewish restraint after A.D.70, leaving the Johannine community with Gentile self-identification, was the decisive step which ensured that Jesus was hailed as God, and genuinely treated as different in nature from the rest of us, not just exalted in functions.

Polytheism was not in any way involved in this process, because the rise in the status and function of Jesus gave no motivation for hailing Zeus, Moses or anyone else as God. On the contrary, the separate identity of the Christian community ensured that no such thought or feeling was entertained. Rather, the community took the most functional path of raising only Jesus to deity and doing so in such a way that it could perceive itself as having transformed traditional Jewish belief: "the Jews", on the other hand, were bound to perceive the community's faith as not monotheistic and consequently reject it, thereby excluding themselves from salvation. As the Johannine Jesus puts it, "No-one comes to the Father except by me" (14.6): "He who hates me also hates my Father" (15.23). As we have seen, chapters 5 and 10 both present the point of objection as the deity of Jesus. Moreover, the use of pre-existence in this way in the debate about Abraham in chapter 8, and the equation of sonship with deity, are both probably due to the setting of such debates in a situation where the Johannine community believed in the pre-existence, sonship and deity of Jesus alone. The subordinationist trend comes from the same social nexus, for it presents the Johannine claim that the Jewish God was wholly responsible for Jesus' mission. Hence for example in chapter 5, immediately following the evidently correct charge that Jesus was making himself equal to God, "The Son cannot do anything of himself except what he sees the Father doing.... For the Father does not judge anyone, but has given all judgement to the Son, so that everyone should honour the Son as they honour the Father. He who does not honour the Son does not honour the Father who sent him ... I cannot do anything of myself. I judge as I hear, and my judgment is righteous, because I do not seek my own will but the will of Him who sent me."

Thus the final redaction of John 1-20 gives us the first evidence of the deity and incarnation of Jesus. This development took place in the latter part of the first century in a community which had Gentile self-identification. This Gentile self-identification was a result of the crisis in Jewish identity which had been building up over the years as an increasing number of Gentiles joined the Christian community, and which was exacerbated by the war with the Romans and the destruction of Jerusalem. This Gentile self-identification was a necessary cause of belief in the deity of Jesus, a belief which could not be held as long as the Christian community was primarily Jewish. But why was Jesus the central identity factor of the Christian community in the first place? And what do we know of the earlier stages of development? To answer these questions, we must drive back though the synoptic Gospels to the Jesus of history, and trace the earlier stages of the christological developments which began during his ministry.

1. Cf E.M.Sidebottom, *The Christ of the Fourth Gospel* (1961); G.Sevenster, "Remarks on the humanity of Jesus in the Gospel and Letters of John", in Studies in John Presented to Professor Dr.J.N.Sevenster, NT.S 24 (1970), 185-93; W.A.Meeks, "The Man from Heaven in Johannine Sectarianism", *JBL* 91, 1972, 44-72; U.B.Müller, *Die Geschichte der Christologie in der johanneischen Gemeinde*, SBS 77 (1975); B.L.Mastin, "A Neglected Feature of the Christology of the Fourth Gospel", *NTS* 22, 1975-6, 32-51; M. de Jonge, *Jesus: Stranger from Heaven and Son of God* (1977); D.M.Smith, "The Presentation of Jesus in the Fourth Gospel", *Interp.* 31, 1977, 367-78; D.L.Mealand, "The Christology of the Fourth Gospel", *SJTh* 31, 1978, 449-63; C.K.Barrett, *Essays on John* (1982); J.D.G.Dunn, "Let John be John", in *Das Evangelium und die Evangelien,* ed P.Stuhlmacher (1983), 309-39; W.G.Loader, "The Central Structure of Johannine Christology", *NTS* 30, 1984, 188-216; P.Pokorny, "Der Irdische Jesus im Johannesevangelium", *NTS* 30, 1984, 217-28; R.Kysar, "The Fourth Gospel: Recent Research", *ANRW* II.25.3 (1985), 2389-2480, esp. 2443-9; W.E.Sproston, "'Is not this Jesus, the son of Joseph?' (John 6.42). Johannine Christology as a Challenge to Faith", *JSNT* 24, 1985, 77-97.
2. Cf infra, 166.
3. On this reading, cf Mastin, op.cit.
4. Cf. especially J.A.T. Robinson, " The New Look on the Fourth Gospel, *St Ev, TU* 73, 1959, 338-50, reprinted in J.A.T. Robinson, *Twelve New Testament Studies*, SBT 34 (1962), 94-106; C.H. Dodd *Historical Tradition in the Fourth Gospel* (1963); L.L.Morris, *Studies in the Fourth Gospel* (1969); L.L.Morris, *The Gospel*

according to John (1971); D.A.Carson, "Historical Tradition in the Fourth Gospel: After Dodd, What?", in *Gospel Perspectives,* ed R.T.France and D.Wenham, vol II (1981), 83-145; J.A.T.Robinson, *The Priority of John* (1985); J.F.Coakley, "The Anointing at Bethany and the Priority of John", *JBL* 107, 1988, 241-56. For a different view, J.L.Martyn, *History and Theology in the Fourth Gospel* (1968).

5. Cf infra 44-6, 106, 148-9.

6. On the Johannine epistles, infra 156-9.

7. Pseudepigraphy among Jewish people has been regarded as especially characteristic of Apocalyptic, and a more correct understanding is still emerging. Cf particularly M.Smith, "Pseudepigraphy in the Israelite Literary Tradition", with discussion, in *Pseudepigraphie I. Entretiens sur l'Antiquité Classique* 18, 1971, 191-227; M.Hengel, "Anonymität, Pseudepigraphie und 'Literarische Fälschung' in der jüdisch-hellenistischen Literatur", with discussion, ibid., 231-329; I.Gruenwald, "Jewish Apocalyptic Literature", *ANRW* II.19.1 (1979), 89-118, esp 97-102; D.G.Meade, *Pseudonymity and Canon* WUNT 39 (1986).

8. I cannot discuss here detailed source and redaction theories, none of which I have found convincing. Cf Kysar, op.cit., 2391-2411.

9. For this and other reasons, there have been numerous attempts to argue that the term "Jews" in John means something else, especially "Judaeans" and "Jewish leaders". A critical discussion of the secondary literature cannot be offered here. Cf especially W. A. Meeks, "Am I a Jew? Johannine Christianity and Judaism", in J. Neusner (ed), *Christianity, Judaism and Other Greco-Roman Cults: Studies for Morton Smith,* vol I (1975), 163-86; M.Lowe, "Who were the Ioudaioi?", *NT* 18 (1976) 101-30; J.Townsend, "The Gospel of John and the Jews: The Story of a Religious Divorce", in A.T.Davies (ed), *Anti-Semitism and the Foundations of Christianity* (1979) 72-97; U.C. von Wahlde, "The Johannine 'Jews': A Critical Survey", *NTS* 28 (1982) 32-60; J.E.Leibig, "John and 'the Jews': Theological Antisemitism in the Fourth Gospel", *JES* 20 (1983) 209-34; J. Ashton, "The Identity and Function of the Ioudaioi in the Fourth Gospel", *NT* 27 (1985) 40-75; S.Freyne, "Vilifying the Other and Defining the Self. Matthew's and John's Anti-Jewish Polemic in Focus", in J. Neusner (ed), *To See Ourselves as Others See Us. Christians, Jews, "Others" in Late Antiquity* (1985),117-43.

10. The suggestion that the "other sheep" are diaspora Jews is remote from John's environment. For such interpretation of this and similar passages, J.A.T.Robinson, "The destination and purpose of St John's Gospel", *NTS* 6, 1959-60, 117-31 reprinted in J.A.T.Robinson, *Twelve New Testament Studies* SBT 34 (1962), 107-25; J.A.T.Robinson, *The Priority of John* (1985), 60ff. See further, in addition to the standard commentaries, O.Hofius, "Die Sammlung der Heiden zur Herde Israels (John 10.16, 11.51ff)", *ZNW* 58, 1967, 289-91; S.Pancaro, "'People of God' in St John's Gospel", *NTS* 16, 1969-70, 114-29; H.B.Kossen, "Who were the Greeks of John XII.20?", in A.Geyser et al., *Studies in John :Presented to Dr J.N.Sevenster on the occasion of his Seventieth Birthday* NT.S XXIV (1970), 97-110; S.Pancaro, "The Relationship of the Church to Israel in the Gospel of St John", *NTS* 21, 1974-5, 396-405; J.Painter, "The Church and Israel in the Gospel of John: A Response", *NTS* 25, 1978-9, 103-12.

11. For full discussion, W.Horbury, "The Benediction of the *Minim* and Early Jewish-Christian Controversy", *JThS* 33, 1982, 19-61. Cf also Townsend, op.cit.; F.Manns, "L'Evangile de Jean, réponse chrétienne aux décisions de Jabne", *SBFLA* 30, 1980, 47-92; R.Kimelman, *"Birkat Ha-Minim* and the Lack of Evidence for an anti-

Christian Jewish Prayer in Late Antiquity" in E.P.Sanders et al., *Jewish and Christian Self-Definition*, vol 2 (1981), 226-44; F.Manns, "L'Evangile de Jean, réponse chrétienne aux decisions de Jabne. Note complémentaire", *SBFLA* 32, 1982, 85-108; S.Freyne, "Vilifying the Other and Defining the Self: Matthew's and John's Anti-Jewish Polemic in Focus", in J.Neusner (ed), *To See Ourselves as Others See Us. Christians, Jews, "Others" in Late Antiquity* (1985), 117-43; W.Horbury, "Extirpation and excommunication", *VT* 35, 1985, 13-38.

12. See further infra, 121-3.

13. Cf J.Neusner, "'Pharisaic' - Rabbinic Judaism: A Clarification", *HR* 12, 1973, 150-70 =*Early Rabbinic Judaism* SJLA 13 (1975), 50-70, ="The Formation of Rabbinic Judaism: Yavneh (Jamnia) from A.D.70 to 100," *ANRW* II.19.2 (1979), 17-42; S.J.D.Cohen, "The Significance of Yavneh: Pharisees, Rabbis and the End of Jewish Sectarianism", *HUCA* 55, 1984, 27-53.

14. Supra 13, 15-6.

15. Supra, 16.

16. Cf E.G.Turner, "Tiberius Julius Alexander", *JRS* 44, 1954, 54-64.

17. Cf supra, 23-4.

18. Cf esp Martyn, Manns, Muller, Townsend, op.cit.; J.L.Martyn, "Glimpses into the History of the Johannine Community: From its Origins through the Period of Its Life in which The Fourth Gospel was Composed", in M. de Jonge (ed), *L'Evangile de Jean. Sources, rédaction, théologie*, BEThL 44, (1977), 149-75, also J.L.Martyn, *The Gospel of John in Christian History* (1978), chapter 3; R.E.Brown, *The Community of the Beloved Disciple* (1979).

19. Cf especially R.E.Brown, op.cit.

20. Supra, 13-6.

21. Cf supra, 26.

Chapter 4
Messiah, Son of God and Son of Man

1. Introduction

The titles of Jesus have been a significant aspect of orthodox christology for centuries. Much recent scholarship[1] has however argued that Jesus himself did not use the most important of them, except for "son of man", which is exceptionally difficult to understand. The purpose of this chapter is to examine the three major titles found in the synoptic tradition, to determine how far they help us to recover Jesus' understanding of himself, and how far they are developments for which the early church was responsible.

2. Messiah

"Christ", the Greek translation of "messiah", or "anointed", was virtually a name of Jesus already in the New Testament period. It is very common in the Pauline epistles, and it is used of Jesus in every New Testament document except 3 John. Our oldest Gospel sources, however, display a different picture. Mark's seven occurrences do not include a single example of Jesus using the term with reference to himself, and the word "Christ" does not occur in Q. That takes us straight to two of our main conclusions: Jesus did not apply the term "messiah" to himself, and the early church applied it to him abundantly.

Did Jesus then not believe that he was "the Messiah"? Traditional scholarship has affirmed that he did, and has used Mark's Gospel as the basis of an explanation of why he did not use the term itself. The confession of Peter has been fundamental to this view. In response to Jesus' question, "Who do *you* say that I am?", Peter is reported to have declared "You are the Christ" (Mk 8.29). Mark does not record Jesus saying either "I am" or "I am not", but continues "And he sternly charged them to tell no-one about him." Anderson expresses briefly, though with caution, the essence of the traditional view: "On the lips of Peter the title 'Christ' would have referred to the messianic Son of David.... The coming of a Davidic Messiah, who would restore the political fortunes of Israel and establish her national supremacy over the world, was a widespread hope.... The political implications of the title probably explain why Jesus does not appear to have appropriated it during his ministry."[2] Many scholars have argued that the "political implications" of "the title" constituted the sole and sufficient reason for Jesus not to have used it. He did not want to be misunderstood, he did not want to cause a Zealot revolt. Therefore he did not openly accept the title until the time of his humiliation when he could safely and rightly claim it in front of those who would not believe him, let alone revolt for him: "Again the high priest asked him and said to him, 'Are you the Christ, the Son of the Blessed?' But Jesus said, 'I am, and you will see the Son of man sitting on the right of Power and coming with the clouds of heaven'" (Mk 14.61-62). Even here, the acceptance of the title "messiah" or "Christ" is at once modified by Jesus' characteristic use of the term "Son of man".

This view has often been challenged from a more radical perspective. In view of the absence of the term from the earliest sources of Jesus' teaching and the repeated injunctions to silence in Mark's Gospel, it has been argued that Jesus did not believe that he was the Messiah, and that the "messianic secret" was a device used by Mark to explain why Jesus was not recognised and confessed as Messiah during his ministry.[3] The radical view has never been able to explain why the church proclaimed Jesus as Messiah so soon, with a term which was clearly widespread, and the conservative view has been rendered increasingly vulnerable by recent research.[4] What is now clear is that "the messiah" was not a title in Second Temple Judaism, and the term "messiah" or "anointed" on its own was not specific enough to refer to the messianic son of David, nor indeed to any single individual at all. Anointing was not confined to Davidic kings: priests and prophets could be anointed as well. For example, at 1 Kings 19.16 Elijah is instructed by God to anoint Elisha as a prophet instead of himself: at Leviticus 4.3 the high priest is called "the anointed priest"; and at Isaiah 45.1 the Persian king Cyrus is referred to as "his anointed", that is, God's anointed. Thus it is natural that in the Second Temple period both the future Davidic king and other figures could be referred to with the term "messiah", or "anointed". For example, the Qumran community expected an eschatological high priest as well as a king of David's line, and they could refer to them both together as "anointed ones" (or "messiahs") "of Aaron and Israel"(1 QS IX,11). Old Testament prophets could be referred to as "anointed ones" (1 QM XI,7, cf CD VI,1), while in 11Q Melchizedek a figure subordinate to Melchizedek is referred to as "anointed".

We must deduce from this general usage that anyone who wanted to refer to the Davidic messiah would have to do more than use the word "messiah" to make his meaning clear. For example, "Whenever Israel rules, there shall [not] fail to be a descendant of David upon the throne. For 'the ruler's staff' is the covenant of kingship, [and the tribes] of Israel are the 'feet', until the messiah of Righteousness, the branch of David, comes" (4Q Patr, commenting on Gen 49.10). Here, after setting up "descendant of David upon the throne" with great clarity in the context, the author still felt the need for a run of full four words to identify "the messiah of Righteousness, the Branch of David". In the face of evidence like this, we should interpret in the most straightforward and literal manner two well-known facts about the usage of "messiah" in Jewish documents of the Second Temple period. Firstly, the term is not commonly used with reference to the future redeemer of Israel: secondly, the absolute title "the Messiah" does not occur in non-Christian Jewish documents at all. The reason for this is that "anointed" or "messiah" was not specific enough to refer to the

Davidic king without further qualification. This situation changed after the destruction of Jerusalem in A.D.70, when Judaism no longer had any prophets nor any anointed high priests officiating in the Temple, and her hopes of deliverance crystallized around the traditional expectation of a future Davidic king: after years of this, Jews did eventually call this figure who would deliver them "King Messiah", or even "the Messiah."

This provides us with a straightforward explanation of the fact that Jesus did not apply the term "messiah" to himself. The term was not sufficiently meaningful on its own, and it was not necessary for a figure who was playing a fundamental role in the salvation of Israel to produce a longer formulation containing it. We must therefore accept the radical view that passages such as Mark 8.29-30 and Mark 14.61-62 were produced by the early church. Peter cannot have said "You are the Anointed" as a major confession of Jesus' position because the term "the Anointed" was not specific enough to be used in such a confession. The confession has however an excellent *Sitz im Leben* in the early church. The messianic secret in Mark's Gospel solves the problem of why this central term is absent from Jesus' own teaching. Peter's confession corrects the authentic and favourable verdicts of outsiders that Jesus was Elijah or one of the prophets, and balances the account of Jesus' rebuke of Peter in the following verses. Mark's welding together of these scenes does not go further than the limits conventional among ancient historians, who put words into the mouths of their characters when they knew more or less what they must have said.[5]

A similar kind of explanation must account for Mark 14.61-62. The High Priest is said to have asked "Are you the Messiah, the Son of the Blessed?" This question is hardly specific enough to have been used like this, but it has an excellent *Sitz im Leben* in the early church, for Jesus' reply "I am" has him claim both the Church's major titles for himself, thus bringing to an end Mark's "messianic secret" which had characterized his ministry. The rest of Jesus' reply is a *midrash* created on the basis of Daniel 7.13, Psalm 110.1 and probably Zechariah 12.10, and when we look at the term "son of man", we shall see that there are other reasons for not attributing it to him.[6] It contains nothing to account for his being found guilty on a charge of blasphemy under Jewish law (cf Mk 14.63-64). But we know from the epistles that the early church searched the scriptures for evidence of Jesus' speedy return, and Jewish opponents of Christianity will have found Jesus' reply blasphemous in the popular sense of that term. We must deduce that there was no authentic tradition of Jesus' condemnation because none of his sympathisers were there. Mark has therefore put into his mouth the sort of thing he knew he must have said.

One question remains outstanding. If the radical view is right in this instance, how do we explain the widespread and early application of "Christ" to Jesus? It is not sufficient to refer here to Jesus' condemnation as "king of the Jews" (cf Mk 15.2ff, esp 15.26).[7] This was the "charge" fixed on his cross, and it represents a successful charge of sedition before the Roman governor. We should probably also accept the authenticity of Mark 15.32. Jesus' opponents used the term "anointed" in a way that makes perfectly good sense. In their expression "the anointed, the king of Israel", the words "king of Israel" provide precisely that definition so conspicuously absent from passages such as Mark 8.29. This is not however sufficient to explain why the disciples should have taken up the term and used it so much after Jesus' death and resurrection. On the contrary, only the general use of "anointed" noted above prevents this from being a reason why they should have avoided it. A full solution to this question requires an overall theory to explain why christology developed.[8] We shall see that the driving force is not specific to the term "messiah" or "Christ", but rather of the general kind which necessitated the use of whatever term the community could find, and it is this which explains why there are no particular features of Jesus or "messiah" that seem to demand the early use of "messiah" as a title for him.

3. Son of God

All four Gospels use the term "the Son", or "the Son of God", as a major christological title. We have seen that this is secondary in the fourth Gospel, whose 28 examples belong to the christology of the Johannine community.[9] I noted also the rarity of the term in our earliest sources: Jesus refers to himself as "the Son" only once in Mark, and three times in a single saying in Q. The synoptic evangelists have more examples than are found in the teaching of Jesus in Mark and Q, but fewer than John. Mark himself has seven examples, Luke 12, and Matthew 17. These basic facts further clarify the tendency of the tradition to insert a title which Christians were using by the time that the Gospels were written. Matthew can be seen at work: four of his 17 examples are inserted into passages of Mark which he largely copied (Mt 14.33; 16.16; 27.40,43). Thus the observable tendency of the tradition confirms the evidence of the distribution of this term, and its known *Sitz im Leben* in the early church, to show that as a christological title it belongs to the early church rather than the Jesus of history.

These overall factors must not be lost sight of when we consider the two sayings which are attributed to Jesus in Mark and Q. Both use the term "the Son" in an absolute sense as an exalted christological title. If Jesus had held this belief and found this usage appropriate, he was bound to have used the term more often, and a church which can be shown to have increased such usage within the synoptic tradition would not have failed to transmit a larger number of genuine sayings. Moreover, both sayings have an excellent *Sitz im Leben* in the early church. Mark 13.32 arose from the delay of the parousia: "But concerning that day or that hour no-one knows, neither the angels in heaven nor the Son, but only the Father." In its present context this saying clearly refers to the time of the End, and it is difficult to see that it could ever have referred to anything else. The standard defence of its authenticity is that the church would not have produced a saying which asserts the ignorance of Jesus.[10] This defence fails to take seriously both the distribution of the term "the Son" and the situation with which the church was confronted. We know from the epistles that some Christians had been expecting the End to come immediately for some years. In this respect they continued the expectation of Jesus himself, and we shall see that this view arises naturally out of the dynamics of Jewish expectation of the kingdom.[11] Such expectation often had to cope with the fact that God had not intervened as people had hoped. The Qumran community reacted to this situation by interpreting the prophetic tradition with mystified reverence: "God told Habakkuk to write down what would happen to the last generation, but he did not make known to him the completion of the end ... the end time will be prolonged, and will exceed all that the prophets have said, for the mysteries of God are astonishing...."(1QpHab VII, 1-8). Here the community has reacted to the incorrectness of its own predictions by supposing that Habakkuk could not tell the time of the End and that the prophets did not get it right. Their complete reverence for scriptural prophets could not prevent them from doing this, because of the obvious fact that the final age had not come to an end.

The church's reaction was of a basically similar kind, but the church had a single figure central to its identity, and they transmitted his words as well as those of scripture. It was these words which predicted the End soon, without giving any precise date: the church was therefore bound to deduce that the Son had not known the time, provided only that they could face this information. In those days, the Son's ignorance was much easier to face than the delay of his parousia. No-one had yet produced the idea that the Son knew everything. The delay of the parousia, however, confronted the church inescapably. Mark 13.32 meets this as well as possible. The Son is mentioned after the angels as the highest possible figure, the use of the absolute term "the Son" balancing, as well as could be, the assertion of his ignorance. The view that the church would not have produced a saying which asserted the ignorance of Jesus is remote from the christology of the earliest period. Matthew, faced likewise with the delay of the parousia, accepted the ignorance of the Son into Matthew 24.36, but Luke dropped the saying; having dealt otherwise with the problem of the delay of the parousia, he could afford not to believe in the Son's ignorance.

Matthew 11.27/Luke 10.22 is also untypical of the teaching of Jesus. The Matthean form may be translated, "All things have been given to me by my Father, and no-one knows the Son except the Father, nor does anyone know the Father except the Son and anyone to whom the Son wishes to reveal him." As with Mark 13.32, the use of the absolute term "the Son" shows that the saying has its *Sitz im Leben* in the early church. Some aspects of it are strongly reminiscent of the fourth Gospel, especially the correlation of the Son with the Father and the position of the Son as the unique and necessary revealer of the Father. These aspects probably indicate some use of the Wisdom tradition.[12] At Job 28, Wisdom "is concealed from the eyes of all the living" (vs 21), while "God understands the way to it and he knows its place"(vs 23). If Job 28 tells us that only God knows Wisdom, Wisdom 9 tells us that only Wisdom knows God: "For which man shall know the counsel of God?... For the reasonings of mortals are worthless and our ideas are fallible.... Who got to know your counsel unless you gave him Wisdom...?" (Wsd 9.13,14,17). Matthew 11.28-30 continues with another passage which has a very close parallel at Sirach 51.23-27.

Parallels of this kind do not however provide a proper explanation of the origin of Matthew 11.27/Luke 10.22. For this, we must look to its function. It declares that knowledge of God is impossible except through Jesus. This view does not have a satisfactory *Sitz im Leben* in the teaching of the historical Jesus, for it necessarily implies that diaspora Jews did not know God. After the successful Gentile mission, however, one of the main needs of the churches was the belief that Christians rather than Jews formed the covenant community, and hence that Jesus was essential for salvation. In that setting, this is what the saying expresses. Christians know the Son, and therefore also the Father, while Jews who do not know the Son do not know the Father either. Non-Christian Jews are therefore rejected. We shall see that the term "the Son" became a significant christological title at the time of the Pauline epistles, when the churches contained both Jews and Christians. We must infer that this saying is a product of the early church, and not a very early one. The diverse forms of Matthew and Luke show that it was still the object of creative editing when it was written down.[13]

While these two major sayings are not authentic, there is some evidence that this term began to be used during the historic ministry. For example, at Mark 5.7, a very difficult demoniac declares, "What have you to do with me, Jesus son of God Most High? I adjure you by God, do not torment me." Here the demoniac's term for Jesus, "son of God Most High", fits perfectly well into the use of terms such as "son of God" for wise and righteous individuals.[14] Such evidence is sufficient to show that Jesus could have been called a son of God by anyone who thought that he was a particularly righteous person: given his ability as an exorcist, people who believed themselves possessed by evil might well use the term of so obviously holy and effective a figure. The early church, on the other hand, was not likely to put any declaration of its own in the mouth of demoniacs unless it had a tradition of such declarations. The evidence of the narrative of Mark 5.7 is amplified by the summary statement of 3.11, and the confession of the centurion at Mark 15.39 is approximately at the same level. These examples are from the lips of outsiders. The only possible genuine use by Jesus is the purely parabolic Mark 12.6.

We must conclude that the beginning of the use of terms such as "son of God" goes back to the period of the historic ministry, but that we still have to account for its development into a title used to indicate Jesus' unique status. As with the term "messiah", we shall find that the reasons for this development are not specific to the term "son of God", but belong rather to the community's need to develop its central identity factor.

4. Son of Man

The term "son of man" is of fundamental importance for our understanding both of Jesus himself and of the christology of the earliest church.[15] As the Gospels now stand it is much the commonest title of Jesus, and it is the term which he characteristically uses to refer to himself. It occurs 69 times in the synoptic Gospels, and 13 times in John. Our oldest Gospel has 14 examples in the teaching of Jesus, and when all parallels are discounted, the three synoptic Gospels still produce 38 independent sayings. At least some of them must go back to Jesus, for the following reasons. The term occurs very frequently: it is found in all Gospel sources - Mark, Q, the separate traditions of both Matthew and Luke, John, and some non-canonical traditions: the early sources attribute it almost exclusively to Jesus himself: it is not normal Greek, a fact which we can explain only if it originated as a translation of the Aramaic expression *bar nash* or *bar nasha:* and the early church did not use it in any of its confessions nor in any New Testament epistle. This combination of reasons should be regarded as decisive: Jesus certainly used the term "son of man".

So far, so good, but we cannot go further without meeting serious problems. The Aramaic term *bar nash(a)*, "son of man", was a normal term for "man": further, it now seems clear that it was not also a title in the Judaism of the time of Jesus.[16] The mere fact that it was a normal term for man means that sentences containing *bar nash(a)* would not have sufficient referring power to denote a single individual, unless the context made this reference clear. This means that *bar nash(a)* was a generally unlikely term for an author or a social group to select for use as a major title. The general improbability that *bar nash(a)* would be selected for use as a messianic title is supported by the empirical data: there is no satisfactory documentary evidence that any social group took this improbable step.

In the Gospels, however, the term "son of man" does not function as a normal term for "man" at all: it functions as a title, and it generally refers to Jesus alone. Jesus cannot have used the term like this. If it was not a title, he cannot have used it to refer to a known figure, "the Son of Man", whether he is supposed to have identified himself with such a figure or not. Nor can he have produced it as a title for the first time. The fact that it was a normal term for "man" means that he is unlikely to have wanted to use it as a title. Had he used it as a title, he would have had to make it clear from the context that he was doing so, but the "son of man" sayings in the Gospels do not do this. Had he been obscure enough to use it as a sort of title without making clear that he was doing so, his sentences would not have made proper sense or would have made the wrong sense, his disciples would have been puzzled, and we should have traces of this in the tradition.[17] In fact, some "son of man" sayings are not satisfactory sentences when they are reconstructed in the original Aramaic, but people appear to understand them without difficulty as references to Jesus alone.

Mark 8.31 illustrates several of these points: "And he began to teach them that the son of man must suffer many things, and be rejected by the elders and the chief priests and the scribes, and be killed, and after three days rise. And he spoke the word openly." This saying cannot be turned into a satisfactory Aramaic sentence. It contains a general term for man which does not refer clearly to Jesus, yet it makes precise reference to the elders and chief priests and scribes, that is, to the specific circumstances of Jesus' death and not to the death of men in general. Peter is none the less portrayed as understanding this saying very clearly. "And Peter took him on one side and began to rebuke him. But he turned and, seeing his disciples, rebuked Peter and said, 'Get behind me, Satan, for your mind is not set on the will of God but on the concerns of men.'" So serious a criticism of Peter would not be found in Mark's Gospel if it did not represent approximately what Jesus said. But if Peter's reaction is authentic, he must have had something like Mark 8.31 to react to. There are, therefore, good reasons why Mark 8.31 must be authentic, and good reasons why it cannot be. This is how the "son of man" problem has appeared insoluble, with the straightforward application of apparently firm criteria leading to opposite conclusions from the equally straightforward application of other apparently firm criteria.

The key to a solution was provided by Vermes in his seminal paper, first published in 1967.[18] Vermes argued that, in addition to being a normal term for "man", the Aramaic *bar nasha,* "son of man", was also a conventional substitute for the first person pronoun, "I". This would, in a sense, solve the problem, in that it would explain why Jesus used the term "son of man" to refer to himself. Vermes' interpretation of the Aramaic evidence has not, however, convinced most scholars who can read the Aramaic sources. Also, if this were no more than a well-established Aramaic idiom, we might reasonably have expected bilingual translators to render *bar nash(a)* with the Greek word for "I", but there are only two known examples of this (Mt 10.32-3) to set against all the "son of man" sayings in the Gospels. I have therefore proposed a more complex theory which is partly based on the evidence which Vermes collected and presented.[19] The rest of this discussion is an updated summary of this theory.

Genuine sayings will be examined first. These belong to an Aramaic idiom, in accordance with which a speaker might use a general statement primarily in order to say something about himself. In general, he might do this in order to avoid sounding arrogant, self-centred, unusual or humiliated. We have similar idioms in English, using "a man", "we", "you", "one", "everyone" and other terms of this kind. Aramaic examples include a saying of R.Simeon ben Yohai, who lived in a cave for 13 years at the end of the Bar-Cochba revolt. When he was wondering whether it was safe to come out, he saw birds being hunted. Some were captured, others escaped, and he declared, "A bird is not caught without the will of heaven; how much less the soul of a son of man". (Gen.R.79,6). R.Simeon then emerged from the cave. It follows that he intended to apply the statement to himself, but it does not follow that it is nothing more than a substitute for the first person pronoun. On the contrary, the first sentence, "A bird is not caught without the will of heaven", is quite clearly a general statement: the second must be interpreted in the same way, because we already know that "son of man" was a general term for "man", and this ensures that "how much less the soul of a son of man" balances and follows from the general statement about birds. The general statement may be used to refer to more people than the speaker. In this version of the story, R.Simeon has his son with him, and since they both emerge from the cave, the general statement is clearly intended to refer to them both. The idiom may therefore be defined as follows: In Aramaic, a speaker might use a general statement, in which the general term was *bar nash(a),* "son of man", in order to say something about himself or a group of people including himself. He would normally do so in order to avoid being and sounding unduly arrogant, self-centred or humiliated.

Aramaic examples of this idiom may use either the indefinite state, *bar nash,* or the definite state, *bar nasha.* Examples translated into Greek in the Gospels consequently use the Greek definite article, which may be either genuinely definite, the equivalent of the English definite article "the", or it may be generic. Owing to differences in the structure of Greek and Aramaic, this results in two articles in Greek, one before "son" and one before "man". In the following examples from the Gospels, I use the indefinite English article "a", to make the point that the original sayings were general statements: there is no way that they can be translated without some distortion of this kind.[20] The conventional use of "the" for the first article, before "son", is merely a conventional distortion. I follow the convention of omitting the second article, before "man", for this is clearly generic.

This idiom accounts for about a dozen sayings in the synoptic Gospels. One of the more straightforward examples is Mark 2.28, which concludes a dispute between Jesus and the Pharisees.[21] Some of Jesus' disciples had been going along a path through the fields, plucking the grains of corn, an action to be expected of poor and hungry people taking *peah*. Jesus' disciples were however doing this on the sabbath, and for this reason the Pharisees objected. Jesus warded off the Pharisees' criticism with two arguments, the second of which may be rendered, "The Sabbath was created for man, not man for the Sabbath. So, you see, a son of man is master even of the Sabbath!" The general nature of Mark 2.28 is guaranteed by the general statement of 2.27. This idiom, in which a general statement is deliberately used to divert attention from the speaker, is the only use of "son of man" that makes proper sense of both sentences. Otherwise, the statement that a son of man, or the Son of Man, is lord or master of the sabbath does not follow from the obviously general declaration that the sabbath was created for man, not man for the sabbath. This declaration looks back to God's purpose at creation, when he made man effectively lord of the creation, provided that he remains obedient to God (cf Gen 1.26,28; Ps 8.6-9; 2 Esdras 6.54; 2 Bar 14.18). Thus the general statement of Mark 2.28 includes the disciples, who as masters of the sabbath were entitled to take *peah* on it. It is an indirect way of making clear that Jesus did have the authority to take the halakhic decision that they were entitled to take *peah* on the sabbath. Jesus' general statement is a dramatic one, but no more dramatic than that of Rabbi Aqiba, who settled another small point of sabbath law with the declaration "Profane the Sabbath, and don't depend on people"(bT Shabb 118a/bT Pes 112a). Thus at Mark 2.28 Jesus declared his right to fend off unwanted sabbath *halakhah*, indirectly claiming his prophetic ability to interpret the will of God, but not using any christological title.

A more serious conflict with orthodox Jews arose over Jesus' healing ministry. Scribes who came from Jerusalem accused him of casting out demons by means of Beelzebub. Jesus replied in a number of sharp sayings, one of which may be reconstructed from the differing versions in Mark and Q, the strongest possible combination of sources for a dispute which followed inevitably from the differing life-stances of Jesus and the most orthodox Jews: "Everyone who speaks a word against a son of man shall be forgiven, and everyone who speaks a word against the Spirit of holiness shall not be forgiven" (cf Mk 3.28, Mt 12.32/Lk 12.10).[22]

Jesus was famous for his preaching of forgiveness to sinners, and the first part of this saying, "Everyone who speaks a word against a son of man shall be forgiven", has a straightforward general level of meaning. At the same time, this part of the saying was spoken with reference to Jesus himself, and therefore appears to offer forgiveness even to his most vigorous opponents. In fact it sets up the second part, in which the orthodox attack on his healing ministry is repudiated in the strongest possible terms, yet without directly mentioning it. "Everyone who speaks a word against the Spirit of holiness" refers to anyone who criticizes God in action. This is precisely what Jesus believed that orthodox Jews were doing when they accused him of casting out demons by means of Beelzebub. Jesus effectively told them that they had committed an unforgivable sin. His use of indirect expressions, "everyone" instead of "you" or "scribes and Pharisees", "son of man" instead of "me", "the Spirit of holiness" instead of "God, who has given me power to cast out these demons", all are due to the highly charged nature of the situation, which led Jesus to eschew direct polemic, and to make a statement which would have commanded widespread agreement at its general level. Its application to him will not have been in doubt, and, as at Mark 2.28, there is an implicit claim that Jesus, unlike his orthodox opponents, was acting with divine authority, a fundamental claim made without the use of any christological title.

Another saying which can be reconstructed from varying forms in Mark and Q also dealt with commitment and opposition to Jesus' ministry. "Everyone who confesses me before men, a son of man will confess him before the angels of God, and everyone who denies me before men, a son of man will deny him before the angels of God"(cf Lk 12.8-9/Mt 10.32-3, Mk 8.38).[23] This saying uses the imagery of the divine court. It was conceived in terms modelled on a human court, so it assumes that individual people stand up and testify for or against anyone who is judged. The saying is more direct than the previous example, in that Jesus uses the first person pronoun for himself as the object of witness, but he uses a general statement to say indirectly that he will respond to earthly witness now by speaking for or against people when the divine court meets. Thus the saying indirectly assumes, without using any title, that Jesus will soon be one of the most powerful people in the universe, but he avoided saying this directly by making a general statement, which assimilates his position in the divine court to that of a witness like everyone else.

One of the Q examples of this idiom belongs to a more mundane level of experience: "Jackals have holes, and the birds of the air have roosts, but a son of man has nowhere to lay his head"(Mt 8.20/Lk 9.58).[24] This saying belongs to the migratory phase of Jesus' ministry, and contrasts the divine provision of natural haunts for animals with the lack of such provision for men, who have to build houses to live in. The reference will have been in the first place to Jesus himself, for he had nowhere to go as he moved about, and he could not provide for his disciples. This would be a humiliating thing to say, and consequently Jesus used an indirect way of saying it. The general level of the saying also takes in the disciples, especially the one who had just declared that he would follow Jesus wherever he went (Mt 8.19/Lk 9.57).

These four examples illustrate Jesus' use of this idiom. He used it in the same way as such idioms generally are used, to declare his own exalted status and function only indirectly, and to avoid direct mention of a humiliating situation. Both these feelings were involved in his predictions of his death and resurrection.[25] It is simplest to start at the Last Supper, where Mark 14.21 goes straight back into Aramaic without much modification: "A son of man goes as it is written of him, but woe to that man by whom a son of man is betrayed: it would be good for that man if he had not been born." The first general statement, "a son of man goes as it is written of him" depends on the universal fact that people die, recorded in scriptural passages such as Genesis 3.19 and Isaiah 40.6. At this general level, the "son of man" statement is obviously true, and the function of its being obviously true was to make it easier for his disciples to accept the application of it to Jesus himself. At a second level, the saying is a prediction of Jesus' forthcoming death. There should be no doubt that Jesus did interpret scriptural passages of himself and his ministry, though we do not have much reliable evidence as to which ones. It is not difficult to suggest some possible interpretations.[26] For example, Mark 14.18 implies the use of Psalm 41, and Jesus might have seen God's support and vindication of him in this understanding of the Hebrew text of Psalm 118.14-17: "The Lord is my strength and song, and he is for me, for Jesus.... The right hand of the Lord raises up.... I shall not die because I shall live." This was one of the psalms set for singing at Passover (cf Mk 14.26).

The first part of Mark 14.21 also helps to set up the condemnation of Judas Iscariot. This begins with a second "son of man" saying: "Woe to that man by whom a son of man is betrayed". This can be understood as a general condemnation of traitors, a highly functional level of meaning because it would command almost universal assent. The application of this saying to Jesus himself will however have been perfectly clear. The verse ends with a quite indirect condemnation of Judas: "it would be good for him if that man had not been born." This is also perfectly comprehensible in the general terms of the previous sentence - it is generally accepted that traitors should come to a sticky end. Throughout this verse, the general level of meaning functions to enable the vigorous condemnation of Judas Iscariot to be accepted without objection, and the references to Jesus' own death are made easier to mention by means of the two idiomatic uses of the term "son of man".

We can now return to Mark 8.31. It is not possible to reconstruct a satisfactory Aramaic version of this. The editing of the predictions by Matthew and Luke shows a pronounced tendency to expand them with reminiscences of the passion, and we may suspect the same tendency in some of the other predictions in Mark, notably 10.33-4. We must therefore see whether we can reconstruct an original general statement which could have been modified in the same way to produce Mark 8.31. I have suggested something on the following lines: "A son of man will die, and after three days he will rise." This is a sound general statement. The first part of it is obviously true, because we all die, and this is the key to its function. It is because we all know that all of us die that Jesus' first effort to tell the disciples that he intended to die is couched in such a general form. In this situation, reference to resurrection was essential. Death might be interpreted as rejection by God: resurrection was the culturally relevant form of vindication. "After three days" is both a general term for a short interval, and long enough, in a literal sense, to ensure that he was really dead.[27] When this prediction was translated into Greek, "die" was rendered as "be killed" because Jesus was killed. The rest of Mark 8.31 consists of details added from the events themselves, or from scripture.

A third authentic prediction of Jesus' death is to be found at Mark 10.45: "a son of man comes not to be served but to serve, that is, to give his life as a ransom for many."[28] In Aramaic, "come" was used with reference to the purpose of life, and "give one's life" could cover devoting or risking one's life, not only being killed. The saying has a general level of meaning which fits well into its context: the purpose of life is service, even to the point of death. The application to Jesus will also have been clear, the idiomatic use of "son of man" being set up in the context. Jesus had just predicted his death indirectly at Mark 10.38, when he challenged the sons of Zebedee, "Can you drink the cup which I drink, or be baptised with the baptism with which I am baptised?" Since they accepted this challenge, the "son of man" saying necessarily includes a reference to them as well, but this in no way undermines its clarity as a prediction of Jesus' death.

This gives us three authentic "son of man" predictions from which Mark 9.31 and 10.33-4 have been formed. This mixing in the tradition is understandable, for the clarification of sayings by means of scripture, tradition and the actual events was natural in a culture accustomed to midrashic expansion. Mark needed to record predictions of Jesus' death. It was a drastic event which could have been interpreted as God's condemnation of him: the only alternative to that view was the positive evaluation of it that we find in the early church. We must deduce from the arrangement of Jesus' teaching in Mark's Gospel that Mark did not know when most of the teaching was given. He therefore placed the predictions which he had, and perhaps developed and clarified, at regular stages in the build-up towards the final events. Thus the additional and clarified predictions have an excellent *Sitz im Leben* in the post-Easter church, which needed their content, and in the composition of Mark's Gospel, which needed the dramatic build-up of the series. The "son of man" passion predictions therefore give us two insights. They show us part of the origin of christology in Jesus' declaration of his forthcoming death, its significance as an atoning sacrifice, and his confidence in his vindication by God. The second insight is into the work of the early church, who took up the predictions in the light of scripture and subsequent events, expanding them in the manner of Jewish *midrash* to make their meaning clearer, and arranging them in a feasible sequence in the structure of our earliest Gospel.

The predictions of the parousia give us more insight into the work of the early church. Some are patently not authentic. For example, Luke 17.24 cannot be reconstructed in feasible Aramaic. There are however predictions of the parousia which make use of Daniel 7.13, and the authenticity of some of them must be seriously considered. Mark 14.62 is usually regarded as the outstanding example. In response to the High Priest's question, Jesus replied, "I am, and you will see the Son of Man sitting on the right of Power and coming with the clouds of heaven." Here Daniel 7.13 is combined with Psalm 110.1, and perhaps with Zechariah 12.10. While the Aramaic is not that of the idiom which we have largely been considering, it is feasible Aramaic. A virtual quotation from a scriptural text referred by a speaker to himself cannot be excluded as unidiomatic in a culture where it was relatively normal to apply scriptural texts to contemporary and future events. The saying should none the less be regarded as the midrashic work of the early church, for reasons which I have set out at length elsewhere and summarize now.[29]

Firstly, this is one of a small group of sayings which speak of the "Son of Man coming". Only this group of parousia sayings can be authentic, because only if there is a clear reference to the scriptural text (Dan 7.13) can the Aramaic be regarded as feasible. Further, if a large group of such sayings are regarded as authentic, we cannot explain why the expectation of the kingdom of God and the parousia of the Son of Man are always separate, except in the editorial work of Matthew (Mt 13.41; 16.28). On this ground also, therefore, the group of authentic sayings must be small. Furthermore, half of this small group of sayings must be secondary for quite separate reasons. Matthew 16.28 is one such saying: "Amen, I tell you, there are some of those standing here who will not taste death until they see the Son of Man coming in his kingdom." This is an edited version of Mark 9.1. The earlier Marcan saying does not contain the term "son of man", and Matthew's editorial work has produced the combination of son of man and kingdom that we would expect in the teaching of Jesus if this group of sayings were authentic. When other sayings are removed for detailed reasons of this kind,[30] we are left with only four (Mk 13.26, 14.62; Mt 24.44/Lk 12.40; Mt 10.23).

The next peculiarity is the purely scriptural basis of Jesus' references. Several New Testament writers refer to the second coming of Jesus in a variety of ways, but in the synoptic Gospels, where the influence of Daniel 7.13 is clearly found (Mk 13.26/Mt 24.30, Mk 14.62/Mt 26.64), this event is almost invariably referred to in terms of "the Son of Man" coming. This consistency is striking, and can be explained only by the influence of this text. But we cannot explain why the Jesus of history should depart from his normal practice of teaching clearly with authority, whether openly to the crowds or in private to the disciples, in favour of indirect references to a scriptural text which he is never said to have quoted. We should not connect this with any motif of secrecy, because the Gospel writers do not treat these sayings as in any way ambiguous. Further, in Aramaic as in Greek and English, these sayings could not easily be understood as references to Jesus, who would have had to explain at some stage that it was his own coming to which he was referring. But of confusion and explanation there is no trace. Two of these sayings are not just references to one biblical text: Mark 13.26 and 14.62 lie in combinations of Old Testament allusions, a mode of preaching not generally characteristic of our records of the teaching of Jesus. Nor can we explain why the predictions of Jesus' second coming are never associated with the predictions of his resurrection. Both sets of predictions declare God's forthcoming vindication of him - why does the Son of Man never rise from the dead *and* come on the clouds of heaven?

On the other hand, all these sayings have an excellent *Sitz im Leben* in the early church. We know from Acts and the epistles that they eagerly awaited his return, and that they searched the scriptures for evidence and interpretation of the events of salvation history. We have seen that there is other evidence that they produced some sayings of this group. For example, the same evidence which shows that Matthew 16.28 is not in its present form an authentic saying of Jesus, also demonstrates that it was produced by Matthew. The group of parousia sayings which cannot be reconstructed in feasible Aramaic are important again here too. The evidence which shows that Luke 17.24 is not an authentic saying of Jesus, also shows that the early church secondarily attributed to Jesus a "son of man" saying which predicts his parousia. The same goes for all sayings in this group.

There are additional reasons for doubting the authenticity of Mark 14.62, the saying most frequently defended, and containing perhaps the clearest reference to Daniel 7.13. It occurs in the context of equally unsatisfactory use of the terms "messiah" and "son of the Blessed", and it does not give grounds for conviction on the legal charge of blasphemy indicated at Mark 14.63-64. It has also a particularly good *Sitz im Leben* in the Gospel of Mark. It brings the messianic secret to an end, declaring Jesus' future vindication with all three of the major christological titles used by St Mark.[31] It explains that Jesus was wickedly condemned because he said who he really was and how God would vindicate him, and it thereby condemns his judges. We must conclude that Mark 14.62 and the other "son of man" parousia sayings were produced by the early church. In these sayings, "son of man" is a title. A Greek-speaking audience would understand it as indicating that Jesus was the outstanding member of mankind, and with "son of God" in the tradition, the understanding of "son of man" as a reference to Christ's human nature could not fail to occur eventually. Christians who did not speak Aramaic would be likely to assume that the term "son of man" was a title in the translated versions of authentic sayings too.

5. Conclusions

It remains to summarize the results of this study of the major christological titles in the synoptic Gospels. All three owe their appearance as titles to the early church, though they have some connection with the historic ministry. Terms such as "son of God" were occasionally applied to Jesus as a holy but not unique person: "messiah", or "anointed", was used by those who mocked him on the cross with reference to the "anointed king of Israel": "son of man" was used by Jesus, but not as a title. As well as producing titles, the early church expanded and developed the genuine predictions of Jesus' death, and they created a group of sayings about his parousia, including some which employed Daniel 7.13. We have not however explained why the early church produced all this material. This is a much more complex task, attempted in chapters 5-9, where I shall also fit the synoptic developments into the overall patterns of the development of the christology of all New Testament writers. The study of the major christological titles also gives us some insight into the ministry of Jesus. While he did not use christological titles, some genuine "son of man" sayings show that he did preach with authority, and with total confidence in the divine authorisation of a mission in which he brought the good news of forthcoming salvation. We must now turn to his life and teaching as a whole, and see what it was about him that formed the origin of New Testament christology, and how far he contributed to the forces which generated later developments.

1. See in the general bibliography s.v. Cullmann, Dunn, Fuller, Hahn, Marshall; TDNT s.vv.; G.Vermes, *Jesus the Jew* (1973), chs 6-8; and for "son of man", infra n.15.
2. H. Anderson, *The Gospel of Mark*, New Century Bible (1976), 214.
3. For a survey of the specific debate begun by Wrede, J.D.Kingsbury, *The Christology of Mark's Gospel* (1983), ch 2. Cf H.Räisänen, *Das Messias-geheimnis im Markusevangelium* (1976); C.Tuckett (ed), *The Messianic Secret* (1983); F.Watson, "The Social Function of Mark's Secrecy Theme", *JSNT* 24, 1985, 49-69.
4. Cf especially M. de Jonge, "The Use of the Word 'Anointed' in the Time of Jesus", *NT* 8, 1966, 132-48: id., "The Earliest Christian use of Christos. Some Suggestions", *NTS* 32, 1986, 321-43.
5. For Jewish rewriting of history, cf supra, 27.
6. Infra, 53-4: Casey, *Son of Man*, ch 8, esp. 182-3, 213-8. The historical problems posed by Mark's account at this point are notorious. Cf J.Blinzler, *The Trial of Jesus* (1959); D.R.Catchpole, *The Trial of Jesus. A Study in the Gospels and Jewish Historiography from 1770 to the Present Day* (1971); J.R.Donahue, *Are You the Christ? The Trial Narrative in the Gospel of Mark*, SBL.DS 10 (1973); P.Winter, *On the Trial of Jesus*, 2nd ed., rev. and ed. T.A.Burkill and G.Vermes (1974); J.R.Donahue, "Temple, Trial and Royal Christology (Mark 14:53-65)", in W.Kelber (ed), *The Passion in Mark* (1976), 61-79; D.R.Juel, *Messiah and temple: the trial of Jesus in the Gospel of Mark* (1977); O.Betz, "Probleme des Prozesses Jesu", *ANRW* II.25.1 (1982), 565-647; D.Hill, "Jesus before the Sanhedrin - On What Charge?", *IrBS* 7, 1985, 174-86.
7. Cf N.A.Dahl, "The Crucified Messiah", rev ET in *The Crucified Messiah and Other Essays* (1974), 10-36.
8. Infra, 105-6.
9. Supra, 25, 27.
10. See e.g. V.Taylor, *The Gospel according to St.Mark* (1959), ad. loc. For the more radical view, cf e.g. E.Schweizer, *TDNT* VIII, 372; C.K.Barrett, *Jesus and the Gospel Tradition* (1967), 24-26.
11. Infra, 58-9.
12. Cf infra, 88-90, 115-7, 144, 151, 157.
13. Cf further supra, 37-8; infra, 134-5, 143-5, 148-9, 151, 156-9.
14. Infra, 79.
15. For recent surveys, Dunn, *Making,* ch III; W.O.Walker, "The Son of Man: Some Recent Developments", *CBQ* 45, 1983, 584-607; J.R.Donahue, "Recent Studies on the Origin of Son of Man' in the Gospels", *CBQ* 48, 1986, 484-98. Of the massive secondary literature, cf especially G.Vermes, "The Use of br nš/br nš" in Jewish Aramaic", Appendix E in M.Black, *An Aramaic Approach to the Gospels and Acts* (3rd ed., 1967), 310-28; G.Vermes, *Post-Biblical Jewish Studies* (1975), 147-65; Casey, *Son of Man;* R.Kearns, *Vorfragen zur Christologie* (3 vols. 1978-82); B.Lindars, *Jesus Son of Man* (1983); M.Müller, *Der Menschensohn in den Evangelien*

(1984); M.Müller, "The Expression 'the Son of Man' as Used by Jesus", *StTh* 38, 1984, 47-64; O.Betz, *Jesus und das Danielbuch. II. Die Menschensohnworte Jesu und die Zukunftserwartung des Paulus (Daniel 7,13-14)* (1985); P.M.Casey, "The Jackals and the Son of Man", *JSNT* 23, 1985, 3-22; R.Kearns, *Das Traditionsgefüge um den Menschensohn*. Ursprünglicher Gehalt und älteste Veränderung im Urchristentum (1986); G.Schwarz, *Jesus, "der Menschensohn"* (1986); P.M.Casey, "General, Generic and Indefinite. The Use of the Term 'son of man' in Aramaic Sources and in the Teaching of Jesus", *JSNT* 29, 1987, 21-56; A.Y.Collins, "The Origin of the Designation of Jesus as 'Son of Man'", *HThR* 80, 1987, 391-407; R.Kearns, *Die Entchristologisierung der Menschensohn. Die Übertragung des Traditionsgefüges um den Menschensohn auf Jesus* (1988); V. Hampel, *Menschensohn und historischer Jesus: Ein Rätselwort als Schlüssel zum messianischen selbstverständnis Jesu* (1990); P.M. Casey, "Method in our Madness and Madness in their Methods: some Approaches to the Son of Man Problem in Recent Scholarship", *JSNT* (1991).
16. This is still controversial, but the matter is too complicated to enter into here, and I have discussed it elsewhere: *Son of Man,* esp chs 2 and 5. On the Similitudes of Enoch, infra 87-8.
17. For more detailed discussion of these effects, with reconstruction of possible and impossible Aramaic sentences, Casey, *JSNT* 29, 1987, 21-56, esp. 34-6, 47-50.
18. Vermes, op. cit.
19. Casey, op. cit.; cf especially Lindars, op. cit.; Müller, op. cit.
20. For detailed discussion, *JSNT* 29, 1987, 27-34.
21. For detailed discussion of this pericope, P.M.Casey, "Culture and Historicity: the Plucking of the Grain (Mark 2.23-28)", *NTS* 23, 1988, 1-23.
22. For an Aramaic reconstruction and discussion, Casey, *Son of Man,* 230-1; Lindars, op. cit., 34-8, 178-81; Casey, *JSNT* 29, 1987, 36-7. For an explanation of the conflict between Jesus and orthodox Jews, infra, 62-4.
23. For an Aramaic reconstruction and discussion, Casey, *Son of Man,* 161-4; Lindars, op.cit., 48-56, 181-4; Casey, *ExpT* 96, 1985, 235-6.
24. For an Aramaic reconstruction, with full critical discussion, Casey, *JSNT* 23, 1985, 3-22.
25. For detailed discussion, including reconstruction of Aramaic originals, Casey, *JSNT* 29, 1987, 40-49.
26. Cf Casey, *JSNT* 29, 1987, 41.
27. See further infra, 64-8.
28. For an Aramaic reconstruction, with critical discussion, Casey, *JSNT* 29, 1987, 42-3.
29. Casey, *Son of Man* ch 8, esp. 182-3, 213-8. A hypothetical Aramaic reconstruction is given on p.178.
30. Mk 8.38c; Mt 25.31; Lk 18.8; Casey, *Son of Man,* 161-4, 190-1, 196-7, 201-2.
31. Cf supra, 43.

Chapter 5
Jesus of Nazareth

1. Introduction

Jesus of Nazareth is a major symbol in our culture. Many people know that they have met him personally: many other people know with equal sincerity and conviction that such claims are not merely false but foolish. This makes it difficult to discuss him accurately. There is a second reason why it is difficult to discuss the earthly life which he lived almost 2,000 years ago. Our historical sources are Gospels which were written some 30 odd years after his death, in Greek rather than the Aramaic which he spoke, selecting those aspects of his life which they found significant; two of the three synoptic writers show significant signs of Gentile self-identification, whereas Jesus and the first apostles were Jewish.

Critical scholars have tried to find methods for dealing with the second of these problems, only to run headlong into the first. A striking example of this is the criterion of dissimilarity, still in use despite clear demonstration of its drastic faults.[1] This criterion states that we should not accept the authenticity of any saying of Jesus which can be paralleled in Jewish sources or in the early church. The removal of anything paralleled in our Jewish sources has enabled Gentile scholars to hold the abstract belief that Jesus was incarnate among the Jews, while they have not portrayed him as anything so alien as a Jewish man. Moreover, our Jewish sources are so meagre that the absence of some items from them may be due simply to gaps in the evidence. The removal of sayings paralleled in the early church reduces the contacts between Jesus and the early church, and this makes the origins of Christianity more difficult to explain.

It is natural that there has been a conservative reaction to radical scholarship, but nothing has emerged in the way of agreed methods and results. None the less, I cannot attempt here a full discussion of the authenticity of all the sayings that I use, nor can I discuss all aspects of Jesus' ministry.[2] I have selected those aspects of his life and teaching which seem to me to be the most important for understanding the origins and growth of christology. I have also assumed that both Mark and Q contain a large quantity of authentic source material, much of which was written down in Aramaic by Jews long before the writing of the Gospels, and which can therefore be properly understood only if we apply to it the assumptions of Jewish culture.[3]

2. The Kingdom of God

The preaching of the kingdom of God was one of the central aspects of Jesus' ministry.[4] Mark begins his account of the ministry with a summary which is confirmed by all our evidence: "Jesus came into Galilee preaching the good news of God and saying, 'The time has been fulfilled, and the kingdom of God is at hand: repent and believe the good news.'"(Mk 1.14-15). The kingdom, or kingship, of God was a standard Jewish metaphor used to express the divine status of superiority and the divine functions in the general area of power and rule. It is given cultic expression in the psalms (e.g. Ps 47.2-3), and in the book of Daniel, Nebuchadnezzar, cured because he repented, responded appropriately by praising God: "I blessed the Most High, I praised and glorified Him who lives for ever: his sovereignty is everlasting sovereignty and his kingship is with every generation.... Now I, Nebuchadnezzar, praise, exalt and glorify the King of Heaven, all of whose deeds are right, and his ways are just and he can bring down those whose conduct is arrogant" (Dan 4.34-37). It was none the less clear that God's rule was not wholly effective on this earth now. Sinners flourished, demons caused illnesses, and many Jewish people felt oppressed under the rule of successive foreign powers. In these circumstances, faithful Jews hoped for the establishment or restoration of God's kingdom, and in times of stress they have often expected it to happen in a short time. An old Jewish prayer, the *Qaddish*, expresses the general hope: "May he let his kingdom rule in your lifetime and in your days, and in the lifetime of the whole house of Israel, speedily and soon."

The book of Daniel, which celebrates the permanent and enduring kingship of God in chapter 4, also proclaims the final establishment of the kingdom in the near future. In chapter 2, Nebuchadnezzar is told that God has given him the kingdom, or kingship (2.37): subsequently, however, there will be a second, third and fourth kingdom, and after that, at the time of the real author of Daniel c.164 B.C., "The God of heaven will set up a kingdom which will never be destroyed, nor shall its sovereignty be left to any other people. It will break in pieces all those kingdoms and bring them to an end, and it will stand for ever" (Dan 2.44). Here it is evidently the Jewish kingdom which will be restored: at the same time it is God's kingdom, and the book as a whole is completely committed to the observance of the Law. The same crisis led some faithful Jews to separate themselves from the main body of Judaism to live in purity and holiness in the wilderness of Qumran. The kingdom did not come, despite the promise of Habbakuk; "For there shall be yet another vision concerning the appointed time. It shall tell of the end and shall not lie. If it tarries wait for it, for it will certainly come, it will not be late" (Hab 2.3). The faithful Jews who had retreated to the wilderness to serve God interpreted the delay in the coming of the kingdom as a further indication of the profundity of God, in response to whose commands they kept the Law. One of them commented on the Habbakuk text: "This means that the end time will be prolonged, and will exceed all that the prophets have said, for the mysteries of God are astounding.... The interpretation of this concerns the men of truth who do the law, whose hands shall not slacken in the service of truth when the end time is prolonged. For all the ages of God reach their appointed end as He has determined for them in the mysteries of his prudence" (1QpHab VII, 7-14).

Thus the cultural conditions necessary for a new prophet to declare that the kingdom was at hand were present in the Judaism of Jesus' time. John the Baptist had already made a basically similar declaration that the end was at hand, though he looked for an intermediary figure greater than himself to bring it about (Mk 1.7-8; Mt 11.2-3/Lk 7.18-19). Jesus voluntarily underwent John's baptism (Mk 1.9-11), hailed him as Elijah (Mk 9.12, cf Mt 11.7ff/Lk 7.24ff), and sought to fulfil his prophecy of a coming one (Mt 11.2-6/Lk 7.18-23).

Against this background (cf Mk 11.10; 15.43), those sayings of Jesus which indicate the imminence of the end should be taken quite literally. "The time is fulfilled and the kingdom of God is at hand" (Mk 1.15): "Amen I tell you, there are some of those standing here who will not taste of death until they see the kingdom of God come in power" (Mk 9.1): "Amen I tell you, this generation shall not pass away before all these things come to pass" (Mk 13.30). At the Last Supper, a brief interval is likewise implied with the imagery of the eschatological banquet: "Amen I tell you, I shall certainly not drink of the fruit of the vine until that day when I drink it new in the kingdom of God" (Mk 14.25, cf Lk 22.16). This is what the disciples were to pray for (Mt 7.10/Lk 11.2), the good news which they were to preach when they were sent out on a mission (Mt 10.7/ Lk 10.9). Given this evidence, we must interpret in a similar way the injunctions to watch in case something drastic happens suddenly: "It is like a man away from home, who left his house and gave authority to his slaves, putting each of them in charge of his own work. And he charged the doorkeeper to keep watch. So watch! For you do not know when the master of the house is coming, whether late or at midnight, at two in the morning or when it gets light! Otherwise, he might come suddenly and find you asleep" (Mk 13.34-36, cf Mt 24.50/Lk 12.46; Mt 25.13).

3. The Mission to the Lost Sheep
Jesus took his message to Jews who were not very faithful. The most succinct definition of his normal audience is given in a mission charge to the twelve: "Do not go into the way of the Gentiles, and do not enter a Samaritan city, but go rather to the lost sheep of the house of Israel" (Mt 10.5-6). The accuracy of this summary is confirmed by all our evidence, and it necessitated his constant call to them to return. Our English translations of the Gospels naturally follow the Greek text and translate this as a call to repent, but the usual word for "repent" in Aramaic *(tubh)* is the normal Aramaic word for "return", and it has a very positive content. It does not mean simply regretting the wrong which we have done, though it does involve this. It means, return to the Lord your God. A similar message punctuates the condemnation of Israel at the hand of her prophets (cf Hos 12.6; Is 10.21; Jer 3.12). This is the message which Jesus took to the Jews of his own day, both in his own preaching and by means of the disciples whom he sent out, and this is what the unresponsive cities which he condemned should have done: "If the mighty works done in you had been done in Tyre and Sidon, they would long ago have returned in sackcloth and ashes"

(Mt 11.21/Lk 10.13). In parables such as the prodigal son (Lk 15.11-32), Jesus celebrated in a different way the return of the sinner, sometimes with a hyperbolic contrast directed against those who satisfied the currently accepted legal norms of Israel's religion. The parable of the lost sheep (Lk 15.4-7) provides almost a paradigm of those people whom Jesus saw as the potential recipients of his ministry. Again, "I have not come to call the righteous but sinners" (Mk 2.17).

The terms "sinners" and "lost sheep" point the same way, to Jews who had fallen away from God and who did not observe the Law as they should. Another trajectory is that of poverty.[5] The lost sheep were evidently not rich Jews assimilating into the Greek world in cities like Sepphoris, but poor Jews in the towns and villages of Galilee. Jesus offered them blunt reassurance; "Blessed are the poor, for yours is the kingdom of God" (Lk 6.20, cf Mt 5.3). The seriousness of this economic factor is clear partly from its obverse: when a rich man asked Jesus what he should do to inherit eternal life, Jesus, having failed to satisfy him by telling him to keep the law, next told him to sell all his property, give to the poor, and become his disciple. The man refused, and Jesus reflected, "How difficult it is for those with wealth to enter the kingdom of God!" (Mk 10.23). Then he defused the situation with one of the many jokes that we no longer appreciate; "Its easier for a camel to get through a needle's eye than for a rich man to get into the kingdom of God!" When pressed, he admitted "all things are possible with God" (Mk 10.27), but the difficulty is clarified both by the general social situation, in which the rich oppressed the poor so badly that it is difficult to see how they could have lived in accordance with God's will and remained so rich, and by direct criticism of their attitude to God.

Jews who did return had to be taught. The major thrusts of Jesus' teaching may be seen as a prophetic intensification of certain aspects of Jewish tradition, those which were especially relevant for returning sinners. The fatherhood of God conceptualised a central feeling. "Father" was a traditional Jewish image of God (e.g. Jer 3.9; Sir 23.1; 1QH IX, 35-6), and Jesus intensified it by teaching people to use the familiar term *Abba*, which everyone used for their own earthly fathers.[6] It was the first word of the Lord's prayer (Lk 11.2), and Jesus used it himself when he prayed to be spared his atoning death (Mk 14.36). God's availability and care were also presented in his willingness to answer prayer, as in the following simile from earthly parenthood: "Now which of you, being a father and your son asks for a fish, will give him a snake instead of a fish? So if you, being wicked, know how to give your children good gifts, how much more will your heavenly Father give good things to those who ask him!" (Lk 11.11,13/Mt 7.9-11).

God's care could be presented without the concept of fatherhood: "Don't worry about yourself - what you will eat, or what you will wear on your body. Aren't you more important than food, and your body more important than its clothing? Look at the ravens! They don't sow or harvest or gather into barns, but God feeds them. Aren't you worth more than birds?" (Mt 6.25-6/Lk 12.22-4). The acceptance of the sinner who returns was thus part of an overall pattern of fatherly care, and it was elaborated in parables such as the prodigal son (Lk

15.11-32). The centrality of God could also be presented with the overarching concept of the kingship of God (Mt 13.45-46). The image of entering the kingdom could be used to impart ethical teaching. One passage is an acted parable of the most general kind: "Let the children come to me, don't stop them, for of such people is the kingdom of God. Amen I tell you, whoever does not receive the kingdom of God like a child will certainly not enter it" (Mk 10.14-15).

Concepts and attitudes like this were necessary, but they were not sufficient. Jesus' teaching also included detailed ethical instructions, all of which can be seen, as Matthew saw them, as intensification of certain aspects of the Law. "Do not swear at all" (Mt 5.34): "Whoever strikes you on your right cheek, turn the other one to him" (Mt 5.39/Lk 6.29). It is noticeable that many of these recommendations are ways of telling people not to overreact to the uncontrolled behaviour of their fellow-men and their oppressors, and that forgiveness is a main theme. The same teaching is found in stories and in more general exhortations: "Watch out! If your brother does wrong, rebuke him, and if he repents, forgive him. And if during the day he wrongs you seven times and turns back to you seven times saying 'I repent', you will forgive him" (Lk 17.3-4, cf Mt 18.15, 21-2). A similar injunction is written into the Lord's prayer (Mt 6.12/Lk 11.4). Another general rule intensifies the Levitical command to love your neighbour: "Love your enemies, do good to those who hate you, bless those who curse you, pray for those who abuse you" (Lk 6.27-8, cf Mt 5.44).

Jesus did more than teach returning sinners. In a society with no modern medicine, he undertook exorcisms and healings in a culture in which people attributed illness to the activity of demonic powers. The first recorded healing is an exorcism in a Capernaum synagogue one sabbath (Mk 1.23-27). This was an authoritative act, and it was not accompanied by any significant christological title. Jesus was bound to feel that his abilities in this area were due to divine inspiration, and this is explicit in his reply to John the Baptist's question, "Are you he who is coming, or are we to expect someone else?" (Mt 11.3/Lk 7.19). Jesus' reply may have been somewhat written up in transmission, but it corresponds to his ministry, and, like the question, it lacks features characteristic of the christology of the early church, so it is likely to be substantially authentic: "Go and tell John what you see and hear: blind people see and lame people walk, lepers are cleansed and dumb people hear, dead people are raised and the poor have the good news preached to them: and blessed is he who does not find me a stumbling-block" (Mt 11.4-6/Lk 7.22-3). Awed reactions are reported from those who were present on these occasions. While these may have become somewhat formalized in transmission, they too must be substantially authentic because such events were bound to produce awe in a sympathetic audience, and our reports rarely show features characteristic of the early church.

4. Conflict with the Orthodox

When we consider this ministry as a whole, it is not difficult to see why Jesus' contemporaries thought of him as a prophet and a teacher. None the less, he ran into serious opposition from the orthodox wing of Judaism. The orthodox were devoted to the enactments of the Law.[7] They defended Jewish identity by their commitment to *external* ordinances. The Pharisees were especially prominent on the orthodox wing of the community. They maintained their Jewish identity by their expansion of the *halakhah* and by their insistence on careful observance of the traditions of the elders. This orthodox wing, however, was not, and could not be, the whole of Judaism. The massive stress on external observances, which separated the community into different groups, was bound to produce a prophetic reaction as well. The prophetic tradition was as fundamental a part of Jewish culture as the Law. The prophets of old were revered in our period, and so well entrenched that commentaries on their sacred texts were written in the Law-centred community of Qumran. They were read in the synagogue, and apocryphal stories grew up around them, stories which included the martyrdom of most of them. Moreover, much Pharisaic and Essene legislation was not observable by many people in the towns and villages of Galilee, and the prophetic message was clearly directed at Israel as a whole, not at an elite group who observed large quantities of non-biblical ordinances. As the prophetic reaction called on Israel to return to the Lord, it was bound to perceive a lack of religious profundity among people who observed legal enactments to protect Jewish identity, and the extent to which the return of the people of the land was prevented by laws which they effectively could not observe. Hence both John the Baptist and Jesus preached to Jews as a whole, and intensified the prophetic rather than the legal side of Judaism.

I have noted that Jesus took the good news to sinners. To reach them, it was necessary to ignore orthodox development of purity legislation, for this made it impossible to make contact with Jews who did not maintain a state of ritual purity. The first incident recorded by St Mark shows the irreconcilable nature of the cleavage, though it is relatively mild in itself: The tax-collector Levi son of Alphaeus threw a large party after his decision to follow Jesus,

And many tax-collectors and sinners reclined with Jesus and his disciples, for there were a lot of them and they followed him. And Pharisaic scribes, seeing that he was eating with sinners and tax-collectors, said to his disciples, 'Why is he eating with tax-collectors and sinners?' And when Jesus heard this, he said to them, 'It's not healthy people who need a doctor but the sick! I came to call not the righteous, but sinners' (Mk 2.15-17).

By Old Testament Law, Jesus had done nothing wrong. He might become unclean, if he was not unclean already: but Pentateuchal Law does not object to people becoming unclean in such ways, it tells them how to become clean again. The Pharisees had, however, been active in the orthodox expansion of purity legislation, maintaining Jewish identity by keeping themselves in a state of purity whenever possible, a process which served to separate them from sinners. We can see this most clearly in later orthodox sources. For example, we read that the clothes of one of the "people of the land" convey touch uncleanness to Pharisees (M.Hag.II,7). Again, it is characteristic of an "Associate" that he undertakes not to make ready his ritually prepared food with one of the "people of the land", and to eat ordinary food in a state of purity (T.Demai II.2). All this was perceived to be obedience to the Law of God himself, revealed to Moses on Mt Sinai, and since Jesus had a reputation for piety, the scribes expected him to obey the purity laws. We can however see from the story of Levi that these purity laws were contrary to the centre of Jesus' mission. Further, their very function in separating some people from others was contrary to the prophetic tradition, which called upon the whole of Israel to return to the Lord. Sooner or later, Jesus was bound to attack the orthodox tradition for the separation which it enforced: the parable of the good Samaritan (Lk 10.30-37) is extraordinarily sharp in this respect.

The means used by orthodox Jews to extend purity legislation derived in considerable measure from their attempts to observe in daily life the standards of purity laid down for priests in the Temple. The selection of a priest and a Levite to go past on the other side from the wounded man intensifies the attack by ignoring the difference between a priest and a lay person: what should have been done by a priest or Levite in a state of cleanness should *a fortiori* be done by anyone else. The "reason" for ignoring the victim was to avoid incurring corpse uncleanness if he were dead. Corpse uncleanness is contrary not to Pentateuchal Law, which necessarily allows for the burial of the dead, but to an attempt to maintain a state of purity appropriate to priests in the Temple. The Samaritan, who adhered only to the laws in the Pentateuch, was for that reason able and willing to help. The parable thus attacks the orthodox expansion of the oral law by showing how strict application of it in separating oneself from uncleanness could lead to the violation of what is agreed by our most orthodox Jewish sources to be one of the most fundamental commandments of the written Law, "Love your neighbour as yourself" (Lev 19.18, quoted and discussed at Lk 10.25-29). At this level, Jesus' attack on scribes and Pharisees is the necessary obverse of his taking his prophetic message to the lost sheep of the house of Israel.

A more general attack on externality ensued. "And when you pray, you will not be like the actors, for they love to stand and pray in the synagogues and on the corners of the street, so that people see them" (Mt 6.5). From a different perspective, externality could be regarded as functional. Praying openly, like purity laws and lengthening of phylacteries, meant that a person visibly embodied Jewish identity. From the individual's point of view, careful observance of the law will have made him feel more Jewish and hence more righteous. The polemical description of orthodox Jews as "hypocrites" also hit at the same external mode. It was probably not even an Aramaic word. Faced with Pharisees who made an open display of Jewishness against the threat of Hellenism, Jesus seems to have picked the Greek word for "actor" as his main label for them. The orthodox stress on externality could not have been hit with a sharper label.

Conflict of this kind could only grow. If orthodox Jews sought reassurance in Jesus' ethical teaching, they did not find it. Having from their perspective breached the purity laws in order to reach the sinners and call upon them to return, Jesus did not then demand that they kept the Law.[8] At least, not from an orthodox perspective. From his perspective, he did. Indeed, in some respects he intensified the Law's demand, interpreting "love your neighbour" as meaning "love your enemies" (Mt 5.44). But that could not satisfy the orthodox perspective, from which he no more demanded the observance of purity laws from others than he kept them himself. Then there was the sabbath, one of the main identity factors of Judaism. Of course he kept the sabbath from his perspective, but from an orthodox perspective he violated it, chiefly by healing on the sabbath, once also in defending his poor and hungry disciples who were plucking the grain left for the poor at the edges of the field (Mk 2.23-28).[9] What then of Jesus' mighty works? They could not be divinely inspired because he broke the Law so much. In that culture, there was only one other possibility: "And the scribes who came down from Jerusalem said, 'He has Beelzebub', and 'He casts out demons by the prince of demons'" (Mk 3.22).

Jesus hit back with a series of analogies, and an indirect but real claim of direct divine inspiration: "If I by the finger of God cast out demons, the kingship of God has come upon you" (Mt 12.8/Lk 11.20). This is the same use of the concept of God's kingship as we found in Nebuchadnezzar's celebration of his healing (Dan 4.34-37).[10] It is not inconsistent with the hope that God will finally establish his kingdom soon: it means that God's power is visible in Jesus' exorcisms. It was the scribes' denial of this that led him to the equally indirect but equally real accusation that they had committed an unforgivable sin (cf Mt 12.32/Lk 12.10, Mk 3.28).[11]When Jesus said this, no-one will have been in any doubt that it was the scribes who had spoken against the Spirit of holiness by accusing Jesus of casting out demons by Beelzebub. When the dispute between Jesus and the orthodox was so clear and irrevocable, Jesus let fly with attacks of a general kind which need the whole background to become comprehensible: "Woe to you, scribes and Pharisees, hypocrites, for you bar the kingdom of God before men. For you do not enter it yourselves, nor do you allow those who are entering it to go in" (Mt 23.13).

5. Death and Vindication

It was against this background that Jesus went up to Jerusalem for the last time, knowing full well that he was going to die. His clash with orthodox Jews, the execution of John the Baptist, and his intention to "cleanse the Temple" gave him quite sufficient grounds for expecting to die, apart from the theological reasons with which he understood and explained his death. There are several predictions. In their original forms, none of them has a satisfactory *Sitz im Leben* in the early church, and all of them are indirect, a natural feature of the speech of a would-be martyr, not the voice of the early church. I have noted those which use the term "son of man".[12] Mk 10.45 concludes a narrative containing another prediction. When Jacob and John asked to sit on his right and left in his glory, Jesus replied, "You don't know what you are asking for. Can you drink the cup which I shall drink, or be baptised with the baptism with which I am baptised?" (Mk 10.38). The first metaphor, that of the cup, is the same as he was to use in Gethsemane (Mk 14.36), and it was evidently not ambiguous. Nor was the indirect general statement of Lk 13.33: "But today, tomorrow and the next day I shall go on my way, for it wouldn't do for a prophet to perish outside Jerusalem." Here Jesus accepted the popular estimation of himself as a prophet, and used it to predict his death in Jerusalem. Thus his predictions of his death were uniformly indirect but clear (cf also Lk 12.50; 13.32).

When Jesus reached Jerusalem, "He began to throw out those who bought and sold in the Temple. He overturned the tables of the money-changers and the seats of those who sold doves, and he did not allow anyone to carry anything through the Temple" (Mk 11.15-16).[13] These actions could all be perceived as secular activities being carried on in a holy place, the court of the Gentiles. Jesus' quotation of Isaiah 56.17 indicates that his action was directed at restoring the use of the court of the Gentiles to its proper purpose: "Is it not written that my house shall be called a house of prayer for all nations?" (Mk 11.17). Jesus' action was thus both logical and prophetic, but it was violent, and people may also have believed that Jesus had predicted doom for Jerusalem and the destruction of the Temple (cf Mk 13.2, 14.57-9/Mt 26.60-61; Mt 23.37-39/ Lk 13.34-5). It was thus predictable that Jesus' action would lead to a clash with the Temple authorities, and entirely possible that the Romans would be called in. Jesus' fate was partly sealed by his vigorous conflict with orthodox Jews. Hence the immediate sequel to the cleansing, "the chief priests and scribes heard about it, and sought ways of destroying him" (Mk 11.18, cf 14.1). Some of the "scribes" will have been Pharisees whose opposition to Jesus was already implacable before he cleansed the Temple, others will have been orthodox Jews totally devoted to the doing of all the enactments of the Law, and just as outraged as any Pharisee by such factors as Jesus' contempt for the expansion of the purity laws. This outrage of the life-stance of orthodox Judaism was more basic than the percentage of scribes who had joined the Pharisaic sect. Once Jesus' perceived attack on the Temple had put the Sadducean aristocracy against him too, an alliance between "scribes" and "chief priests" was inevitable.

If, then, Jesus anticipated his death, how did he interpret it?[14] The passion predictions use the metaphors of "cup", "baptism" and "completion", give his role as a prophet, and declare his death to be written in scripture, a form of service and a ransom for many; he would be vindicated by resurrection, and his future position would be a glorious one in which God could decide whether particular people might sit on his right or left. At the Last Supper, Jesus effectively said that his sacrificial death would in some sense bring about the redemption of Israel: "This is my blood, it is of the covenant, shed for many" (Mk 14.24).[15] He continued with a saying which implies a short interval before the coming of the kingdom (Mk 14.25). We should deduce that Jesus' mind was working on the same basic lines as those who meditated on the deaths of the innocent Maccabean martyrs, and who concluded that their deaths were an expiatory sacrifice which assuaged the wrath of God and enabled him to deliver Israel (cf 2 Macc 7.37-8; 4 Macc 17.20-22). Jesus' death likewise was to be an expiatory sacrifice which assuaged the wrath of God and enabled him to redeem Israel despite her faults.[16]

It follows that Jesus expected God to vindicate him. To understand this, we must consider contemporary Jewish beliefs in survival after death.[17] Jewish documents of our period put forward more than one view of survival after death, and their comments appear to be related to the situation which they consider, rather than to concepts held by them. They tend to put forward something like a view of resurrection when they consider the general resurrection at which Israel or the righteous will finally be vindicated. When they consider the fate of individuals at death, however, they generally make comments which are more akin to our concept of immortality.

For example, Daniel 12.1-2 portrays the end of all things, and envisages the resurrection of many people at a single moment of time. The reference to their sleeping in the dusty ground implies that their graves will be empty, though this is not explicitly stated. This event is placed in the future, though in apocalyptic literature this means in the very near future. Contrast Josephus' account of the belief of the Pharisees, when he considers the fate of people at death. "They hold a belief that souls have power to survive death, and under the earth there are rewards and punishments for those who have led lives of virtue or wickedness. Some receive eternal punishment, while others pass easily to live again" (A.J.XVIII, 14). Here we find no mention of the resurrection of the body, but only the continued existence of souls. There is no indication of any kind of pause after death before a final judgment: the natural interpretation is that the soul goes to its eternal fate at once.

Some documents imply both an immediate and a final judgment. 1 Enoch 22 classifies the dead in terms of righteousness and wickedness, including one group of sinners in a particular compartment for those who have already been punished. There will none the less be a final judgment, when other sinners will enter very great torment, but those who have already been punished will not rise. Some documents introduce clear concepts to deal with specific problems. For example, IV Ezra has the disembodied souls of the righteous received at once by God, spend seven days contemplating their fate and the universe, and then go to chambers in the underworld to await their resurrection and vindication at the last judgment. As a document, however, IV Ezra is hardly consistent on its own major problem, the salvation of the chosen people. The agonizing chapters 3-10 imply the damnation of most Jews because they have not kept the Law up to orthodox standards, while the visions of chapters 11-13 resolve this problem by their vigorous portrayal of the salvation of Israel. Evidence of this kind should lead us to a more general conclusion. The concepts which Jewish people used at the time of Jesus to cope with death and with the destiny of Israel were variable, and liable to a degree of obscurity, change and inconsistency beyond those which modern scholars regard as tolerable when they see them in others.

The meagre evidence of the Gospels suggests that Jesus shared the attitude to resurrection and immortality characteristic of Jews who believed in survival after death. For example, in answer to an awkward question from the Sadducees, Jesus assumed that there will be an occasion when the dead rise, commenting, "For when they rise from the dead they neither marry nor are given in marriage, but are like angels in heaven" (Mk 12.25). The natural assumption is that they rise on a particular occasion, and Jesus conspicuously fails to say that they will not have bodies at a point where such a conception would have been helpful to his argument. On the other hand, the parable of the rich man and Lazarus (Lk 16.19-31) pictures the fate of the righteous and the wicked at death. Consequently, there is no pause in time before they pass to bliss and torment respectively, and it is clear they have not left their tombs empty. Nor presumably did father Abraham, who was already in the next world with powers to send a messenger from the dead if he wished, a process described as "going from the dead" at Luke 16.30 and "rising from the dead" at 16.31. The strength of Jesus' belief in survival after death is illustrated by his supposedly crushing argument against the Sadducees, who did not hold any belief of this kind. He argued from the nature of God himself. God is so clearly the God of the living (cf Jer 10.10) that his declaration to Moses "I am the God of Abraham and the God of Isaac and the God of Jacob" (Ex 3.6, 15, 16) is held to demonstrate the survival of Abraham, Isaac and Jacob, and thereby the raising of the dead.[18]

Most of Jesus' comments about his own fate are not very specific. Mark 14.25 implies his survival and vindication, and a short interval of time before he drank new wine in the kingdom. The passage is however typical in that it says nothing about resurrection or immortality, that is, it gives no details about the mode of survival. The same applies to Mark 10.40, where Jesus accepted that people will sit on the right and left of him in his glory, but he did not respond with any details of his or their mode of existence. A few other sayings likewise imply that Jesus will have a significant position in the kingdom, from which we must infer Jesus' vindication and survival (cf Mk 9.1; 10.29-30; Luke 12.8-9/ Mt 10.32-3, with Mk 8.38). The one saying that predicts instead of assumes Jesus' survival is that which lies behind Mark 8.31, 9.31 and 10.33-4. I have argued that the original form of this prediction was a general statement such as "A son of man will die, and after three days he will rise".[19]

The Aramaic word for "rise" can only have been *qum*. This is the most general word for "rise", and could refer to what we might call either resurrection or immortality. An interpretation of "after three days" may be deduced from midrashic sayings which declare that Israel, or the righteous, will not be left in distress for more than three days, a view supported with several passages of scripture (e.g. Jon 2.1; Hos 6.2).[20] One such occasion is the last days, when deliverance will be by means of the resurrection. If "three days" is interpreted like this, the general resurrection could be expected "after three days". Three other sayings of Jesus use the three-day interval in a similar metaphorical sense (cf Mk 14.58; Lk 13.32, 33). At a more literal level, three days is just long enough to ensure that a person was really dead (cf Jn 11.39; bT Sem VIII,1; Lev R. XVIII,1). We may conclude that, in the original saying, Jesus probably meant that he would be vindicated in the general resurrection, which would take place after a short interval.

There is thus ample evidence that Jesus expected God to vindicate him after his atoning death. One saying implies that this would be in the first instance at the general resurrection, which was to be expected shortly. Other sayings look to the kingdom of God, in which Jesus and his disciples would be prominent.

6. Prophet and Teacher

It should be clear even from this brief summary of Jesus' life and teaching that he worked with massive personal authority. He did not use the major christological titles. Rather he acted out his prophetic conviction that he was called by God to bring back the people of Israel to the Lord, the last messenger to bring the good news that the kingdom of God was at hand, to warn them of destruction if they did not return, and finally to take upon himself the wrath of God which they deserved. In the course of this mission he healed the sick, and vigorously condemned many of the nation's other leaders. Only two minor christological terms are known to have been used by him, "prophet" and "teacher", neither of them with any frequency.[21] I have noted "prophet" at Luke 13.33, where it enabled him to refer indirectly to his forthcoming death in Jerusalem. The only other example is Mark 6.4, where he sought to explain his inability to heal the sick in Nazareth with another general statement indirectly referring to himself. The single example of "teacher" is hardly more than a password (Mk 14.14).

There is ample evidence that both his own circle of disciples and other people addressed Jesus as "rabbi", the conventional address for teachers (e.g. Mk 9.17; 11.21). The appropriateness of the category of "prophet" is confirmed by the few known comments of outsiders. Mark 6.15 reports some people as saying that he was Elijah, others that he was a prophet like one of the prophets. The view that he was Elijah shows a heightened awareness of the eschatological role that he sought to play (cf Mal 4.5; Sir 48.10). Herod is reported as declaring that he was John the Baptist raised from the dead (Mk 6.14). This is the same kind of judgement, with stress on Jesus' prophetic eschatological role. Similar verdicts from unknown people are recorded at Mark 8.28. Herod apart, these outside verdicts show us the impression which Jesus made on Jews who were favourably disposed towards him, but who did not belong to the inner circle of disciples.

No significant conclusions should be drawn from the use of "Lord" with reference to Jesus. At one level, it was no more than a polite form of address. At this level, it may have been used during the ministry more often than our oldest sources suggest (cf Mk 7.28; Mt 7.21-2; Lk 6.46). Most examples in the synoptic tradition are however secondary. They owe their origin to the fact that the term "the Lord" was a title of majesty which the early church commonly used of Jesus.[22]

7. The Jesus Movement

One other aspect of the historic ministry, fundamental for understanding the origins and early growth of christology, is the community which formed round Jesus.[23] The twelve apostles were at the centre of this group. Their number corresponds to the twelve tribes, and one saying declares that they will sit on twelve thrones judging the twelve tribes of Israel (Mt 19.28/Lk 22.30). Mark gives their purpose on earth as "to be with him, and so that he might send them out to preach and to have power to cast out demons" (Mk 3.14-15). He records just one such mission (Mk 6.7-13). The longer accounts of Matthew and Luke specify the preaching of the kingdom (Mt 10.7; Lk 10.9), and Luke gathered together some of the missionary material under the heading of a separate mission by 72 people (Lk 10.1-20).

The church also remembered the sudden calling of some of the twelve, including Simon Peter, and Jacob and John, the sons of Zebedee (Mk 1.16-20). The circumstances of these calls have been lost in the transmission of the narratives, but all our evidence coheres with the inference that Jesus called the inner circle of disciples to leave their regular occupations and follow him in a migratory ministry of preaching and exorcism. For example, Mark follows the opening incidents in Capernaum with a summary account of such a ministry throughout the towns and villages of Galilee (Mk 1.38-39). A group of women played a significant role in supporting the ministry. Mary Magdalene was one of them. She went up to Jerusalem for his final Passover, and was among the witnesses of his crucifixion (Lk 8.2-3; Mk 15.40-41,47). We are also told that Jesus preached to large crowds, and that he was at times so popular in Galilee that it was difficult for him to move about normally (cf Mk 2.2; 3.7-10; 4.1).

The social bonding of the inner group of disciples was very tight. Their acceptance of harsh conditions of existence is a straightforward indication of this. There is ample evidence that the ministry was migratory, and that Jesus took his disciples with him. This could mean sleeping rough. As one Q saying puts it, "Jackals have holes, and the birds of the air have roosts, and a son of man has nowhere to lay his head" (Mt 8.20/Lk 9.58).[24] When the 12, and perhaps the 72, were sent on their own mission, they were not to take any food or money, nor a second tunic (Mt 10.9-10; Lk 9.3). Existence in these circumstances could be precarious. The intensity and urgency of commitment required is also shown by Jesus' reaction to a potential disciple who wanted to go and bury his father: "Follow me, and let the dead bury the dead" (Mt 8.21-22, cf Lk 9.59-60). The burial of the dead was a religious duty as well as a social custom: this saying declares that it should be set aside by the immediate needs of the mission.[25] The migratory ministry could also mean long absences from home. Peter is recorded as telling Jesus, "Look, we have left everything and followed you" (Mk 10.28). Jesus' reply accepts that people leave brothers, sisters, mother, father, children and fields: he promises that they will receive one hundredfold in this age, and eternal life in the age to come. Thus the community could itself be presented as a reward for leaving conventional life to join it (cf Mk 3.31-35), and the promise of future reward was closely related to the social bonding of the community in the present.

Some sayings effectively call for complete self-sacrifice (cf Mk 8.34-5). One saying ties eschatological vindication directly to a person's attitude to Jesus' ministry (Lk 12.8-9/Mt 10.32-3, cf Mk 8.38).[26] Those who left everything, followed him and listened to his preaching, will have been particularly confident that they had fulfilled the conditions necessary for entering the kingdom. Exorcisms and healings will have reinforced their conviction that Jesus' ministry was wholly in accordance with the will of God. For example, Luke records that he cast seven demons out of Mary Magdalene (Lk 8.2). She must have been very dependent on him, and a constant reminder to others of the divine power which he could exercise.

8. The Jewish Identity of the Jesus Movement

We must consider next the identity factors of the Jesus movement. Jesus apart, they were largely the same as those of Judaism itself. Of the eight identity factors isolated in chapter 2, seven were clearly maintained, six of them without dispute. Ethnicity was taken for granted: there was no mission to the Gentiles during the historic ministry, and Gentile faith was regarded as remarkable (cf Mt 8.10/Lk 7.9; Mk 7.24-30). The authority of scripture was beyond question (e.g. Mk 2.25-6; 12.26-7), being put forward as decisive evidence even at a point where a Mosaic enactment was held to permit an unsatisfactory attitude to God and to people (Mk 10.2-9, citing Gen 1.27 and 2.24). Monotheism was unquestioned. When a scribe asked him which is the most important commandment of all, Jesus cited the *Shema*ᶜ(Deut 6.4-5, slightly expanded at Mk 12.29-30). Conventional monotheism was intensified by Jesus' teaching on the fatherhood and kingship of God. He put the distance between himself and God with especial clarity when he was addressed as "good rabbi": "Why do you call me good? No-one is good except the one God" (Mk 10.18). Circumcision, dietary laws and the major festivals were so taken for granted that they do not emerge for serious discussion. The importance of Jesus' final Passover is especially clear, since he went up to Jerusalem for it with his disciples, and used the occasion of the Passover meal to explain something of the significance of his forthcoming death.

Sabbath and purity are the only two identity factors which led to disputes, and of these two, there is no doubt that sabbath observance was upheld by Jesus and his followers. One dispute concerns the right of poor and hungry disciples to pluck grain (Mk 2.23-28), and all the others concern Jesus' right to heal on the sabbath. In all these cases, Jesus disagreed with orthodox Jews as to *how* the sabbath should be observed, but he did so within a framework in which observance itself was beyond question. Jesus himself attended the synagogue on the sabbath (e.g. Mk 1.21ff), and had he infringed the sabbath limit or carried burdens on the sabbath, the inevitable disputes would certainly have been transmitted to us. His disciples likewise observed the sabbath. After his first sabbath healing, other sick people were brought to him. Mark's note of time is very careful: "When evening came, when the sun had set" (Mk 1.32), that is, when the sabbath was clearly over. This makes sense only if Mark's source made the standard Jewish assumption that we do not carry people on the sabbath under the rubric of not carrying burdens (Jer 5.21-2). Neither healing nor plucking the grain left for the poor on the sabbath was in this category: there was no known regulation against doing either.[27]

Details of this kind were generally established by analogical arguments from existing tradition, and Jesus' position inside Judaism is well illustrated by his use of similar arguments (though, naturally enough, they do not always correspond to later rabbinical rules). For example, at Mark 3.4 he defends his healing by analogy from the general principle of doing good and the specific *halakhah* of saving life overriding the sabbath. Similarly, at Mark 2.25-28 he defends his disciples plucking grain by arguing from the scriptural example of David, and with reference to the divine purpose in creating the sabbath as known to everyone from the opening of the book of Genesis. There would have been no need for any of these arguments if Jesus believed he was breaking the sabbath. His actions were however wholly within a reasonable understanding of biblical law. They were disputed only by the orthodox, who were committed to the observance of expanding *halakhah*. We must conclude that Jesus and his followers upheld the observance of the sabbath.

The purity laws are the only identity factor of Judaism which Jesus might be thought not to have wholly maintained. I do not want to follow here the general trend of exaggerating Mark 7.15: "There is nothing outside a man going into him that can defile him, but the things going out of a man defile him." It is understandable that Gentile Christians have perceived this as undermining the whole of Jewish purity and dietary laws, especially as Mark's editorial comment "cleansing all foods" (Mk 7.19) is part of the sacred text.[28] Jesus cannot however have meant that it was all right to eat pork and other forbidden food, because this would have caused disputes which would have been preserved, and Peter would not have needed a vision to make him eat Gentile food (Acts 10.9-16; 11.1-18, cf Gal 2.11-12). We must therefore interpret this saying as a vigorous rejection of the orthodox view that people should wash their hands before meals (Mk 7.2ff). In a normal Jewish environment, everything going into a man was kosher food touched by unwashed hands, as Matthew evidently realised (Mt 15.20).

Moreover, Jesus' teaching nowhere suggests that, for example, people do not become unclean by touching a corpse, or that they should not cleanse themselves before going into the inner courts of the Temple. He is also reported to have told a leper whom he had healed to follow the legal procedure for becoming clean (Mk 1.44). On the other hand, Jesus' comments on purity testify to consistent and thoroughgoing opposition to contemporary developments of purity law. The vigour of Mark 7.15 could come only from someone whose rejection of the orthodox expansion of purity regulations was very committed. Q contains equally vigorous attacks on scribes and Pharisees, which assume that their view of purity is in itself reprehensible (Mt 23.25-27/Lk 11.39-41,44). I have noted the similar thrust of the parable of the good Samaritan (Lk 10.29-37). We have also seen that Jesus' behaviour conformed to his teaching, for he had to breach the orthodox view of purity in order to preach the good news to sinners (cf Mk 2.15-17; Lk 7.36-50; 11.38).

We must draw two straightforward conclusions from the attitude of the Jesus movement to the identity factors of Judaism. Firstly, the Jesus movement was thoroughly Jewish, taking most of the identity factors for granted and intensifying some of them. Secondly, the Jesus movement was on the opposite end of a spectrum from orthodoxy. Sabbath and purity are two areas of *halakhah* where we can document a large increase in enactments in the Second Temple period,[29] and these are the two identity factors which occur repeatedly in the disputes between Jesus and the scribes and Pharisees. In other words, the majority of arguments were caused by Jesus' opposition to the orthodox expansion of the *halakhah*: he was not opposed to what he and the majority of Jews perceived the law to be. Virtually all the other conflict material is on the same trajectory. Jesus objected to the Korban regulations (Mk 7.9-13), and to the neglect of central matters brought about by too much stress on the tithing of herbs (Mt 23.23-4/ Lk 11.42). Hence also the general criticism of the scribes and Pharisees for laying burdens on people and doing nothing to help them (Mt 23.4/Lk 11.46). The fact that the Jesus movement was on the opposite end of a spectrum from orthodoxy means that conflict with orthodox Jews was functional, because it reinforced a different view of Judaism. This different view of Judaism was conditioned by the positive centre of the movement in the prophetic tradition.

9. Jesus as the Embodiment of Jewish Identity

All the basic aspects of Jesus' life and teaching may be perceived to embody Judaism as a religion. They form a resurgence of aspects which, John the Baptist apart, had not been prominent in the immediately preceding period. The centre of the ministry was the prophetic call to Jewish sinners to return to the Lord.[30] This was central to Jewish religion. God had made his covenant with the *whole* of the people of Israel. This is writ large in the Law (e.g. Ex 19.3-8; Deut 6.1-9). Jewish tradition also records the rebelliousness of Israel, both in the wilderness and later (e.g. Ex 32; Neh 9.16ff, 26ff; Ps 78). Against that background, the prophets constantly called upon her to return (e.g. Hos 14.2-3; Is 49.5; Jer 3.12-14, 22-3). At the time of Jesus, these many declarations were part of the sacred text. Jesus' ministry embodied and recreated them. The centrality of God drove the resurgence.

We can see this both in imagery and in practical action. The fatherhood and kingship of God are Old Testament images. God was conventionally thought of as king in the Old Testament, and this is the proper background for Jesus' use of the term "kingdom", or "kingship".[31] It is the recreation of an Old Testament idea, embodied in incidents such as Mark 10.13-31, and in exorcisms interpreted as at Matthew 12.28/Lk 11.20. His preaching that the kingdom was at hand recreated the prophetic promise that God would deliver his people (e.g. Is 11.10ff; 40.1ff; Am 9.11-15; Jer 31.31-34). The description of God as Father is an Old Testament image, one which was taken up in the intertestamental period. This means that Jesus' preaching of the fatherhood of God recreated and intensified existing tradition.[32]

At a more practical level, Jesus' healing ministry embodied the power of God in action, as in the mighty acts of Jewish history and in stories such as the healings performed by Elisha (cf 2 Kings 2.19-25; 4-7). His concern for the poor also took up the prophetic tradition (cf e.g. Am 2.6-7; Is 1.16; 61.1; Jer 22.16; Ezek 22.29; also e.g. Ps 9.18; 1QH V, 22).[33] The same goes for the whole of his ethical teaching, which may be seen as the amplification and expansion of an ethical tradition centred in the Levitical command to love one's neighbour as oneself (Lev 19.18). Nowhere is this clearer than in his amplification of the theme of forgiveness, in which the return of Israel to God was mirrored in private life by the forgiveness to be shown to those who do us wrong.

Thus the whole of Jesus' ministry could be perceived as the embodiment of Judaism as it should be. This is evident also in some of the reactions of the disciples. The inner group accepted Jesus' call to leave their everyday lives and follow him. This entailed harsh conditions of existence, and we must infer their acceptance of the promise of the community itself, and of eschatological triumph, as a reward for their participation in the community now.[34] At this level, we should not be contemptuous of unfulfilled promises to die with Jesus (Mk 10.38-9; 14.29-31). No-one gives such an undertaking without a very high level of commitment, and shock at Jesus' fate will have led to mutual support, not to abandonment of the Jesus movement. During the ministry, the apostles also went out on missions two by two, preaching to the lost sheep of the house of Israel and healing the sick (cf Mk 3.14-15; 6.7-13; Mt 10; Lk 9.1-6; 10.1-20). They thus carried Jesus' embodiment of Judaism into their own lives, and they transmitted it to others. They too might be perceived to have embodied Judaism as it should be. Positive reactions to Jesus' teaching and healing ministry are important here too, for they show acceptance of him among Jews who did not necessarily belong to the movement (cf e.g. Mk 1.27-8, 32-3; 2.12; 3.20).

A second outstanding quality on this trajectory was the difference between Jesus' ministry and the conventions of orthodox Judaism. This further explains the appeal of Jesus' ministry to many Jews. Non-observance of the Law is a permanent feature of Jewish life, and the more orthodox our perspective, the more prevalent this feature appears. At the time of Jesus, the orthodox view of Judaism was just as alien to many Jewish people as the orthodox movement is now. If returning to the Lord meant keeping oneself in a permanent state of purity, or learning all the traditions of the Pharisaic elders, many inhabitants of Galilean villages had no hope of returning to the Lord. Jesus offered people the spiritual centre of Judaism instead. Like the whole prophetic tradition, his adherents would keep the sabbath and circumcise their sons, but the centre of life would be love of God and other people, not the detailed regulations of the orthodox. In practice, this meant that returning to the Lord was feasible.

It follows that conflict with the scribes and Pharisees was highly functional for the Jesus movement. When Jesus' adherents heard him attack scribes and Pharisees for their purity laws, they knew that the non-biblical regulations of an elite group had prevented them from returning to the Lord, and that Jesus' rejection of those regulations now enabled them to return to the Lord. When he defended his right to heal on the sabbath, he defended the demonstration of God's power against those who sought to restrict it by means of a non-biblical regulation, and he used arguments drawn from central Jewish tradition. His defence of poor disciples plucking grain on the sabbath, against Pharisees who did not mind them being hungry (Mk 2.23-28), embodied his concern for others and the prophetic tradition of the defence of the oppressed. Parables such as that of the good Samaritan did the same. Scribes from Jerusalem, who alleged that he cast out demons by means of Beelzebub, could only confirm that the perception of Judaism in terms of the traditions of the elders in Jerusalem was a gross distortion of the real Judaism which was always present in word and action before people's eyes.

Thus the social bonding of the Jesus movement was extremely tight. It was bound together by the identity of Judaism itself, and it embodied the Jewish identity of the disciples. What, then, were the *specific* identity factors of the

Jesus movement? It existed at this stage wholly within Judaism - what marked it off from the rest of Judaism? There is only one answer to that question - Jesus himself. This is expressed in a few of the sayings attributed to him: "He who is not for me is against me, and he who does not gather with me scatters" (Mt 12.30/Lk 11.23). The central importance of Jesus was implicit in the significance of his death, and it could be pushed home with eschatological vindication (Lk 12.8-9/Mt 10.32-3, cf Mk 8.38).[35] Jesus' position in the movement was more central than the implication of individual sayings. He led the movement and taught his followers. He was himself the visible embodiment of Jewish identity, and the source of the recreation of the Jewish identity of his disciples. Consequently, the disciples could not abandon Jesus' view of Judaism when he was put to death. It was not just a question of the abandonment of the Jesus movement itself, though its social bonding was tight enough to make that in itself improbable. The nature of Jesus' message as the embodiment of Judaism means that the disciples could not abandon his message without abandoning Judaism, thereby abandoning God and themselves.

This was the cultural setting for the development of christology after Jesus' death. His execution, so far from being a disadvantage to it, was a catalyst, in the first place because it required interpretation. Jesus had already supplied some interpretation of it in terms of an atoning sacrifice, with God's vindication of him by means of resurrection, and this gave the disciples a key to interpret his fate. The only feasible alternative interpretation of his death in that culture was that he had been condemned by God as well as by the Sanhedrin, and since he embodied the identity of Judaism itself, that view was not a live option for his disciples. The only live option was therefore further development. From some perspectives, Jesus' death was more extreme than the crucifixion of 800 Pharisees by Alexander Jannaeus (cf Jos A.J. XIII, 380-3). This event is none the less relevant because it did not provoke the reaction that these men were accursed of God. That was the fate of most people who were hung on a tree, because that was the fate in store for an apostate, and he truly was accursed of God because he was apostate (cf Dt 21.23; 11Q Temple 64.6-13; Gal 3.13).[36] When 800 Pharisees were crucified, their fate was so obviously unjust that they were to be avenged (cf A.J. XIII.410ff). The Maccabean martyrs are more clearly relevant, because of the reactions to their unjust deaths, albeit not by crucifixion. Their death was interpreted as an atoning sacrifice by which Israel was delivered, and some faithful Jews believed that they had been vindicated by being taken immediately to eternal life.[37] Jesus' crucifixion was even more fertile than the fate of the Maccabean martyrs, for he was not only innocent - from the disciples' perspective he was the embodiment of Judaism itself. This guaranteed more dramatic interpretation of his role than is found in any of the other cases.

Jesus' death also permitted some other developments. It removed him as a possible source of objections to his increasing status (cf Mk 10.18), and it gave him the potential for having a range of redemptive, heavenly and abstract theological functions which could not be attributed to a human being who was visibly present among first century Jews. Neither the slaughtered lamb of Revelation nor the heavenly high priest of Hebrews could readily be developed to describe a person still visibly present, nor could Christ be perceived as the end of the Law if he and his followers visibly observed it. One further precondition was necessary if rapid christological growth was to take place in the early church: the processes involved in it had to be culturally normal. We must therefore examine the development of messianic and intermediary figures in Second Temple Judaism, in order to establish that it was a culture in which the processes involved in christological growth were already well-established processes visible in the development of other figures.

1. M.D. Hooker, "Christology and Methodology", *NTS* 17, 1970-1, 480-7.
2. For general treatments, cf C.G.Montefiore, *Some Aspects of the Religious Teaching of Jesus*, Jowett Lectures (1910); G.Bornkamm, *Jesus of Nazareth* (1956. ET 1960); C.H.Dodd, *The Founder of Christianity* (1971); J.Jeremias, *New Testament Theology I: The Proclamation of Jesus* (ET 1971); G.Vermes, *Jesus the Jew* (1973); J.Riches, *Jesus and the Transformation of Judaism* (1980); G.Vermes, *The Gospel of Jesus the Jew* (Riddell Memorial Lectures, 1981); A.E.Harvey, *Jesus and the Constraints of History* (BaL 1980. 1982); E.P.Sanders, *Jesus and Judaism* (1985).
3. These views cannot be justified here. For a discussion of small pieces of material from this point of view, P.M.Casey, op.cit., *Son of Man* chs 8 and 9; *JSNT* 23, 1985, 3-22; *JSNT* 29, 1987, 21-56; *NTS* 34, 1988, 1-23; "The Original Aramaic Form of Jesus' Interpretation of the Cup", *JThS NS 41, 1990, 1-12*. More generally, M. Black, *An Aramaic Approach to the Gospels and Acts* (3rd ed. 1967); M. Wilcox, "Jesus in the Light of his Jewish Environment", *ANRW* II.25.1 (1982), 131-95; G.Schwarz, *"Und Jesus sprach": Untersuchungen zur aramäischen Urgestalt der Worte Jesu* (BWANT VI, 18. 2nd ed., 1987).
4. In addition to the works cited in n.2, cf J.Weiss, *Jesus' Proclamation of the Kingdom of God* (1892. ET, with critical and historical introduction by R.H.Hiers and D.L.Holland. 1971); R.Schnackenburg, *God's Rule and Kingdom* (1959. ET 2nd ed., 1968); G.E.Ladd, *Jesus and the Kingdom* (1964), 2nd ed., *The Presence of the Future. The Eschatology of Biblical Realism* (1980); J.Gray, *The Biblical Doctrine of the Reign of God* (1979); J.Schlosser, *Le Règne de Dieu dans les dits de Jésus* (1980); G.R.Beasley-Murray, *Jesus and the Kingdom of God* (1986).
5. Cf L.Schottroff and W.Stegemann, *Jesus and the Hope of the Poor* (1978. ET 1986); E.Lohse, "Das Evangelium für die Armen", *ZNW* 72, 1981, 51-64.
6. Cf Vermes, *Jesus the Jew*, 194-9; *The Gospel of Jesus the Jew*, 25-28 also *Jesus and the World of Judaism*, (1983), 39-43. The importance of *Abba* is real, but has been exaggerated: Vermes, op. cit.; J.Barr, "Abba isn't Daddy", *JThS NS* 39, 1988, 28-47.
7. Supra, 17-20.
8. I cannot enter here into detailed debate with E.P.Sanders, "Jesus and the Sinners", *JSNT* 19, 1983, 5-36; *Jesus*, ch 6. It will be apparent that I do not accept the equation of the sinners with the wicked. I none the less agree with many of his arguments, and put forward an alternative view when I do not. Cf J.D.G.Dunn, "Pharisees, Sinners and Jesus", in J.Neusner et al.(ed), *The Social World of Formative Christianity and Judaism*. Essays in Tribute to Howard Clark Kee (1988).

9. For full discussion of this pericope, P.M.Casey, op.cit., *NTS* 34, 1988, 1-23.

10. Supra, 58.

11. Supra, 49-50.

12. Supra, 51-2.

13. Cf e.g. V.Eppstein, "The historicity of the Gospel account of the cleansing of the Temple", *ZNW* 55, 1964, 42-58; J.D.M.Derrett, "The zeal of thy house and the cleansing of the temple", *DownR* 95, 1977, 79-94; Sanders, *Jesus*, esp ch 1; R.Bauckham, "Jesus' demonstration in the temple", in B.Lindars (ed), *Law and Religion* (1988), 72-89.

14. Cf Jeremias, op.cit., 276-99; R.Pesch, *Das Abendmahl und Jesu Todesverständnis* (1978); H.F.Bayer, *Jesus' Predictions of Vindication and Resurrection*, WUNT 2.20 (1986).

15. Cf P.M.Casey, op. cit., *JThS NS* 41, 1990, 1-12.

16. Cf infra, 90-1; C.K.Barrett, "The Background of Mark 10.45", in *New Testament Essays: Studies in Memory of T.W.Manson*, ed. A.J.B.Higgins (1959), 1-18; J.Downing, "Jesus and Martyrdom", *JThS NS* 14, 1963, 279-93; Jeremias, op.cit., 276-99; T.E.Pollard, "Martyrdom and Resurrection in the New Testament", *BJRL* 55, 1972-3, 240-51.

17. For this, I am indebted to S.H.Schagen, "Concepts of Resurrection and Immortality in Intertestamental Judaism and in the New Testament" (Diss., PhD, Nottingham, 1985). Dr Schagen is not however responsible for the use which I have made of her work.

18. Cf F.G.Downing, "The Resurrection of the Dead: Jesus and Philo", *JSNT* 15, 1982, 42-50; P.Lapide, *The Resurrection of Jesus* (1984), 59-63; O.Schwankl, *Die Sadduzäerfrage (Mk 12, 18-27 parr)* (1987).

19. Supra, 51-2: *JSNT* 29, 1987, 43-47.

20. Cf H.K. McArthur, "On the Third Day", *NTS* 18, 1971, 81-86.

21. Cf C.H.Dodd, "Jesus as Teacher and Prophet", in G.K.A.Bell and A.Deissman (ed), *Mysterium Christi* (1930), 53-60; D.Hill, *New Testament Prophecy* (1979), ch 2; D.E.Aune, *Prophecy in early Christianity and the ancient Mediterranean world* (1983), chs 5-7; R.A.Horsley, "'Like One of the Prophets of Old': Two Types of Popular Prophets at the Time of Jesus", *CBQ* 47, 1985, 435-63.

22. Infra, 110,113-4,133,150-1.

23. Cf G.Theissen, *The First Followers of Jesus: A Sociological analysis of the earliest Christianity* (1977. ET 1978); G.Lohfink, *Jesus and Community: The Social Dimension of the Christian Faith* (1982. ET 1985), chs 1-2.

24. Supra, 50.

25. We should not however exaggerate - there is no indication that anyone felt this to be a violation of the fifth commandment. Pace M.Hengel, *The Charismatic Leader and His Followers* (1968. ET 1981), 3-15. Cf Sanders, *Jesus*, 252-5.

26. Supra, 50.

27. Cf Vermes, *Jesus the Jew*, 25; D.A.Carson, "Jesus and the Sabbath in the Four Gospels", in D.A.Carson (ed), *From Sabbath to Lord's Day* (1982), 57-97, esp 58-60, 69-71; Casey, op. cit., *NTS* 34, 1988, 1-23; infra, n. 29.

28. Alternatively, critical scholars have argued that it is not an authentic saying. Cf recently H.Räisänen, "Zur Herkunft von Markus 7,15", in J.Delobel (ed), *Logia: les paroles de Jésus* (1982); H.Räisänen, "Jesus and the food laws; reflections on Mark 7.15", *JSNT* 16, 1982, 79-100; J.D.G.Dunn, "Jesus and ritual purity: a study of the tradition history of Mk 7,15", in F.Refoulé (ed), *A Cause de L'Evangile: mélanges*

offerts à Dom Jacques Dupont, LeDiv 123 (1985), 251-76; R.P.Booth, *Jesus and the Laws of Purity. Tradition History and Legal History in Mark 7,* JSNT.SS 13 (1986); B.Lindars, "All foods clean: thoughts on Jesus and the law", in B.Lindars (ed), *Law and Religion* (1988), 61-71.

29. Cf S.T.Kimbrough, "The Concept of Sabbath at Qumran", *RQ* V, 1964-66, 483-502; J.Neusner, *The Rabbinic Traditions about the Pharisees before 70* (3 vols, 1971); J.Neusner, *The Idea of Purity in Ancient Judaism,* SJLA 1 (1973); L.H.Schiffmann, *The Halakhah at Qumran,* SJLA 16 (1975); Schürer-Vermes-Millar II, ch 28; C.Rowland, "A Summary of Sabbath Observance in Judaism at the Beginning of the Christian Era", in D.A.Carson, op.cit., 43-55.

30. Supra, 59-60.

31. Cf supra, 58-9.

32. Supra, 60-1.

33. Cf *TDNT* VI, 39-40, 324, 888ff, 902-7; E.Lohse, op. cit., esp 55f; Horsley, op. cit., 17ff..

34. Supra, 69.

35. Supra, 50-2, 64-8.

36. Cf Fredriksen, *From Jesus to Christ,* 147-8.

37. Infra, 90-1.

Chapter 6
Messianic and Intermediary Figures
in Second Temple Judaism[1]

1. Introduction

The development of New Testament christology is significantly parallelled by a process of development of purely Jewish figures. I have called them "messianic and intermediary figures", an expression which I define rather broadly to ensure that we do not leave out relevant evidence. Three groups of beings are included: One group consists of human beings who are given a status and function beyond the ordinary run of humanity. They include Moses and the future Davidic king. A second group are abstract figures, such as Wisdom and the Word of God. Here it is especially important to keep our definition broad enough, for too strict a definition of "intermediary" would lead us to omit these figures when they are merely aspects of the deity himself, an omission which would obscure the developmental process. The third group are purely supernatural beings. They were mostly regarded as angels.

It is not possible to offer here a complete description of all these figures.[1] I propose to isolate those factors which are important for explaining the growth of christology. I do this under two headings, "static parallels" and "dynamic parallels". By "static parallels" I mean discrete items of known Jewish belief about intermediary figures which are found also as beliefs about Jesus: these items may have been simply transferred to him from another figure. The importance of these static parallels is that they show that Second Temple Judaism already contained some of the beliefs which were taken up into the developing christology of the churches, and this means that they could have been transferred to Jesus very quickly. Static parallels which occur in documents later than the time of Jesus are also relevant. So few documents are known from the earlier period that the absence of a static parallel from earlier documents may be due to the small quantity of surviving evidence, and the fact of the occurrence of any item in a Jewish document shows that it could occur in a Jewish environment.

By a "dynamic parallel", I mean evidence that an intermediary figure was involved in a process which increased its status, or function, or both. Dynamic parallels show that the process of the development of intermediary figures was well established in the Judaism of our period, and at one level this is the pattern into which the development of christology fits.

2. Static Parallels

Three of the major titles, "Lord", "Messiah" and "Son of God", have a significant Jewish background. "Lord" had a very wide range, running from the equivalent of the English "sir" up to the designation of God. It was occasionally used at the bottom end of its range to address the historical Jesus.[2] The early formula *maranatha*, "Come, Lord" (1 Cor 16.22), illustrates how easily the content of the term could slide upwards if the community did no more than continue to address Jesus, now that they believed him to be in heaven. Angels are similarly addressed in Jewish texts (e.g. Zech 4.4-5).

The term "messiah", or "anointed", though not yet a full title, was already used with reference to both the expected Davidic king and the expected Levitical priest, and it was more broadly used with reference to prophets.[3] For example, after a lengthy description of the Davidic king, Psalms of Solomon 17.32 calls him "the Lord's anointed" or "the Lord's messiah", while the Qumran community waited for the coming of "the messiahs of Aaron and Israel" (1QS IX, 11). The term itself was thus already present in Jewish culture to be applied to Jesus. The crystallisation of messianic expectation into a single figure, together with the absence of other anointed figures in the immediate environment, appear to have been the only necessary conditions required for the emergence of the title "the Messiah". This took place in rabbinical Judaism as well as in early Christianity.

"Son of God" was already in use by occasional outsiders during the historical ministry to indicate an exceptional human being.[4] Jewish parallels include its use of wise and righteous individuals. For example, Jesus son of Sirach exhorts, "be like a father to orphans, and be in place of a husband to widows; then God will call you 'son', be gracious to you and save you from destruction" (Sir 4.10). The most striking example is rabbinical in date, though it says nothing that could not have been said in Judaism at the time of Jesus: "The whole universe is sustained on account of my son Hanina, and my son Hanina is satisfied with a kab of carobs from one Sabbath eve to another" (bT Taan 24b/bT Ber 17b/bT Hull 86b). Interpreted in isolation, this might create the impression that Hanina was the son of God in a special or even unique sense, but its cultural context dictates the interpretation that Hanina, being a son of God like so many other people, is being singled out for especial praise, not ontological uniqueness. The same applies to the patriarch Joseph, who is described in *Joseph and Asenath* as the first-born son of God (18.11; 21.4). Pre-Christian examples of people singled out as son of God include Levi and a Hasmonean king (T.Levi 4.2; 4Q ps-Dan).

Some beings seem to be of almost divine status. At Wisdom of Solomon 7.21ff, Wisdom is described in such terms. In 11Q Melchizedek, Old Testament passages containing two of the words for God (El at Ps 7.8-9, and Elohim at Ps 82.1) are interpreted of Melchizedek. Both *Elim* and *Elohim* are used with reference to angels in 4Q Shir Shabb. Philo describes Moses as "God and king of the whole nation" (*Life of Moses*, I, 158), and the *logos* as "the second God" (*Qu in Gen* II, 62). At 3 Enoch 12.3-5, God crowns Metatron, who is enthroned in heaven, and calls him "The lesser YHWH".

Pre-existence is easiest to parallel in hellenistic Judaism, where everyone's souls were believed to exist before they entered bodies, and this belief is probably predicated of all the righteous in the Similitudes of Enoch (cf 1 En 39.4ff; 70.4). Pre-existence in a stronger sense was attributed to Enoch himself, who was named and hidden before the creation of the world (cf 1 En 48.3,6; 62.7). Wisdom was created before everything else already at Proverbs 8.22f, while at Wisdom 7.21 she is the agent of creation. Pre-existent beings who subsequently dwell on earth become perceptible in descent-ascent patterns. The clearest examples are angels who live in heaven and descend temporarily for a specific purpose, as does Raphael in the book of Tobit. The pattern must be deduced in the case of Enoch in the Similitudes, and it is explicit for Wisdom at 1 Enoch 42, while elements of it are applied to Wisdom elsewhere (cf Wsd 9.10; Bar 3.37-38). The presence of these partial elements reflects the fact that the complete pattern may be made up of similar elements in the case of another figure, and need not be taken over in one piece.

When we look for parallels to Jesus' fundamental role in salvation history, we must note that the future Davidic king, Michael, Melchizedek, Moses, Enoch and Wisdom were believed to play a fundamental role in bringing salvation to Israel, while Asenath plays a similar role for proselytes in *Joseph and Asenath*. The details of such a role differ from one figure to another. The Davidic king was sometimes expected to deliver Israel by military and political means, while Michael and Melchizedek seem to have been expected to act in a purely supernatural way (cf Dan 12; 11Q Melch). Moses had already been the lawgiver. Enoch was expected to perform as an eschatological judge, and in the Similitudes this is so important that the righteous are saved in his name (1 En 48.7). At Wisdom 10-11, Wisdom's leading role includes the deliverance of Noah from the flood and the Exodus of Israel from Egypt: equally, men may be saved by Wisdom in that they have become wise (Wsd 9.18). Asenath could be perceived as responsible for the salvation of proselytes, who were initiated into a form of Judaism in which she and her husband Joseph were central.

The miraculous birth of Melchizedek is recounted at 2 Enoch 71. Noah is born fully formed with miraculous accomplishments in 1 Enoch 106, and a similar event is indicated in the fragmentary account of 1QGen Ap II, where Lamech worries that Noah's father may be one of the Watchers or Holy Ones or one of the giants.[5] In the prayer of Manasseh, we are told that Abraham, Isaac and Jacob did not sin: the future Davidic king was also expected to be pure from sin (Ps Sol 18.36). Joseph and Moses are set forth as models for ethically sound behaviour,[6] and the righteousness of Enoch is such that sin does not appear to come into question. The function of revelation performed by the twelve patriarchs and others, especially Enoch, also provides some parallel to the position of Jesus as the revealer. The death of martyrs was believed to have atoning significance (cf 2 Macc 7.37-8; 1 En 48.4; 4 Macc 17.20-22). There is also some evidence that martyrs were believed to have gone straight to heaven (e.g. 4 Macc 13.17). The Binding of Isaac was interpreted as a voluntary act on his part, and in due course it was thought to have atoning value.[7]

Abel, Abraham, Elijah, Enoch, Melchizedek, Michael, Moses, Wisdom and others were variously believed to be in heaven: Enoch, later Metatron, was enthroned there (cf e.g. 1 En 62; 3 En 10), as was Abel (T.Abr. 13) or David (R.Aqiba at bT Hag 14a/bT San 38b). Angels who were normally believed to dwell in heaven might descend to earth. They are frequently portrayed as appearing to people in dreams and visions (e.g. Dan 7-12). Sometimes they appeared like men in normal life, as Raphael does in the book of Tobit. The kings and mighty were expected to supplicate Enoch at the last day (1 En 62.9), when all who dwell on earth would fall down before him (1 En 48.5). The eating of a meal is a significant event in the appropriation of salvation in *Joseph and Asenath*. The Davidic king, the Levitical High Priest, a prophet, Elijah, Enoch and Moses were variously expected to come at the last day: at this time Abel (T.Abr.13) or Enoch (1 En 62; 69.16ff) was expected to play an active role as an eschatological judge. Enoch was also expected to be not only "a staff to the righteous" but even "a light to the Gentiles" (1 En 48.4). OT passages are applied to several figures. Examples include the interpretation of the man-like figure in Daniel 7.13f as Enoch, with consequent use of the term "son of man" in the Similitudes, and the interpretation of this same text as a symbol of the future Davidic king in 4 Ezra 13. The transference to Wisdom of actions which are explicitly actions of God in a scriptural narrative is found at Wisdom 10-11.

These static parallels to New Testament christology are substantial and extensive. Most of them are also well enough known to conventional scholarship, which frequently stops its analysis of them at this point. One may then point out that, if we look at New Testament christology as a whole, many aspects of Christ's finished work have no parallel. Moreover, to find all these parallels, we have had to look at several different Jewish figures, and it may be asserted that Jesus is quite remarkably unique, since he has taken up all these different figures into himself.[8] This kind of view may then be used to support the belief, usually the Gentile Christian belief, of the observer, whose own intellectual habits appear however to be the reason for the static mode of analysis first employed. This is hardly satisfactory. When an analytical mode proves too limited to explain a development, we should try more flexible modes of analysis, and if these lead to more explanatory theories, they must be regarded as more appropriate modes. I turn next to "dynamic parallels".

3. Dynamic Parallels

All the more outstanding of these figures are significantly unique, and the elaboration of them bears witness to a dynamic creative process within Judaism. Not less than 16 figures, the future Davidic king, an eschatological High Priest, Abel, Abraham, Asenath, Elijah, Enoch, Isaac, Jacob, Joseph, Melchizedek, Michael, Moses, Wisdom and Word, all these were held by some Jews of the Second Temple or early rabbinical periods to be of unusually elevated status and to have performed or be about to perform some function of evident significance. The ascription of significant new functions to these figures, and the dynamic parallels thus provided, are of greater importance than static parallels. They testify to the existence of a developmental process, and the variability of this developmental process shows that when another intermediary figure is elaborated, we should not expect it to conform to any existing figure. We must look at some examples in more detail: I take first a brief look at four of these figures, the future Davidic king, Michael, Moses and the Word of God.

The hope for deliverance by a king of David's line goes right back into the Old Testament (e.g. Jer 23.5-8; Mic 5.1-3). This hope became part of Israel's identity, and its development in our period includes lengthy expositions in Psalms of Solomon 17 and 4 Ezra 13.[9] Two developments may be thought especially notable. One is his increasing righteousness, which reaches a climax in the declaration that he will be "pure from sin" (Ps Sol 17.36; cf T.Judah 24.1). Another is the isolation of the title "King Messiah", or more simply "the Messiah". This title could be used without any need for prior identification of this figure in the context, and it appears to have resulted from the crystallization of messianic hopes into one figure after A.D.70, when the other main anointed figures, priests and prophets, ceased to function.[10]

In some documents, the future Davidic king maintains his traditional military functions, as when he slays some of the nations at 2 Baruch 72.2,6. However, careful analysis of the lengthy expositions of his actions in both Psalms of Solomon 17 and 4 Ezra 13 shows that, despite the extreme vigour of the imagery, he achieves everything by peaceful means: *"At his rebuke* nations shall flee from him" (Ps Sol 17.25): "and then he shall destroy them *without labour by the Law,* which is *compared* to fire" (4 Ezra 13.38). This shows considerable reinterpretation of the kingly tradition. It must be attributed to the need of the Jewish community to envisage deliverance when the Romans were unimaginably more powerful than they were. It was consequently easier for some Jews to envisage deliverance by supernatural means, than to imagine the messiah leading an army to defeat the nations by human force.

In 4 Ezra, the messiah is very probably pre-existent (12.32; 13.26, 52; cf Sib Or V, 414ff). 4 Ezra 13 also gives him the function of gathering together the lost ten tribes (4 Ezra 13.12-13,39-47). At 2 Baruch 30, he is expected to return to heaven before the general resurrection of the dead, and later developments include the expectation that he will rebuild the Temple (Tg Is 53.5, cf 52.13).

In spite of this tradition of deliverance by a Davidic king, R.Aqiba hailed Simeon son of Kosiba as "King Messiah" (pT Taan IV, 5, 68d). Simeon was not of Davidic descent, but he led a revolt against Rome, describing himself as "Prince of Israel" on his coins. This further illustrates the flexibility of this hope, and the extent to which it could be reinterpreted in the light of events. If Simeon was leading Israel to victory, he *must* be the King Messiah! Rabbinical exegesis was flexible enough to deal with the matter of Davidic descent, though Aqiba's exegesis of relevant texts has not survived - we know only that he saw the coming of Simeon predicted in the non-Davidic Numbers 24.17. The reinterpretation of the hope for a Davidic king in terms of Jesus of Nazareth is not *precisely* paralleled here. What is paralleled is the vigour and flexibility of reinterpretation, in the light of commitment to a particular figure and the needs of the community.

Michael was the most outstanding figure in a whole supernatural world of angels.[11] Belief in this supernatural world was part of the surrounding culture which Israel had inherited centuries ago (cf 1 Kings 22.19). In our period, we find an established dualistic system in which angels are counterbalanced by evil angels, or demons, and there are a few outstanding figures who have a high status and particular functions. Michael is the most prominent, and at Daniel 12.1 he is described as "the great prince who stands on behalf of the sons of your people". Since his standing up at the time of great distress is immediately followed by their deliverance, he must be at least partly responsible for their deliverance, though the way this works is not spelt out. He has already been mentioned as fighting on their behalf, apparently in heavenly warfare (Dan 10.13; 11.1). He is evidently Israel's own special angel, a fact related to his emergence as the chief angel of all.

At 1QM XVII, the world of good angels is described as "the kingdom of Michael", opposed to the kingdom of wickedness and in contrast to the realm of Israel, who form the earthly realm of the holy ones. As the chief angel, Michael performs an intercessory function with God. At Testament of Levi 5.6-7, he is presumably the angel who is said to intercede for the people of Israel and for all the righteous. At 3 Baruch 11ff he takes the prayers and merits of the righteous to God. He is also the victor over the forces of evil, especially in the last times; at 1 Enoch 54 we are told that he, with Gabriel, Raphael and Phanuel, will cast the hosts of Azazel into hell at the last day.

Michael is thus the chief of a whole class of beings who perform some of the same functions as the deities of the surrounding culture. They are not gods, because monotheism was an identity factor of the Jewish community. They are not worshipped, for the worship of several gods and goddesses had long been characteristic of Gentiles. Nor do they usually indulge in any kind of sexual behaviour, because the restriction of sexuality to the needs of procreation within marriage was characteristic of the public identity of the Jewish community. The exception to this was the widespread speculation on the descent of the sons of God, who mated with the daughters of men and produced the race of giants (cf e.g. Gen 6.1-7; 4Q Giants). This is explicitly regarded as evil, sometimes indeed as the origin of evil (e.g. 1 En 6-10). The angelic world as a whole supplied the need to picture a heavenly realm corresponding to that of earth, and to explain some of the fundamental facts of life. Within it, Michael functioned as Israel's own angel, especially liable to undergo important development because he was part of her identity.

Moses was already a significant intermediary figure in the Old Testament, where he spoke with God face to face and received the Law. As the Law became more and more important because it displayed the identity of the Jewish community as a whole, so the position of Moses was further developed.[12] At Testament of Moses 1.14 he is pre-existent at least in the sense of being foreseen, while Ps-Philo declares that he was born circumcised (Ant.Bib. IX,13). Ezekiel portrayed him dreaming that he sat on the throne of God (Eus. *Praep.Ev.* IX, 29), and Josephus has him disappear in a cloud rather than merely die (A.J. IV,326). Josephus also reports that the Essenes venerated him most after God himself, and that they punished blasphemy against him with death (B.J. II,145, cf 152). Further material was attributed to him, part of a process of declaring that legal judgements and associated material belonged to the same authoritative traditions as the written law itself. This included the expanded version of part of the Pentateuch written in Jubilees, said to have been revealed by the angel of the Lord to Moses on Mt Sinai. This traditional role led to the description of Moses as "mediator of his covenant" (T.Mos. 1.14). In the *Testament of Moses* he also reveals the present suffering and forthcoming deliverance of Israel. Eupolemus tells us that he invented writing (Eus. *Praep.Ev.* IX, 26), Artapanus that he also taught Orpheus (ibid., IX, 27), and he was often thought to have originated Greek philosophy (cf e.g. Jos., *c.Apion* II, 168; 281).

Philo's life of Moses offers an idealised portrait of "the greatest and most perfect of men", who "displayed the beliefs of philosophy in his everyday behaviour", and was outstanding as king, law-giver, high priest and prophet (*Life of Moses* I,1; I,29; II,3). He is set forth as a human being whose life was so superior that he ought to be copied. God is said to have given him the whole world as an heir so that all the elements obeyed him, and he is described as "God and king of the whole nation" (I, 155; 158). Development of the figure of Moses continued into the rabbinical period. Isaiah 53.12 was applied to him by R.Simlai (bT Sotah 14a), and some Jews expected him to return to lead the people with the messiah in the last days (e.g. Tg Neof I, Ex 12.42).

The Word of God was to begin with no more than an aspect of the divine action.[13] The Old Testament, however, already has examples of its use in sentences which could be interpreted as references to a separate being, and which indicate the potential for further development. For example, Psalm 33.6 says of the creation, "By the Word of the Lord were the heavens made." Prophets declared that the Word of Yahweh had come to them, using expressions such as "The Lord has sent a word into Jacob" (Is 9.8). Significant further development is certainly found in hellenistic Judaism. At Wisdom 18, the Word is portrayed like a separate being of great power. The context is the action of God against the Egyptians at the time of the Exodus:

> your all-powerful word from heaven, a relentless warrior, leapt from your
> royal throne into the midst of that doomed land, bearing the sharp sword
> of your unmistakeable command, and stood and filled everything with
> death. He touched the heaven, yet stood on earth (Wsd 18.15-16).

This portrays the Word as a separate being, and gives it a soteriological function which is that of God himself in a scriptural narrative (Ex 14.24-31). We should also note the anthropomorphic presentation of a basically abstract entity, which indicates that no hard and fast line was necessarily felt to exist between what we perceive as human and abstract beings.

In Philo's works, the *logos*, or Word, of God is used in a vigorous and varied way. Perhaps its most important function is to solve the paradox of transcendence and immanence. Philo absorbed enough Greek philosophy to feel that God was too transcendent to be knowable, but he was so Jewish that he believed in a knowable and active God. The *logos* effectively functions as the aspect of God by which people know him. He can therefore be called "God", without a definite article, at Genesis 31.13 (*On Dreams* I, 227ff), and he can be identified as the intelligible universe. Thus he is sometimes described as if he were a being separate from God. For example, he is God's "firstborn son" (*De Agr* 51), "the eldest of the angels, as it were their ruler, who has many names. For he is called 'beginning' and 'Name of God' and 'Word' and 'the Man after his Image', and 'He who sees', that is, Israel" (*De Conf Ling* 146). In discussing the creation of man in the image of God, Philo even describes the *logos* as a second God (*Qu in Gen* II, 62). This indicates that the theoretical limit of Jewish monotheism may appear to be breached by an occasional sentence, but these sentences should not be removed from their cultural context. Philo did not believe in two Gods, nor did he believe that the Word of God was a genuinely separate being forming a sort of binity with the Lord. Rather his description of the *logos*, depending on two cultural traditions both of which exalted it greatly and one of which (the Greek) was not fully monotheistic, is dramatic and vigorous.

Developments are also found in Aramaic-speaking Judaism, though perhaps not before the rabbinical period. Some of the Aramaic translations of the Old Testament have actions done by the Word of God when the Hebrew text has them done by God himself. For example, at Genesis 1.3, Codex Neofiti I reads, "And the Word (Memra) of the Lord said, 'Let there be light', and there was light according to the decree of his Word." Like the developments of human beings and of supernatural figures, the developments of the Word of God are rooted deeply within Jewish tradition, so that they may be perceived as literary developments of an aspect of Jewish identity.

These figures are generally representative of the development of messianic and intermediary figures as a whole. Most of them were closely associated with the identity of the Jewish people, and they underwent striking developments of their status and functions during the Second Temple and early rabbinical periods. These developments seem to be inhibited only by monotheism, which was itself an identity factor of the Jewish community. The developments thus exemplify a common process. Whether these figures are human, supernatural or abstract, additional status and new functions might be attributed to them if some members of the community needed to visualise them like that. Consequently, the developments are most vigorous in cases where the needs of either the community or of a subgroup within it were especially great. There are two cases where a social subgroup can be detected which was responsible for particularly dramatic developments of well-known figures. These two figures are Enoch and Wisdom.

4. Enoch and the Chosen

The earliest recorded mention of Enoch is at Genesis 5.24, where we are told that "he walked with *Elohim*; and he was not, for *Elohim* took him." This must mean that he was with God, or the angels, during his earthly life, and that he did not die.[14] More extensive material, which cannot be later than the third century B.C., presents him as a heavenly scribal figure who receives and transmits revelations. These revelations include wisdom material, such as information about the heavens gathered by Enoch on his heavenly journeys, as well as elaborated versions of old stories about the fall of the angels. In second century documents, his revelations include the final events of human history, which were expected in the immediate future. His scribal function is further developed in 1 Enoch 13-14, where he performs an intermediary function between God himself and the sons of heaven: he takes their petition for forgiveness, conveys the message of judgment back to them and reprimands them for their wickedness. 1 Enoch 14 includes a description of him rising directly into the presence of God.

From the orthodox wing of Judaism, Jubilees 4.16ff presents Enoch as a major source of revelation, knowledge and wisdom, who spent almost 300 years with the angels. His revelations included the correct calendar, and future history until the day of judgment. He is said to have been translated to the garden of Eden, where he acts as heavenly scribe, writing down the condemnation and judgment of the world. He also burnt the incense of the sanctuary before the Lord (4.25).

At a more popular level, the book of Giants portrays Enoch as the heavenly scribe who mediates divine judgment. In 1 Enoch 83-90, Enoch sees the whole of world history, and tells how he went with Judas Maccabaeus and three angels to see the final judgment (1 En 90.31). Also from the less strict wing of Judaism comes 2 Enoch, where Enoch is again primarily the heavenly scribe, author of 366 revelatory books. 2 Enoch consists mostly of the mysteries of the universe, including the ultimate destiny of the righteous and the wicked. It ends with Enoch's translation, and 2 Enoch 64.5 describes Enoch's position after this: "For you will be glorified before the Lord's face for all time, since the Lord chose you, rather than all men on earth, and designated you writer of all his creation, visible and invisible, and redeemer of the sins of man, and helper of your household." In 3 Enoch, he is transformed into the mighty angel Metatron, enthroned and crowned by God, and named "the lesser YHWH" (3 En 4-15). On the hellenized but faithful wing of Judaism, the Wisdom of Solomon accepts the general view that Enoch was exceptionally righteous and consequently translated to heaven (Wsd 4.10-14). Further along that end of the spectrum, ps-Eupolemus records the opinion that Enoch discovered astrology (Eus. *Praep. Ev.* IX.17).

This vigorous development of the figure of Enoch forms the cultural background to two works which provide evidence of an Enoch circle, a subgroup within Judaism characterized by their attitude to Enoch. 1 Enoch 91-93 consists of a revelation by Enoch, in which the whole of world history is divided into ten "weeks". Aramaic fragments from Qumran have confirmed that our Ge'ez manuscripts are corrupt and dislocated, though they represent the approximate contents of the original work. The title highlights a particular social group: "Concerning the sons of righteousness, and concerning the chosen of the world who have grown up from the plant of righteousness and uprightness, I will speak." This isolates Israel, and a subgroup within Israel. The election of Israel is at the end of the third week, when "a man will be chosen as the plant of righteous judgment, and after him will come the plant of righteousness for ever." After the exile, an apostate generation shall arise in the seventh week, a view which shows that this author was out of sympathy with the Second

Temple and its hellenized priesthood. At the end of the seventh week, "the elect shall be chosen from the eternal plant of righteousness as witnesses to righteousness, and to them shall be given sevenfold wisdom and knowledge" (93.10). This is our subgroup, and it is clear from the account of the eighth week, in which a sword is given to the righteous to execute judgment on the sinners (91.12), that a major reason for the composition of this document was to assure this subgroup that they would win soon, in the first place by military victory. This group were faithful Jews, opposed to the drastic hellenization of the period, but there is nothing to place them on the orthodox wing of Judaism. The only perceptible identity factor marking them off from their fellow Jews is their view of Enoch, whose revelations were perceived as the source of the sevenfold wisdom and knowledge which they believed themselves to possess.

Once such a subgroup existed, there was potential for further development. This is found in the crown of this literature, the Similitudes of Enoch (1 En 37-71). It has been a difficult work to interpret. It survives only in late and corrupt Ge'ez manuscripts, which show the same kind of dislocation as the Ge'ez manuscripts of 1 Enoch 91-93. It has three expressions for "son of man", and Gentile Christian scholars who have read it in the hope that it would illuminate the Gospels have supposed that this is the title of the powerful eschatological judge, in spite of his identification as Enoch at the end of the work. Like "son of man" elsewhere in Aramaic documents, it should rather be understood as an ordinary term for "man", and it is not used in any unusually idiomatic way.[15] The work has two major themes. One is the respective fates of the righteous, holy and elect on the one hand, and the sinners, who are by and large the kings and mighty, on the other. The second theme is the identity of the eschatological judge. This permeates the structure of this work from the opening of the second similitude onwards, and the revelation that Enoch is this person forms the climax of the work in chapter 71. The two themes are related to each other because of Enoch's role as the eschatological judge.

The newness and significance of the revelations given in the Similitudes are indicated in the introduction: "Until now there has not been given by the Lord of Spirits such wisdom as I have received...." (1 En 37.4). The veiled revelation of the eschatological judge begins in chapter 46. "And there I saw one who had a head of days, and his head was white like wool; and with him there was another, whose face had the appearance of a man, and his face was full of grace, like one of the holy angels" (46.1). Enoch's response is natural, and essential for the structure of the work: "Then I asked one of the angels, one who went with me and showed me all secrets, concerning that son of man, who he was, where he was from, and why he went with the Head of Days" (46.2). These two verses allude to Daniel 7.9-10,13-14, where "one like a son of man" is given power and kingship, but is not identified. Thus "that son of man" is seen as revealed in scripture - to those who can interpret scripture correctly. The angel's answer to the question of this figure's identity is remarkable, for it does not reveal his identity: "This is the son of man who has righteousness; righteousness dwells with him, and he reveals all the treasures of that which is hidden, because the Lord of Spirits has chosen him, and his lot is pre-eminent before the Lord of

Spirits in uprightness for ever" (46.3).

This lack of identity is deliberate, and it is reinforced by the author's practice, throughout the remainder of the work, of referring to this figure as "that son of man" or "the chosen one". The climax of the work is kept for the very end. Here Enoch, translated to heaven without dying, as in the old traditions about him, is taken before God himself and greeted, "You are the son of man who is born of righteousness. Righteousness dwells in you, and the righteousness of the Head of Days will not leave you" (1 En 71.14). This is a clear reference back to 46.3, which requires something like this at some later stage. The structure emphasizes the great importance of this revelation, which mirrors the situation of the community; they will have been well aware that other Jews did not believe that Enoch was so fundamental to salvation as this. Hence also the theme of veiled revelation occurs elsewhere in this work. Enoch was chosen and hidden before the Lord of Spirits before the creation of the world (48.6). At 62.7, this is given as the reason for the recognition scene in which the kings and mighty discover in terror who the chosen one is, as well as the fact of imminent judgment: "For from the beginning the son of man was hidden, and the Most High kept him in the presence of his power, and revealed him to the chosen." The expression "the chosen" can only be a reference to the subgroup who were ultimately to produce the Similitudes.

Much of the Similitudes is taken up with exposition of Enoch's role as eschatological judge. He will condemn and punish the mighty kings and the exalted, who will fall down before him and petition for mercy from him (62.9). Indeed, all those who live on earth will fall down and prostrate themselves before him (48.5). He will judge not only human beings, but also the holy ones in heaven above (61.8). As the eschatological judge, he will sit on a throne in heaven (e.g. 55.4). He will be the light of the nations and the hope of those who grieve in their hearts (48.4, using Is 42.6; 49.6), and in his name the holy and righteous will be saved (62.13). After his final judgment, evil will be abolished and the righteous will live with Enoch in paradise (71.16-17).

This remarkable development of Enoch was carried out during the Second Temple period by a group of faithful and oppressed Jews. Like their predecessors in 1 Enoch 91-93, they did not belong to the orthodox wing of Judaism, a negative correlation which should probably be seen as fundamental to the development of their only specific identity factor. They found him in scripture, and implied by a longstanding and widespread tradition. This led them to put him forward as the agent of their imminent vindication by God, a change of perception primarily due to the needs of a grievously oppressed community.

5. Wisdom and the Wise

The development of Wisdom[16] was also related to the existence of a social subgroup. She is already a pre-existent figure in the book of Proverbs (8.22f), where she is a staff of life to all who grasp her (3.18). She is probably also the agent of creation (cf 3.19, 8.27f). There is a more highly wrought picture of her in Ecclesiasticus, where she makes a considerable speech "in the assembly of the Most High ... and in the presence of his host" (Sir 24.1):

I came forth from the mouth of the Most High and covered the earth like a mist. I dwelt on high, and my throne was in a pillar of cloud. Alone I made a circuit of heaven and walked in the depth of abysses. I ruled over the waves of the sea, the whole earth, and every people and nation (24.3-7).

This description portrays a separate heavenly being, of the greatest possible authority and power. Ecclesiasticus also gives a picture of full-time wise men, highly educated professional people for whom wisdom was the centre of life (39.1-11). The figure of Wisdom was highly developed because she embodied these people's identity, and the identification of her with the Law brings her within the culture of faithful Jews (Sir 24.23; cf Bar 4.1; 2 Bar 38.1-4; 4 Macc 1.17; 5.35). At a practical level, this identification was facilitated by an overlapping body of ethical teaching. At the mythological level, she is also identified with the creative word spoken by "the Most High" (Sir 24.3), another development which presents her as Jewish while keeping her on a cosmic scale.

There is further evidence of the work of a social group of wise men. For example, at Daniel 11.33 we are told, surely by a wise man, that the wise men of the people will give guidance to the many at the time of the Maccabean revolt. Their eschatological vindication follows at Daniel 12.3. At Qumran, they are identified as people who expound the Law (CD 6,2-5; 11QPsa XVIII, 5-14). In Enoch literature, as in the book of Daniel, Wisdom traditions were taken by wise men into apocalyptic literature. The Similitudes are described as a "vision of Wisdom" (1 En 37.1). The Wisdom content and terminology in this work form significant background to the myth of 1 Enoch 42, where Wisdom's dwelling is in heaven. She came down to earth to live among the sons of men, but found nowhere to stay, so she returned to heaven and took her seat among the angels (1 En 42.2; cf Bar 3.29, 38).

Wisdom is almost unique among these figures in being feminine. Philo calls her the daughter of God, a perpetual virgin, though he explicitly demythologises his own language (*De Fug* 50-52). She is the mother of all things (*Qu in Gen* IV,97), in particular the mother and nurse of the wise (*De Conf* 49: *Det* 116). In view of her creative function, she may be called "divine" (*Her 199*). Her femininity is remarkably developed in the original version of Sirach 51, now extant as a separate Wisdom poem (11QPsa XXI). Its imagery is full of erotic double meanings. The only feasible parallel to this is the wicked woman of Proverbs 9.13ff and 4Q 184, who might be thought of as an anti-Wisdom figure rather than simply a wanton female. Of other feminine figures, only the human being Asenath is vigorously developed, and that happens only in *Joseph and Asenath.*

In the hellenized Wisdom of Solomon, Wisdom is again completely central, and even more elevated. She is not however identified with the Law. This is not because the author does not expect Jews to obey the Jewish Law. It is rather that the focus of attention is broader, and Wisdom rather than the Law is the centre of the author's life-stance (cf 6.17-21). Being wise is virtually equated with being righteous. Wise men are a distinct group, and their significance is summed up at 6.24: "a multitude of wise men is the salvation of the world." The wisdom of these people embraced virtually the whole of knowledge. It is said to include justice and law (Wsd 9.4), the purposes of God (9.17), and the subjects listed at 7.17f:

> the structure of the world and the operation of the elements, the beginning, end and middle of epochs, the alternating solstices and the changing of the seasons: the revolution of the year and the positions of the stars: the nature of animals and the behaviour of wild beasts; the violent force of winds and the arguments of men; the varieties of plants and the powers of roots.

This description of wisdom, the daily preoccupation of the author and his fellow wise men, leads straight into the declaration of the exalted position of Wisdom: "I learnt both what is secret and what is obvious, for Wisdom, who made everything, taught me" (7.21). She is presented as very nearly divine:

> For Wisdom is more mobile than motion, she pervades and permeates all things because of her purity. She is the vapour of the power of God, a pure emanation from the glory of the Almighty, so nothing defiled gains entrance to her. She is the effulgence of eternal light, a spotless mirror of the activity of God and an image of his goodness (7.24-26).

Further details of her functions are given: she enters holy souls, and makes them God's friends and prophets. Finally, "she spans the world robustly from end to end, and controls all things benevolently" (8.1). In chapters 10-11, the author attributes to Wisdom the major events of salvation history, so that she plays the role given in the Old Testament account to God. Thus Wisdom is almost divine, but she is not hailed as a goddess, for this would have violated Jewish monotheism. The final elevation of her to the point which she occupies in the *Wisdom of Solomon* should be related positively to the existence of a group of professional wise men, and negatively to the fact that this work does not belong to the orthodox wing of Judaism.

6. The Maccabean Martyrs

One group of figures deserves our attention because of the known reaction to their fate. In the persecution of Antiochus Epiphanes, Jews were for the first time tortured and killed *because* they observed the Law. The problem of the righteous dead therefore became pressing.[17] This led to the first clear declaration of the resurrection of the dead, in a document from the period itself (Dan 12.2-3). Belief in the heavenly vindication of these martyrs was therefore an almost immediate development. Later sources sometimes indicate the immediate transfer of the martyrs to heaven. One of the clearest examples is 4 Maccabees 13.17, which presupposes the present existence of Abraham, Isaac, Jacob and other patriarchs in a place of bliss, to which the martyrs will go when they die. There is no indication that anyone's tomb will be empty.[18]

The book of Daniel shows the first signs of belief in the atoning death of these martyrs. At Daniel 11.35, some of the wise "will stumble, to refine among them and to purify and to make white." Later documents assert more clearly that the deaths of the martyrs were an atoning sacrifice which assuaged the wrath of God and enabled him to deliver Israel (2 Macc 7.37-8: 4 Macc 17.20-22).

In this case, therefore, the shameful deaths of the righteous were coped with by positive thought about the function of their deaths in God's plan, and by unverifiable belief in their immediate survival in heaven. These thoughts enabled the Jewish community to continue to exist under pressure, and to cope with the violent death of the righteous. Some developments took place at once, and others followed later. All this forms a closer parallel to the interpretation of the death of Jesus than could be provided by most of the traditional figures of Israel's history.

7. On the Fringe

On the fringes of Judaism lie some unusual developments which should be considered briefly. The most interesting of these came to be called the two powers heresy.[19] Elisha ben Abuya, a rabbi of the early second century, is reported to have said, during a vision in which he saw Metatron, that there are two powers in heaven (bT Hag 15/ 3 En 16). We must note that Elisha became apostate. The second significant point is that whenever the heresy appears, it is regarded as beyond the boundaries of Judaism. For example, at Mekh *Bah* 5 (Ex 20.2), "the nations of the world" and "heretics (minim)" are the two groups of people who say there are two powers. The heresy cannot be shown to have been at all widespread. We must observe also that the second power was not incarnate. Moreover, this development does not appear to have occurred until the second century, some time after the development of the deity of Jesus in the fourth Gospel. It is probably the reason for rabbinical rejection of R.Aqiba's exegesis of Daniel 7.9, according to which there were two thrones in heaven, one for God and the other for David (bT Hag 14a/bT San 38b).

Thoughts of this kind have always occurred on the fringes of the Jewish community. As the identity factor of monotheism has intensified, they have more clearly led to exclusion from that community. Jeremiah objected to the worship of the Queen of heaven, but worshipped she was (Jer 44), and at Elephantine she was associated with Yahu. After the exile and the Maccabean conflict, a second deity might still attract occasional Jews, but it led to exclusion from the community. It is thus to be distinguished from the occasional use of the term "God" for an intermediary, as we see it in 11Q Melchizedek, Philo and perhaps Romans 9.5.[20]

Finally, there is a little evidence of more unusual developments from sources which have survived only in quotations by Christian writers. For example, Origen quotes a few lines from the Prayer of Joseph, in which Jacob is presented as "the archangel of the power of the Lord and supreme commander among the sons of God", and "the firstborn of every living thing given life by God". Uriel says of him that he "descended to earth and dwelt among men, and was called by the name Jacob" (*Comm on Jn* II, 31). This is a very elevated figure, and if we do not define incarnation so strictly as to include only fully divine beings who are born as people, this figure may be perceived as an incarnate angel during his earthly life.[21] Fragmentary works of this kind must, however, be handled with great caution. It is not only that they may date from a time later than that of Jesus. The main problem concerns the information from a church father that such a work is "Jewish", or "in circulation among the Hebrews"

(Origen, loc.cit.). Such a work may be a product of an assimilating group on the fringes of Judaism, whose work consequently appealed to Gentile Christian writers and was not preserved by Jews. In some cases, including this one, the relationship may have been so close, and the date sufficiently late, for the development to have been a result of contact with Christians and their view of Jesus.

These documents should, therefore, be used only to illuminate christological development as it is found in the epistle to the Hebrews and in the Johannine community, whose Jews assimilated out of Judaism. They should not be used in any simple way to illustrate what might happen in the earliest stage of christological development, when Christianity was still a purely Jewish group within Judaism.

8. Analysis

All these figures provide examples of a common developmental feature. This consists of the addition of new items of belief, whether in assertions, semi-poetic passages, scriptural references or stories. This process is the same for human, supernatural and abstract figures, and it did not alter in any fundamental sense when Judaism was hellenised. Some figures show much more development than others. Enoch and Wisdom were developed with especial vigour, reaching an exceptionally high status with unique functions. They have two significant qualities in common. We can detect a social subgroup attached to each of them, and each of them in some way indicates or embodies the identity of that subgroup.

This illuminates the nature of the cause of these developments. They were caused by the needs of the community. The nature of the development of these Jewish figures should lead us to expect that the figure of Jesus would be developed in accordance with the needs of the early Christian community. Furthermore, the nature of the Jesus movement in having Jesus as the embodiment of Jewish identity[22] means that he could function like one of these figures immediately. Most Jewish figures had been significant for centuries because that was the way that Jewish identity was normally formed, with the continual development of several well-known figures in accordance with the needs of the community as a whole. Since however identity was central, it could substitute for age in a case where a subgroup's identity was formed round a more recent figure.

What were the limits to the development of these figures? The only limitation perceptible in our primary sources is Jewish monotheism. The function of this strict form of monotheism as an identity marker of the Jewish community is stated explicitly by ps-Aristeas, who declares that Moses in the law "went on to show that all the rest of mankind except ourselves believe that there are many gods" (ps-Aristeas 134).

This limitation was real and pervasive. To be quite precise about it, we must also note a handful of sentences in our sources which appear to breach it, and which must be interpreted in their cultural context. Philo is the main source, referring to the *logos* (Word) as a second God (*Qu. in Gen* II, 62), and describing

Moses as "God and king of the whole nation" (*Life of Moses* I, 158). There is, however, no doubt that Philo was fully monotheistic in the strictest sense: these passages illustrate what a strict Jewish monotheist could do occasionally when discussing one of these figures. The same is true of 11Q Melchizedek, which applies to Melchizedek some words about God (El) at Psalm 7.8-9 and God (Elohim) at Psalm 82.1. Such references were all the easier to make because scripture was known to be true, and could therefore legitimate expressions which might otherwise not have been felt to be satisfactory. Passages of this kind should therefore be carefully distinguished from the two powers heresy, and from features of Gentile culture, such as the deification of the Roman emperor in the Greco-Roman world. They must also be borne in mind when we consider the supposed deity of Jesus in such passages as Romans 9.5, Philippians 2.6ff, and Hebrews 1.1ff.[23]

No other serious limitation may be observed. In particular, there was no general bar to prevent the transfer of status and functions from one intermediary figure to another. Such transference is not common in purely Jewish sources because there was rarely any need for it. For example, while we cannot detect any particular reason why it should be Penemue who was landed with the responsibility for leading men astray by teaching them how to write with ink on papyrus (1 En 69.8-11), there was no particular reason to transfer this accusation to anyone else. Certain bonds of propriety were inevitable because some functions would be inappropriate to the identity of a given figure. No-one would be motivated to attribute this function to Moses, Raphael or the future Davidic king. It was produced by the need of a conservative Jewish community to object to persecution by people who belonged to the highly literate culture of the Greeks. If the function were perceived to be good, then the matter was somewhat different. Enoch or Moses might be thought to have invented writing, if it were a significant benefit rather than something that led people astray.

Similar remarks may be made about functions and status of more normative and central importance. For example, several sources expect the Davidic king to lead Israel at the last day. A few sources, however, indicate that an eschatological high priest will be of superior status (cf 1Q Sa II.11ff; T.Judah 21.2f), while some of the Targums to Exodus 12.42 have Moses there, as well as the Messiah. In Daniel, however, he is not important enough to mention, while Michael plays a significant role in the redemption of Israel (Dan 12.1). Complexes of material like this can be seen as examples of transference or not, for our sources have no motivation to declare that they are or are not attributing to, say, Michael in heaven a function someone else might have expected to be performed by, say, the future Davidic king on earth. What they have in common is a profound need to visualize the redemption of Israel. So Jews might visualise the Davidic king leading them in battle (2 Bar 72), or simply leading the people by God's power in the last days (Pss Sol 17-18). A priestly community, however, might need to feel that the High Priest would be superior to the Davidic king in the last days, while people who could not imagine a military victory over the armies of Antiochus Epiphanes might prefer to trust that Michael would play the vital role in their deliverance by supernatural means.

When they were contemplating the deliverance of Israel in the Exodus from Egypt, some Jews might well feel it appropriate that Moses would return with the King Messiah when Israel was delivered at the last day.

This began to change when social subgroups formed around single figures, as we have seen in the cases of Enoch and Wisdom. This led to much greater development, including for example the transference to Enoch of the function of being the light of the Gentiles (1 En 48.4, taking the function of the servant of the Lord at Is 42.6; 49.6), and of being the eschatological judge, traditionally a function of God himself. Similarly, Wisdom could take over the functions of God in salvation history (Wsd Sol 10-11), and she could be identified with the Law (Sir 24.23), or with the rock which accompanied Israel in the wilderness (Philo, *Leg. All.* II, 86). Neither the humanity of Enoch nor the femininity of Wisdom formed any bar to these identifications, because all such factors were secondary to the needs of a subgroup of Jews, each with its own strong traditions. If Enoch was the source of revelations which our predecessors had received from time immemorial, he could turn from writing down the judgment to carrying it out. If Wisdom was the centre of daily life for an orthodox community, she had to be domesticated in Israel, and identification with a rock or the law was too plausible to be upset by her traditional femininity.

9. Conclusions

The study of messianic and intermediary figures in Judaism reveals a basic feature, that of adding beliefs and functions in accordance with the needs of the community. The development went ahead most rapidly where we can detect the needs of a social subgroup, for whom a particular intermediary figure was important. The only detectable limitation to development is that of Jewish monotheism. There is also some negative correlation with orthodoxy.

We might therefore expect that the more vigorous and extensive development of the figure of Jesus is to be explained from the more dramatic needs of the early Christian community. We must consider this in detail in chapters 7-9.

1. Cf J.J.Collins and G.W.E.Nickelsburg, *Ideal Figures in Ancient Judaism*, SCS 12 (1980); J.Neusner, W.S.Green and E.Frerichs (ed), *Judaisms and Their Messiahs at the Turn of the Christian Era* (1987); Hurtado, *One God, One Lord*. Further, see notes 6-7, 9, 11-17 infra; M.Smith, "What is implied by the Variety of Messianic Figures?", *JBL* 78, 1959, 66-72; A.Pfeifer, *Ursprung und Wesen der Hypostasenvorstellungen in Judentum*, AzTh I, 31 (1967); M. de Jonge, "The Role of Intermediaries in God's Final Intervention in the Future according to the Qumran Scrolls", in *Studies in the Jewish Background of the New Testament*, ed O.Michel et al., (1969), 44-63; M.Delcor, "Melchizedek from Genesis to the Qumran texts and the Epistle to the Hebrews", *JSJ* 2, 1971, 115-35; F.Horton, *The Melchizedek Tradition*, MSSNTS 31 (1976); P.J.Kobelski, *Melchizedek and Melchiresha^c* CBQMS 10 (1981); G.Schimanowski, *Weisheit und Messias. Die jüdische Voraussetzungen der urchristlichen Präexistenz-christologie*, WUNT 2,17 (1985).
2. Supra, 68. Cf J.A.Fitzmyer, "The Semitic Background of the New Testament *Kyrios-*

Title", in J.A.Fitzmyer, *A Wandering Aramean*, SBL.MS 25 (1979), 115-42.

3. Cf supra, 41-4.

4. Cf supra, 44-6. Further, Vermes, *Jesus the Jew*, 194-200; Dunn, *Making*, ch III; infra, 148.

5. Cf infra, 152. -

6. Cf B.L.Mack, "Imitatio Mosis. Patterns of Cosmology and Soteriology in the Hellenistic Synagogue", *StPh* 1, 1972, 27-55; H.W.Hollander, *Joseph as an Ethical Model in the Testaments of the Twelve Patriarchs*, SVTP VI (1981).

7. Cf R.Hayward, "The Present State of Research into the Targumic Account of the Sacrifice of Isaac", *JJS* 32, 1981, 127-50 (with bibliography); A.Agus, *The binding of Isaac and Messiah. Law, Martyrdom and Early Rabbinic Religiosity* (1988).

8. Cf e.g. Moule, *Origin*, 150. For creative analysis on more dynamic lines, see now Hurtado, *One God, One Lord*.

9. Cf M.Stone, "The Concept of the Messiah in IV Ezra", in J.Neusner (ed), *Religions in Antiquity*. Essays in Memory of E.R.Goodenough, Numen. SHR XIV (1968), 295-312; J.H.Charlesworth, "The Concept of the Messiah in the Pseudepigrapha", *ANRW* II.19.1 (1979), 188-218; Schürer-Vermes-Millar, vol II ch 29; Davenport and Hultgard in Collins and Nickelsburg, op. cit.; Neusner, Green and Frerichs, op.cit.

10. Cf supra, 42-3.

11. Cf H.Bietenhard, *Die himmlische Welt im Urchristentum und Spätjudentum*, WUNT 2 (1951); D.S.Russell, *The Method and Message of Jewish Apocalyptic* (1964), ch IX; P.Schafer, *Rivalität zwischen Engeln und Menschen*, Studia Judaica VIII (1975), esp 9-40; J.P.Rohland, *Der Erzengel Michael. Arzt und Feldherr* (1977); W.Carr, *Angels and Principalities*, MSSNTS 42 (1981), 25-43; C.Rowland, *The Open Heaven* (1982), ch 4; C.Newsom, *Songs of the Sabbath Sacrifice*, HSSt 27 (1985), esp 23-38; Hurtado, op.cit.

12. Cf H.Cazelles et al., *Moïse, l'Homme de l'Alliance* (1955); W.A.Meeks, *The Prophet-King. Moses Traditions and the Johannine Christology*, NT.S 14 (1967), chs III-V; W.A.Meeks, "Moses as God and King", in J.Neusner (ed), *Religions in Antiquity*, Numen. SHR XIV (1968), 354-71; B.L.Mack, op.cit.; P.W.van der Horst, "Moses' Throne Vision in Ezekiel the Dramatist", *JJS* 34, 1983, 21-9; Hurtado, op.cit., 56-63.

13. Cf B.L.Mack, *Logos und Sophia. Untersuchungen zur Weisheitstheologie im hellenistischen Judentum*, StUNT 10 (1973); L.K.K.Dey, *The Intermediary World and Patterns of Perfection in Philo and Hebrews*, SBL.DS 25 (1975); A.F.Segal, *Two Powers in Heaven. Early Rabbinic Reports about Christianity and Gnosticism*, SJLA 29 (1977), ch 11; Dunn, *Making*, 215-30; R.Hayward, *Divine Name and Presence: The Memra* (1981).

14. Following M.Barker, *The Older Testament* (1987), 16, we should interpret Gen 4.17 as an equally dramatic reference to the same complex of traditions, but the implications of reinterpreting the Hebrew text cannot be pursued here. As well as ch 1 of her book, cf generally P.Grelot, "La légende d'Hénoch dans les apocryphes et dans la Bible: Origines et signification", *RSR* 46, 1958, 5-26, 181-210; M.E.Stone, "The Book of Enoch and Judaism in the Third Century B.C.E.", *CBQ* 40, 1978, 479-92; P.G.Davis, "The mythic Enoch: new light on early christology", *ScRel/StRel* 13, 1984, 335-43; J.C.Vanderkam, *Enoch and the Growth of an Apocalyptic Tradition*, CBQMS 16 (1984).

15. P.M.Casey, "The use of the term "son of man" in the Similitudes of Enoch", *JSJ* 7, 1976, 11-29. I cannot deal here with continued efforts to avoid the plain meaning of 1 Enoch 71.14.

16. Cf W.L.Knox, "The Divine Wisdom", *JThS* 38, 1937, 230-7; J.W.Wood, *Wisdom Literature* (1967), chs 5-7; B.L.Mack, "Wisdom, Myth and Mythology. An Essay in Understanding a Theological Trend", *Interp* 24, 1970, 46-70; Mack, op.cit., *Logos und Sophia;* R.L.Wilken (ed), *Aspects of Wisdom in Judaism and Early Christianity* (1975); Harrington in Collins and Nickelsburg, op.cit.; C.V.Camp, *Wisdom and the Feminine in the Book of Proverbs* (1985); E.J.Schnabel, *Law and Wisdom from Ben Sira to Paul*, WUNT 2, 16 (1985).

17. Cf J.Downing, op. cit., *JThS NS* 14, 1963, 280-4; W.H.C.Frend, *Martyrdom and Persecution in the Early Church* (1965), ch 2; G.W.E.Nickelsburg, *Resurrection, Immortality and Eternal Life in Intertestamental Judaism*, HThS XXVI (1972), ch III; A.P.O'Hagan, "The martyr in the fourth book of Maccabees", *SBFLA* 24, 1974, 94-120.

18. Cf supra, 65-7: infra, 102-3.

19. Cf Segal, op.cit.; Rowland, op.cit., ch 11.

20. Cf supra 79-85; infra, 135-8.

21. For the effect of different definitions of incarnation on the analysis of these figures, infra 166-8. On this piece, J.Z.Smith, "The Prayer of Joseph", in J.Neusner (ed), *Religions in Antiquity*, Numen. SHR XIV (1968), 253-94; J.Z.Smith, *Map is not Territory: Studies in the History of Religions*, SJLA 23 (1978), 24-66.

22. Cf supra, 72-5.

23. Infra 112-7,135-7,144.

Chapter 7
From Jesus to Paul

1. Three Stages of Development

It took some 50 or 60 years to turn a Jewish prophet into a Gentile God. Cultural change was as important as the passage of time. To analyse christological development against this background of cultural change, I use a three-stage model. In the first stage, the Christian community was Jewish, a subgroup within Judaism, as the Jesus movement had been. In the second stage, Gentiles entered the Christian community in significant numbers, without becoming Jewish. In the third stage, Christianity is identifiable as a Gentile religion.

These three stages were not chronologically successive in a simple sense. This three-stage model is useful because it is analytically fruitful, and corresponds to reality in a more complex way. The third stage could not have occurred until after the second, and the second stage could not have occurred until after the first. The succession was not however a simple one. The first stage did not end when the second stage began, nor even when it became well established. Some Jewish Christians continued to perceive Christianity as a Jewish group. In the New Testament period, these included some of Paul's opponents in Galatia, and Jews who decided to remain within the Jewish community when Johannine Christians were thrown out of it. In the patristic period, Jews who perceived Christianity as the true form of Judaism were responsible for writing such works as the Clementine Homilies and the Gospel of the Ebionites. A similar perspective continues today among small groups of Jews, generally known as Hebrew Christians.[1]

To complicate matters further, some ethnically Gentile people, after entering the Christian community in stage two, took on the perspective of stage one. Some of the Galatians came into this category. Having been converted to Christianity, they so perceived it as a form of Judaism that they underwent circumcision and began to observe the sabbath and some festivals (cf. Gal 4.8-10; 5.2-4; 6.13). The polemic of church fathers such as Ephraem and Chrysostom shows that this perspective continued during the patristic period.

When we consider christological development during stage one, the evidence of the development of messianic and intermediary figures considered in chapter 6 is fundamental, because it shows that development during this stage could have been rapid and extensive. This is especially important because of the empirical problems involved in identifying the beginning of stage two. We know that the Gentile mission was under way within a few years of Jesus' death.

We must infer from Acts and the epistles that, by the early 50s, Paul had made a successful stand for the admission of Gentiles to the community without their becoming Jews, and that the numbers admitted were significant. We cannot however measure them, either in numbers, or by cultural background. How many of them had, say, one Jewish grandparent, we have no idea. Moreover, all our New Testament documents were written when stage two of christological development was in full bloom.

We must respond to this lack of information with increased analytical sophistication. It is not of crucial importance that some developments which could have taken place in stage two may have taken place in stage one. Stage one is shown by the purely Jewish evidence considered in chapter 6, and by analysis of the social bonding and developmental needs of the earliest Christian community, to have been a stage when significant christological development could have taken place. This means that early christological developments will have been welcome to observant Jewish members of the community, whether or not they took place when numerous Gentiles had entered it. We must therefore analyse out those developments which could not have taken place until stage two, or which could have assumed an important function only in stage two.

Finally, we must note that stage three, in which Christianity is identifiable as a Gentile religion, is easy to verify throughout the patristic period. I argue elsewhere in this book that this stage was reached when Johannine Christians were thrown out of the synagogue, and that this was a direct cause of the evolution of belief in the deity and incarnation of Jesus.[2]

2. The Vindication of Jesus

At the beginning of stage one, we are confronted with one of the most difficult problems in historical research, the historicity of the resurrection of Jesus.[3] Two significant results have emerged from critical scholarship. The belief that Jesus had risen from the dead was held at a very early date, but this belief was not based on the resurrection appearances now found in the four Gospels. The early date of this belief follows from its presence in our earliest sources. 1 Corinthians 15.3-8 gives us direct Pauline testimony to the early date of its list of appearances. Paul also equates his vision on the Damascus road with a resurrection appearance, and indicates that all the other appearances took place within a relatively short space of time. There is no mention of an empty tomb. Similar belief is implied by the speeches of the first apostles in the earliest chapters of Acts.[4] The tradition that there were resurrection appearances is supported by the fact that all four Gospels report some.

None the less, the resurrection narratives in our Gospels cannot be factual reports, for they do not coincide with each other, and they contain internal inconsistencies. Mark evidently intended to write an account of Jesus meeting the disciples in Galilee (Mk 16.7). Matthew agrees, providing a brief appearance to Mary Magdalene and Jacob's Mary in Jerusalem to reinforce the point (Mt 28.9-10, cf 28.1), and following it with an appearance to the eleven in Galilee (Mt 28.16-20). Luke, however, replaces Mark's prediction of Galilean appearances with a comment about what Jesus said when he was in Galilee (Lk 24.6-7), and gives two appearances in the Jerusalem area followed by Jesus' ascension, leaving no room for any appearance in Galilee (Lk 24.13-53). This is barely consistent with the story of the ascension in Acts 1.3-12, it is not consistent with Matthew, and it was evidently written with the deliberate intention of contradicting Mark's tradition of Galilean appearances. Apart from the location, the stories in Matthew and Luke do not contradict each other so much as give an impression of total dissociation, as if neither of them knew the traditions to which the other had access (apart from the story of the empty tomb, which both of them took from Mark).

John's narrative is different again. As in Luke, there is no command to go to Galilee, and the appearances in John 20 all take place in Jerusalem. The first, to Mary Magdalene (Jn 20.11-18), goes unmentioned by Luke, and hardly overlaps with the appearance to Mary Magdalene and Jacob's Mary at Matthew 28.9-10. There follows an appearance to the disciples unknown to Matthew (Jn 20.19-23), barely overlapping with an appearance to the disciples at Luke 24.36ff. Finally, the appearance to doubting Thomas (Jn 20.26-29) is unique. John 21.1-23 provides a lengthy appearance in Galilee which barely overlaps with anything in Matthew. Nor do the Gospel appearances relate properly to the early tradition found at 1 Corinthians 15.3-8.

There are many more disagreements in detail. For example, at Mark 16.1, Mary Magdalene goes with Jacob's Mary and Salome to the tomb to anoint Jesus' body. At Matthew 28.1, Salome is not mentioned, and the purpose is to see the tomb. In Luke, Joanna replaces Salome, and as in Mark they bring the spices which they had prepared (Lk 24.1,10). At John 20.1, only Mary Magdalene goes. She brings no spices because the body has already been anointed under the guidance of Nicodemus, who is not known to the synoptic writers (Jn 19.39-40). At Mark 16.5-8, the women enter the tomb and see an angel, who tells them that Jesus has risen, but they tell no-one, "for they were afraid" (16.8). At Matthew 28.2, the angel of the Lord descends and tells them he is risen (28.6), so they do not need to enter the tomb, and they go and tell the disciples (as we must infer from 28.7-10,16). In Luke, they enter the tomb and two angels appear to tell them that he is risen (Lk 24.2-6), so they tell the eleven and all the others, or the apostles, who do not believe them (24.9-11). In John, Mary Magdelene merely sees the stone taken away from the tomb (Jn 20.1). She runs to Simon Peter and the beloved disciple, who have a race to get there (Jn 20.2-4). The beloved disciple looks in, Peter goes in, and the beloved disciple comes to faith before any appearances (20.5-8).

These discrepancies are too great to have resulted from accurate reporting of a perceptible event. Moreover, the narratives attribute teachings to Jesus which he did not give during his earthly life, and which has an excellent *Sitz im Leben* in the early church. This teaching legitimates significant aspects of the Christian community's existence. For example, at Luke 24.26 Jesus tells the disciples that the Christ had to suffer. The title "the Christ" was not used by Jesus, but it became central to the Christian community before Luke wrote his Gospel.[5] The suffering of the Messiah became a significant point of dispute (e.g. 1 Cor 1.23), and part of the Christian solution was to see it foretold in scripture. Similarly, Matthew 28.19 authorizes the Gentile mission, and baptism in the name of the Father, the Son and the Holy Spirit. Neither of these activities, nor the title "the Son", featured in the ministry of the historical Jesus.[6] The Johannine community attributed its crucial confession of the deity of Jesus to doubting Thomas (Jn 20.28), portraying the risen Jesus as legitimating their faith with his reply (20.29).

It is, therefore, necessary to explain the secondary generation of legitimating narratives, and give reasons why Jesus' resurrection is central to them. Jesus' embodiment of the identity of Judaism was the original driving force. During the historic ministry, Jesus so recreated the prophetic stream of Judaism that from his disciples' perspective he embodied Jewish identity.[7] The ministry of Jesus was formative for the disciples' own identity. Moreover, the tight social bonding of the Jesus movement means that the disciples received constant confirmation that Jesus' view of Judaism was the right one. It was very controversial, suffering vigorous opposition from the orthodox wing of Judaism. The disciples could not now change sides in this dispute. The unjust death of the righteous embodiment of Judaism could not cause them to abandon their identity.

But it seems a long way from not abandoning Jewish identity to belief that God had raised Jesus from the dead. Jesus' death could have this effect only if the development of belief in his resurrection was in accordance with established cultural features. There were two such features, of which the first may be termed "heavenly vindication".

There is sufficient evidence that Second Temple Jews produced belief in heavenly vindication when their community was under serious threat. The most obvious examples are eschatological ones which first emerged during the Maccabean period. The persecution of Antiochus Epiphanes[8] led the authors of the book of Daniel to predict that within a few months God would deliver his faithful people by supernatural means. The exact calculation was based on sacred numbers, and timetabled so that the persecution would end soon (cf Dan 2.44-5; 7.25-7; 8.13-14, 23-26; 9.2, 23-27; 11.40-12.4,6-7,11-12).

The knowledge that God would deliver soon was produced by the faithfulness of people whose Jewish identity was strongest. Furthermore, monotheism was an identity factor of Judaism. Jews could not give up their faith in God without ceasing to be Jewish. The scriptures told them that if they did not keep the covenant, God would punish them (cf e.g. Deut 8.19-20; 28.15-68; 2 Kings 17.7-23; Jer 7; Ps 78.56-64): this had happened, for hellenizing Jews had abandoned the covenant and severe persecution had followed. The covenant also provided for the salvation of the righteous (cf e.g. Deut 7.9-10; Pss 1; 32), and for the salvation of Israel, particularly when she repented, or when she had been sufficiently punished (cf e.g. Deut 9.25-29; Is 1.24-2.4; 10.20-12; 40.1-11; Jer 31.31-34; Ezek 20.40-44; Hos 14).

In this cultural context, the authors of the book of Daniel incorporated a prayer of repentance in Daniel 9, followed by prayer for deliverance. Daniel's prayer leads directly to reassurance from the angel Gabriel. The controlling factor in this response was the community's need for deliverance. Their criteria were visions, or dreams, and scripture. Visions are narrated in Daniel itself. The use of scripture is especially clear in Daniel 9. This begins with Daniel meditating on the 70 years of Jeremiah 29.10ff. After the invoking of God in the prayer of repentance, Daniel is visited by Gabriel, who gives him details of the 70 *weeks*, that is, the 70 *weeks of years* which Jeremiah is understood to have prophesied. The details show how scripture has been interpreted to speak directly to a community in need of deliverance; the 69th week of years was half-way through when the temple was desecrated.[9]

Scripture and visions are also the source of knowledge in 1 Enoch 83-90 and 1 Enoch 91-93, both of which predict the final intervention of God during the Maccabean period. From the orthodox wing of Judaism, the author of Jubilees foresaw a return to strict keeping of the Law: the Lord would heal his servants, and they would drive out their adversaries (Jub 23.26-31). His modes of vindication were by no means purely eschatological. Faced with the slaughter of circumcised children and their parents, he announced the circumcision of the two highest classes of angels (Jub 15.27). He was determined to have the death penalty for unlawful sexual intercourse, and his expanded *halakhah* prohibited sexual intercourse on the sabbath. The prohibition of sex on the sabbath was, therefore, included in a list of sabbath regulations (Jub 50.8), given to Moses on Mt Sinai. The reinforcement of the death penalty for unlawful sexual intercourse flows from the elaborated stories of Reuben and Bilhah, and of Judah and Tamar (Jub 33.2-20; 41.8-28). Thus heavenly vindication might include events of the past as well as the future, and it might involve changes in accounts of the patriarchs on earth.

During the Roman period, the same feature is visible in two sub-groups, the Qumran community and the Enoch circle. As well as preserving Daniel, 1 Enoch 83-90, 1 Enoch 91-93 and Jubilees, the Qumran community provided a vigorous picture of final deliverance by means of Melchizedek in 11Q Melchizedek. The calculations of the date of the End in some of these works passed without it coming, and the sect's commentary on Habakkuk is a classic example of the faithful reverence with which many Jews have reacted in similar situations.[10] In a community of faithful Jews, no amount of distress would cause loss of faith.

Another sub-group produced the pictures of imminent vindication in 4 Ezra and 2 Baruch. Both documents move from inner convictions in a context of scripture, tradition and visionary revelation. In a profound sense, they were not only writing about the future. They were also vindicating the existence of the orthodox in Israel. At this level, their convictions about God's acts in the future are not significantly different from convictions about past events such as God's rest on the seventh day, a rest which legitimated the observance of the sabbath (Ex 20.11; cf Gen 2.3; Deut 5.15).

These documents have a central feature in common. Jews whose existence or identity were threatened responded by producing new beliefs in modes of heavenly vindication. Some of these referred to past events, such as the circumcision of the highest classes of angels when they were created. Other beliefs referred to current heavenly states: these angels were still circumcised, and they were believed to celebrate the sabbath (Jub 2.17-22). In view of the severe political oppression of Israel, the majority of extant pictures of heavenly vindication have a future reference. These pictures incorporate the most dramatic recent events. They proceeded from an absolute conviction that God would deliver his people, or more particularly the righteous remnant who believed themselves to be the true Israel. These convictions were perceived to be verified from tradition visible in scripture, and from visions.

Early Christian belief in the resurrection of Jesus is another example of heavenly vindication. It vindicated Jesus and his ministry, and assured the earliest Christians that God would shortly deliver them. A function of this set of beliefs was to vindicate the community's identity. The particular form of this resulted from a second significant feature of Jewish culture, the development of messianic and intermediary figures. Chapter 6 described how several of these figures were developed, gaining new roles and functions in accordance with the community's needs. These figures were generally related to Jewish identity. The final developments of Enoch and of Wisdom were each due to a sub-group, for whose identity they were fundamental. This is especially relevant to christological development, because in stage one Christianity was a purely Jewish movement, the identity and existence of which might have been threatened by Jesus' death. In view of the development of these different figures, we must infer that development of the figure of Jesus was a culturally natural response to the attack on the Jesus movement formed by his crucifixion.

These two cultural features overlap. The future Davidic king, Abel, Enoch, the Maccabean martyrs, Melchizedek and Michael all underwent new developments which were related to the deliverance of Israel, or of a subgroup within Israel. The Maccabean martyrs are especially relevant.[11] From a situation in which Judaism was split and the righteous were killed, some people produced the belief that their death had atoning significance and had permitted the deliverance of Israel. The martyrs were also held to have been vindicated by survival in the future life, and this was sometimes believed to have been immediate. The development of past events in this way was not very common, because few events in the current history of an oppressed people were perceived to be salvific, but there was no kind of bar to the positive interpretation of recent events. The consequences of the death of the Maccabean martyrs, like the declaration that the highest classes of angels were circumcised, involved the perceived heavenly reversal of earthly disaster.

One more crucial factor returns us to our main cause, the dependence of the disciples on Jesus for their view of Judaism and thus their own identity. Resurrection is an interpretation of the form of vindication which Jesus predicted for himself. We have seen that, in addition to sayings which assumed his survival and vindication, Jesus made a prediction on these lines: "A son of man will die, and after three days he will rise (qum)."[12] The original reference was probably to the general resurrection, which was expected to happen very soon. This prediction was eminently capable of reinterpretation. It said nothing of the fate of Jesus' body, and it is so general as to be consistent with the assumption that his tomb was empty and with the assumption that it was not.

We must not exaggerate the degree of reinterpretation which was necessary, and we must keep it in its cultural context. We have seen that when Jews considered the deaths of people whose survival they needed to believe in, they might imagine them transported to their eternal fates at once. Jesus had presented his fate as exaltation after a short interval, and this is what his disciples now knew must have happened. Their belief did not require an empty tomb for its verification, partly because the normative modes of verification were dreams or visions and scripture. Moreover, verification was essential for the identity and existence of the community. If the normative modes were visions and scripture, and the survival of people was not dependent on their bodies disappearing, no-one would be motivated to look for the disappearance of Jesus' bodily remains. He had himself assumed survival without an empty tomb in the parable of the rich man and Lazarus (Lk 16.19-31), a normal view in that culture, and necessarily taken over by the disciples and applied to him, because only that view would permit the community to continue and life to be understood. Thus we find in our earliest sources that it is precisely resurrection appearances and the witness of scripture that are put forward as proofs.

It should not be held against this that resurrection appearances are different from dreams and visions. In that culture, the difference could be overridden by the need for supernatural legitimation satisfied by all three. The authors of Daniel 7 do not seem to have minded whether Daniel had a dream or a vision, and they put the interpreting angel inside it. Angels could appear as if they were people, and be entertained unawares (Heb 13.2). At 1 Corinthians 15.3ff, Paul equates his vision on the Damascus road with a resurrection appearance, because of his profound conviction that Jesus had appeared to send him to the Gentiles. We must apply this to the earliest appearances: if people had visions of Jesus, their visions were bound to be interpreted as appearances of the risen Jesus, because this interpretation demonstrated God's vindication of Jesus, and hence his support of the community.

It must be inferred that the story of the empty tomb is secondary. It performs the same legitimating role as in all resurrection narratives of any length. Some Jews did believe that resurrection involved the resuscitation of the earthly body, and this view was functional because of its legitimating role. This is why it eventually became dominant.

We can now work back through the resurrection stories, seeing what they legitimate and what they explain. In John, the new point to be legitimated is the deity of Jesus, declared at 20.28, and accepted by the risen Jesus at 20.29. The layout of the clothes, the fact that Mary did not instantly recognize Jesus, and the appearances through closed doors explain that Jesus' earthly body was transformed into a spiritual one. Chapter 21 reinforces this with another episode in which he is not at first recognized, and deals obliquely with the death of the beloved disciple and the delay of the parousia.

Luke's ascension narrative (Lk 24.50-53) explains why resurrection appearances have ceased. Acts 1.3-11 clarifies this, deals vigorously with the problem of the delay of the parousia, predicts the legitimating arrival of unusually visible Holy Spirit, and commands the Gentile mission. Luke 24.36ff gives the authority of the risen Christ for the specifically Christian interpretation of scripture. It also explains that the risen Jesus was not just a spirit, an obvious interpretation of the being who had appeared on the road to Emmaus. The appearance on the Emmaus road (Lk 24.13-35) legitimates the Christian interpretation of scripture, setting non-Christian and doubtful Jews in their place as foolish and slow in heart to believe what was said by the prophets (24.25). The story also explains that Jesus' risen body was a spiritual one: as in John, disciples who knew him might not recognize him.

Matthew's single appearance in Galilee (Mt 28.16-20) concentrates on legitimation of the Gentile mission. It includes also baptism, the sonship of Jesus, obedience to his teaching, and his continued presence. The account of the guard at the tomb (Mt 28.11-15) shows that the tomb was empty. An appearance to the women reinforces the Galilean tradition of appearances (Mt 28.9-10). Matthew slips in the information that the tomb was new, Luke explains that no-one had yet been laid in it, and John says both (Mt 27.60; Lk 23.53; Jn 19.41). All three make clear that only Jesus' body or bones had to disappear for the tomb to be empty, so no-one could have thought that he had risen because they imagined his remains were those of someone else.

Mark's story of Jesus' burial (Mk 15.42-7) explains that Jesus was really dead. Pilate and the centurion were the best witnesses that Jesus was dead, because they were the authoritative outsiders responsible for his death. A pious Jew was the best owner of the tomb, since he was plausible, none of the disciples had been distinguished or political enough to have got the body, and another person from outside the movement showed that Jesus was really dead and buried. Mary Magdalene and Joseph's Mary saw where he was laid (Mk 15.47), so the women could not have gone to the wrong tomb. In the story of the resurrection (16.1-8), the angel also shows that Jesus' remains had gone from the correct tomb. He points out the part of the tomb where he was laid (16.6), so the women could not have failed to recognize a rotting body and imagined that he had gone from an empty space left for the next one. He also gives the information that Jesus had risen, and legitimates a purely Galilean tradition of appearances (16.7). The women's failure to tell anyone (16.8) explains why the story had not been heard by everyone before. This story as a whole legitimates the uniqueness of Jesus' resurrection in a way that the immortality of his soul could not.

The *Sitz im Leben* of the empty tomb is not in the earliest period of the church. Its presence in all the Gospel stories, together with its legitimating function, means that when we note its absence from 1 Corinthians 15.3ff and the early speeches of Acts, we note a feature of the earliest evidence. Its absence from the earliest sources is complemented by early Christian ignorance of where it was. The significance of its absence from these sources cannot be overthrown by the implications of the beliefs of Paul and Luke. Paul may have believed the tomb was empty, and Luke certainly did. This makes its absence from these speeches all the more striking. We must conclude that Acts 2.31 results from the writing up of a speech with the LXX text of Psalm 16 in mind, as quoted. The original psalm was probably used in the earliest period, in the original text, which implies immortality, not resurrection.

The following conclusions should therefore be drawn. The driving force of early Christian belief in the resurrection of Jesus was his embodiment of Jewish identity during the historic ministry. This ensured the disciples' continued belief that God approved of him. Two features of Jewish culture, heavenly vindication and the development of messianic and intermediary figures, enabled this to take the form of believing that God had raised him from the dead. His prediction that he would rise ensured that it did take that form. This belief was legitimated by means of scripture and visions, because these were the normal modes of verifying revelation in the culture of the first disciples. This belief permitted but did not require people to suppose that his tomb was empty. The story of the empty tomb is a secondary development. It originated among disciples who knew resurrection as the normative form of survival after death, and it eventually became normative because it was the strongest form of legitimation.

It is only at this point that pagan beliefs in dying and rising gods become relevant. They show us that a message centred on a person who had died and risen again appealed to a fundamental need of human beings to believe in survival and redemption. The story of Jesus had the great advantage of being the story of a man who had recently been alive. Gentile converts who had previously known ancient myths could consequently perceive a passage from story to truth, a truth constantly reinforced by their religious experience in the life of the church.

Now that some people had come to terms with Jesus' death by means of their belief in his vindication, christology could only develop further. Our literary sources for this stage of development all belong to stage two of christological development. We must search them for early material.

3. The Early Chapters of Acts

The speeches attributed to the apostles in the early chapters of Acts[13] contain a number of early features. They also have two major titles, "Christ" and "Lord" (Acts 1.6,21; 2.31,36,38; 3.6,18,20; 4.10). "Lord" was an obvious term to use, because of its wide range of meaning. I have noted some evidence of its use by outsiders as a form of address during Jesus' ministry: as an address to him when he was in heaven it has a static parallel in the common habit of addressing angels as "Lord".[14] Its use as a form of address to the risen Jesus is attested for the Aramaic-speaking church by the early formula *maranatha* (1 Cor 16.22; Didache 10.6). The transition to the absolute "the Lord" is a natural one. At Acts 2.36 we are halfway to that with the declaration that God made Jesus both Lord and Christ. There is also evidence of an early Christian confession "Jesus is Lord", but we do not know how early this confession was first used.[15]

The origins of the title "Christ" have been more difficult to explain. I have argued that neither Jesus nor his disciples used the term of him during his historic ministry.[16] None the less its use in these speeches, and its extensive use in the Pauline epistles, combine to show that it was an early title for Jesus. One significant factor was its broad range, because of which it might be used by Jesus' followers at any time, without necessarily carrying connotations of Davidic kingship. We find this use of the verb "to anoint" at Acts 10.38, which introduces a summary of Jesus' ministry by saying that God anointed him with Holy Spirit and power. The decisive factor was Jesus' position as the central identity factor of the Christian community. This is what made a title highly desirable, and in a community where he was superior to other prophets and the high priest was neither near nor highly regarded, this overrode the existence of other figures who might have been thought of as "anointed". There is a dynamic parallel in the crystallisation of the title "the Messiah" for the future Davidic king.[17] Once the title was thought of, it could be found in scripture, as at Psalm 2.1-2, quoted at Acts 4.25-6. The quotation ends, "The rulers were gathered together against the Lord and against his Christ". The actualizing exegesis sets off at 4.27, "There were indeed gathered together in this city against your holy servant Jesus, whom you anointed, Herod and Pontius Pilate."

At Acts 2.36, the messiahship and lordship of Jesus are dated from the resurrection. In its own right, this view is perfectly logical. Jesus could reasonably be perceived as becoming Lord when he was exalted to the right hand of God, anointed to rule and to come again soon for the final deliverance of his people. A similar pinpointing of the resurrection as the moment at which Jesus was placed in his exalted position is found at Acts 5.31, and in the use of Psalm 2.7 at Acts 13.33 (cf Phil 2.9).

This use of the resurrection as the point of entry into lordship, messiahship and so on is evidently of early date. Not only does it occur in early source material, it is a logical development of the situation which the early Christians had to interpret, whereas there was no reason to produce it when later christology had become established. It was particularly suited to that stage of christological development which assumed that Jesus was not more than a man during his earthly life, however important his life might have been.

This view was not, however, likely to survive in a dominant position, because it does not cohere well enough with other developments. In the first place, the term "Christ" was more likely to crystallize eventually round the beginning of the earthly ministry, because of its importance for salvation history. Secondly, as Jesus became the son of God in a special sense and rose towards deity, the pinpointing of the resurrection as his point of entry into lordship was bound to seem less appropriate. In the early speeches of Acts, when pre-existence, sonship and deity had not yet been developed, we find formulations which refer to each possible point of reference correctly left unreconciled.

The earliest period of christological development produced several other terms suitable for describing an outstandingly religious man. Jesus is God's servant (Acts 3.13,26; 4.27,30), as David also was (Acts 4.25). Similarly he is the holy and righteous one (3.14, cf 7.52), and "holy" is used as a creative description of him (4.27,30), and in quotations of Psalm 16.10 (2.27, 13.35). The term "prophet" continued to be used of him, the examples in Acts being quotations of Deuteronomy 18.15,19 (Acts 3.22-3, 7.37). "Leader", or "founder"[18] is a very general term: one of its occurrences refers to Jesus during his earthly ministry (3.15), while the other appears to date his leadership from the time of the resurrection (5.31). The latter passage also uses the term "saviour". All these different terms show that in the earliest period there was vigorous christological development at a level quite remote from unique sonship and deity.

At the same time, a fundamental shift is reflected, in which Jesus replaced the kingdom of God as the centre of the proclamation. This shift took place within an overall framework which remained unchanged. Jesus had expected the kingdom to come, and the first apostles continued to believe that the End was at hand, verifying this afresh from scripture (e.g. Acts 2.16-21, quoting Joel 2.28-32). The need to keep the community together now meant that the preaching had to concentrate on the community's central identity factor. His death and resurrection had to be central to be meaningful, and the widespread expectation of a redeemer figure was shifted straight onto him: "... so that times of refreshment may come from the face of the Lord and he may send the Christ who was appointed for you, Jesus, whom heaven must receive until the times of the restoration of all things, of which God spoke through the mouth of his holy prophets from the beginning" (Acts 3.20-21).

Most other developments at this stage were in the area of function rather than status. With Jesus at the right hand of God, Acts 2.33 holds him in some sense responsible for the events of Pentecost. This is a very elevated function, though we should not regard it as evidence of deity. We have seen abundant evidence that messianic and intermediary figures took on functions which were previously those of God, and that this did not make them divine. This verse occurs in a context where God himself is the overall author of the event. The main importance of this development is that it attributes a perceptible event on earth to the work of Jesus in heaven, thereby validating the community's belief in his exaltation. It illustrates the restructuring of experience carried out with belief in Jesus' exaltation.

A similar function was performed by healing in the name of Jesus. Some comments in the Gospels show that the disciples already healed in Jesus' absence (cf Mk 6.13; 9.28; Lk 10.9), and that they, and indeed an outsider, performed exorcisms in his name (Mk 9.28, 38-9). It follows that when Peter healed the lame man in Acts 3, he was not doing something completely new. The fundamental point is the interpretation put on it: "in the name of Jesus Christ the Nazarene, whom you crucified, whom God raised from the dead, by him he stands before you in good health" (Acts 4.10). The healing thus became another event perceived to be possible only in the light of the resurrection.

The relating of events to the community's sole identity factor was particularly significant in the case of baptism.[19] No such ceremony had been felt to be necessary during the historic ministry. Luke however reports a very early declaration of the centrality of Jesus, "There is no salvation through anyone else" (Acts 4.12). Despite the shift in covenantal nomism involved, this may represent genuinely early tradition. The undermining of the standard form of covenantal nomism had begun in the ministry of John the Baptist. John's message of judgment warned his fellow Jews not to rely on their sonship of Abraham, that is, their membership of the Jewish community (Mt 3.9ff/Lk 3.8ff). This attack was intensified in the ministry of Jesus. He argued vigorously that some people would not enter the kingdom of heaven, and this too made membership of the covenant community insufficient for salvation. His attack on orthodox Jews was sealed by his death, condemned by the Sanhedrin led by Sadducees.[20] Salvation now had to be with one version of Judaism or the other. Since Jesus embodied the true form of Judaism over against scribes, Pharisees and chief priests, it was only a matter of time before one of the disciples made a declaration like Acts 4.12. At about the same time, and owing to the same shift in covenantal nomism, the community needed some form of initiation rite, if it was to hang together as a definable group of Jews. The rite had to be simple enough for Jewish disciples to perceive it as part of their traditional culture, yet powerful enough to symbolize entry to the community as a return to God.

Ritual washing was widespread in the Judaism of this period, and prophets and psalmists had long ago used the act of washing as an image of the removal of sin (e.g. Is 1.15-17; Ps 51.2,7). Washing played a part in the process of admitting people to the Qumran community (1QS III, 8-10). Jesus had been baptised by John the Baptist, as some other members of the earliest community must have been. This baptism symbolized return to God (Mk 1.4-5). Ritual washing was therefore a natural symbol for the earliest Christians to use to symbolise the return of Jews to God when they joined the Christian community. The community, however, needed it to be specific to itself at the same time as it was perfectly Jewish, and this was achieved by doing it with reference to Jesus. The baptism of converts will always have confirmed the faith of members of the community, who had been baptised on previous occasions.

Acts also records the gift of the Holy Spirit, which was especially useful in legitimating the entry of Gentiles into the community (cf 10.44-48; 11.15-18; 15.8-9). Christians are baptised without receiving the Holy Spirit (8.16), or baptised because they have received the Holy Spirit already (10.44-48), and there is some association of the two, with laying on of hands as part of the ceremony (19.5-6, cf 2.38). This variety can only be explained as an accurate record of early Christian experience. The report of Gentiles being baptised because they have received the Holy Spirit shows the need to relate the entrance of people into the community to Jesus. It belongs to the transition from stage one of christological development into stage two.

Another significant experience was the interpretation of scripture. At the intellectual level, the early speeches demonstrated the correctness of Christian claims. For example, Peter's speech in Acts 2 contains a standard Jewish kind of proof of the resurrection of Jesus, based on Psalms 16 and 110. We must deduce from evidence of this kind that the interpretation of scripture was fundamental in confirming faith in God's vindication of Jesus. The other significant level is the experiential one. The effect of finding Jesus prophesied in scripture was not the same as finding a proof of an abstract proposition. It will also have been a religious and emotional experience of new revelation (cf Acts 8.26-40). Social confirmation of christological exegesis will have taken place when Christians met together. Argument about this will also have been very functional. Acts records the use of scripture in arguments with other Jews, and these could only further confirm the correctness of the Christian interpretation and the blindness of Jews who did not agree with them (e.g. 4.12, 23ff).

One other major experience is detectable, namely the celebration of the eucharist. Luke's reports of the "breaking of bread" (e.g. Acts 2.42,46) are too meagre for us to describe accurately the significance of this early custom. We may however infer that the early Christians ate together regularly, in a society where some people would not eat with others, and which distinguished itself from Gentiles by its dietary laws.

We may conclude that the early chapters of Acts give us significant insights into the development of christology in the earliest period. At this stage Jesus was "a man accredited to you by God" (2.22). His life, death and resurrection were fundamental for salvation, but he was not seen as "the Son of God" in any special or unique sense, nor as incarnate or divine. There is nothing in these early chapters that could not be believed by faithful and observant Jews who remained within the Jewish community, as the first apostles did.

4. The Epistle of Jacob

The same trajectory of christological development is found in the epistle of Jacob. This was written to Christians who considered themselves as Jews, and who continued to attend the synagogue (cf 1.1, 2.2), presumably in addition to Christian meetings (cf 5.14-15). Injunctions to keep the Law (e.g. 2.8-11) are an integral part of the ethical exhortations of which the epistle largely consists. It uses two major titles, "Lord" (perhaps four times) and "Christ" (1.1; 2.1), the same two as the earliest chapters of Acts.[21] The continued use of "Lord" as a title for God has made some verses ambiguous to later readers, but we should probably accept 5.7,8 as expressions of the hope of Jesus' return, for which the recipients are to wait patiently, and this suggests that Jesus may be the eschatological judge referred to at 5.9.

This epistle falls well within the scope of its Jewish background: it does not portray Jesus as divine, and it does not contain any belief which could not be accepted by faithful Jews.

5. The Samaritan Mission

Evidence of early Samaritan Christianity is fragmentary and difficult to interpret, but it has been considered important.[22] Acts 8.10 has the dramatic information that a baptized Christian called Simon had previously been hailed as "the Power of God called Great". Justin reports that he was acknowledged as the first God and worshipped (I Apol 26). Simon might therefore be said to have been considered incarnate, even on a rather strict definition of that term. Similar remarks in other late sources include the information attributed to Hegesippus that there was a Simonian sect (Eus. H.E. IV,22).

Most scholars have not been convinced that this information is of central importance in explaining christological growth, and four reasons may be given for this. Firstly, the beliefs about Simon Magus were culturally alien to the early church. We would expect the church to have rejected those beliefs with him, rather than to have borrowed them. Secondly, much of the evidence is of late date, and may be recording late developments. Thirdly, the rest of the New Testament does not confirm a significant Samaritan presence in the early church. Fourthly, Samaria was significantly hellenized, and we do not have sufficient information about the degree of assimilation normal in the sect. Even the dynamic parallel may therefore come from a *Sitz im Leben* alien to stage one of christological development, directly relevant only to the situation in stage two or even the passage to stage three.

Simon should therefore take his place with the messianic and intermediary figures analysed in chapter 6 part 7, as on the fringe of Judaism. He provides another example of a figure which was significantly developed by a particular sub-group, and his rise as well as his influence in a culture similar to that of early Christianity may be explained on the same generative model.

6. Pre-Pauline Formulae

Pieces of old tradition, embedded in the Pauline epistles, form another significant source of information about the christology of the earliest church.[23] Some are evidently formulaic, suitable for repetition. Perhaps the earliest fragment is *maranatha*, "Our Lord, come", preserved in Aramaic (1 Cor 16.22; Didache 10.6; cf Rev 22.20).[24] This locates the hope for Jesus' return in the Aramaic-speaking church. The fact that it is preserved in Aramaic in a Greek epistle shows that it was felt to be part of the church's identity. This continuity was fundamental as the Gospel was preached to Greek-speaking Gentiles, and it shows how much importance was attached to belief in Jesus' return.

This confession also contains the effective origin of the title "Lord".[25] It must be inferred that the term "Lord" was used in the Aramaic-speaking church, before Christianity was significantly hellenized. There is also evidence of its use in a formulaic confession, "Jesus (is) Lord". The existence of this confession must be deduced from Romans 10.8-9, 1 Corinthians 12.3 and Philippians 2.11 (cf 1 Cor 8.6; Col 2.6). We should not try to be too precise about its meaning. It indicates that Jesus was viewed as a superior heavenly being, and a central figure of identity and authority to whom the church was subject. It does not, however, equate him with God. Nor do we know how early it was used. It is extant only in stage two of christological development.

Another pre-Pauline piece already noted is the tradition of resurrection appearances quoted at 1 Corinthians 15.3ff.[26] We have seen that this contains very early tradition. Paul's use of it, together with its formulaic character, shows its importance in maintaining the identity of the developing church with the church of the earliest period. It also illustrates how important faith in Jesus' resurrection was for the church, and how important the appearances were in guaranteeing that faith. The repeated "according to the Scriptures" is a natural development of Jesus' conviction that his death was written in scripture, and a straightforward use of one of the major criteria of revelation. The other significant development is that his death is "for our sins". This was also a natural development, because Jesus had already portrayed his death as a kind of sacrifice, and Jewish sacrifices frequently symbolised the removal of sin or impurity. In the earliest period, such a development was functional because it helped Jesus' death to be seen as necessary. It will have become increasingly functional as the Gospel spread among Jews critical of the Temple worship, diaspora Jews and Gentiles. People remote from the sacrificial system will have experienced the forgiveness of their sins when they contemplated the saving work of Christ's death, and joined in worship where it was celebrated.

The same applies to the other piece of tradition that Paul tells us is early. 1 Corinthians 11.23-5 contains significant development of the authentic tradition preserved at Mark 14.22ff.[27] It uses the title "Lord". The new phrase "for you", qualifying "my body", helps the believer to appropriate the sacrificial death of Jesus. The description "the new covenant" intensifies in Old Testament terms the feeling that the ministry of Jesus was a fresh start in people's relationship with God. The alteration of "this is my blood" will also have been due to natural antipathy to drinking blood. Jesus' words were spoken in a symbolic Passover context, a culturally suitable setting for his dramatic interpretation, and he gave his interpretation *after* the wine had been drunk (Mk 14.23-4). The effect of this timing could not be repeated at a regular ceremony, for people knew beforehand what was going to be said. The new formulation, "This cup is the new covenant in my blood", was ideally suited to the churches' needs when the new symbolic eucharistic context was being established. The repeated command to do this in remembrance of Jesus relates some of the early church's meals to Jesus' own commands when he interpreted his sacrificial death.

In this way the early church maintained its identity, perceiving one of its major events as a continuation of the work of its central identity factor in accordance with his own commands. This legitimation should be regarded as secondary, for if these words had been authentic Mark would have preserved them, and Passover was hardly a suitable occasion for an instruction to repeat a ceremony anything other than annually. The piece is also fundamental at an experiential level. Eating together was an especially significant act in a community some of whose members might otherwise have refused to join in a common meal with Gentiles. The meal will, therefore, have worked to bond the community together in accordance with its own traditions.

Romans 1.3-4 is not marked by Paul as earlier tradition, but it should surely be regarded as such. It dates Jesus' sonship from the resurrection, a fact which raises the arguments for believing it to be an early formula to a very high level of probability.[28] This attribution of sonship is the outstanding development. Jesus had been hailed as son of God in a more conventional Jewish sense at the time of his ministry.[29] As with that usage, and as in Paul's epistles (e.g. Rom 8.14; Gal 3.26), this piece should be understood with the assumption that all faithful members of the covenant community are sons of God. Having been a son of God in this sense, Jesus has been appointed "Son of God in power". The dating of this from the resurrection may be compared with the similar dating of other features in the early speeches of Acts.[30] Like the relatively early 1 Thessalonians 1.10, it shows the need to relate the risen Jesus closely to God himself. It is thus the earliest use of sonship, to be followed by Paul's own use at climactic points with reference to earlier moments of Jesus' existence.[31] This early view was not likely to be a good survivor in churches which believed in the fundamental importance of the historic ministry. Its occurrence some time before an epistle written about A.D.55-57 does not give us an accurate date for it.

The other possible christological development in this piece is Jesus' descent from David. It is difficult to be sure that it is a development because it may have been an historical fact:[32] in that case, however, its position here shows that more significance was being attached to it than during Jesus' ministry. It is likely that this is to be associated with the expectation of the deliverance of Israel by means of a king of David's line. Finally, we should note that Jesus' pre-existence appears not to have developed, and that his virgin birth is not mentioned.

7.Two Pre-Pauline "Hymns"

Two pre-Pauline pieces, Philippians 2.6-11 and Colossians 1.15-20, show massive christological development. Both expound their christology at length, from a biblical basis. Many scholars believe that both pieces are hymns, though criteria suitable for testing such an hypothesis have not been satisfactorily determined.

Philippians 2.6-11 should be understood in the light of the story of Adam.[33] Adam was created in the image of God: he did consider being on a level with God something to be grasped, for he tried to obtain it by eating of the tree of life (cf Gen 3.5,22): he did not empty himself, but was punished by God for his sin, being made to work the ground and to be subject to death. It was also believed that God would highly exalt man with all the glory of Adam. This may be explicit (cf CD III,20; 1QS IV,23; 1QH XVII,15), or it may take the form of the glorification of the righteous (cf e.g. Dan 12.3; Wsd 3.1-9; 4.16; 5.1,15ff; 2 Bar 51). These contrasts are so basic and extensive that they can hardly have been absent from the mind of the author of this piece.

With this in mind, we must consider some details. "In the form of God" indicates a high status, but not necessarily full deity. The words "form" (*morphe*) and "image" (*eikon*) overlap to a large extent, and there were two reasons why the author should not use "image" at this point. Firstly, many Jews believed that man did not lose the image of God at the fall of Adam (cf 1 Cor 11.7). Secondly, "form" is more suitable for drawing the contrast with Jesus "taking the form of a slave" during his earthly life. Further, the form of God included his glory, the visible radiance of light that could be seen at a theophany. It is obvious that man does not possess this (cf Rom 3.23; 3 Bar 4.16; Apc Mos 21.6). The "form of God" was therefore something that Adam could be thought to have lost, and Jesus could be thought to have laid aside when he "took the form of a slave". "Being on a level with God" (*isa theo*) indicates high status, but not full deity. The term *isa* overlaps in meaning with *k*, "like", used at Genesis 3.5,22, where Adam became "like" God when he obtained knowledge of good and evil.

The first act of salvation history follows, each term defining the one that precedes it. "Taking the form of a slave" suggests laying aside the form of God, and this is confirmed by "being born in the likeness of men". Like the following phrase, this implies that in some serious sense Jesus was not just like another man. Later doctrine has combined with Romans 8.3 (cf 2 Cor 5.21) to suggest that he was like us in every way except for sin, but this piece is not so precise.

It should now be clear that Jesus is portrayed as pre-existent.[34] In order to have been in the form of God so that he could choose not to grasp equality with God, before he emptied himself and was born in the likeness of men, Jesus must have existed before his birth. The significant factor that we should deduce from the background of Adam speculation is that the position of Jesus in the opening of this piece does not mean that he is being set forth as ontologically unique, and divine.

This piece continues with aspects of Jesus' earthly life that were considered central to salvation history: "And being found in appearance as a man he humbled himself, becoming obedient unto death, even death on a cross." The first phrase indicates that other people saw him as a man, and sets up his visible act of self-humiliation. As with "likeness" in the previous phrase, the term "appearance" is not inconsistent with genuine humanity, but it is particularly suitable for describing the visible humanity of a being who has been pre-existent "in the form of God". He now had the appearance of Adam after the fall, and he voluntarily humbled himself, whereas Adam was humbled by God, being made subject to death (Gen 3.19, cf Rom 5.12). Hence the need to state "even death on a cross". This penalty was not suffered by Adam, and in the Roman world it was characteristic of slaves (cf 2.7).

The next event is an action of God. "So God highly exalted him and gave him the name which is above every name, so that in the name of Jesus every knee should bow, in heaven, on earth and under the earth, and every tongue confess that Jesus Christ is Lord, to the glory of God the Father." The name given to Jesus is "Lord", described as "the name above every name" because it has been interpreted as equivalent to *Adonai,* the word read aloud where the biblical text used the Name. Again we must describe the exaltation of Jesus with sympathy but without exaggeration. On the one hand, this text does mean that Jesus has been very highly exalted, quite unlike any other person. On the other hand, he is not equated with God the Father, and he is not described as a second deity. It is fruitful to compare Apocalypse of Abraham 10, for here the mighty angel Jaoel has the name of God in him, the name Jah(weh) itself (cf Ex 23.21; 3 En 12.5). This static parallel shows quite how exalted a being could be perceived to be without being thought of as a deity.

After the confession, "Jesus Christ is Lord", God is mentioned as an even higher being, "father" being used here, as "son" is used elsewhere, to mark off the difference.[35] It may be that this piece comes from an environment in which the unique sonship of Jesus had not yet been developed. We must note also that Jesus is not said to be worshipped. On the contrary, the creation shows the traditional sign of respect to a superior being because he has the name of God himself. None the less, the position of Jesus is extremely high. Hailed as "Lord", in possession of the Name, his lordship confessed by the whole universe, he is in a higher position than he had been before he emptied himself and was born in the likeness of men. We should infer that "highly exalted" is to be taken in its full sense, to mean that God exalted Jesus to a higher position than he had in his pre-existent state.

The position of Jesus is on the verge of deity, sufficiently close for anyone involved in Jewish culture to feel that it needed to be legitimated. For this purpose, the author has used the standard Jewish source, scripture. In the first place, this means the Adam story, as we have seen. Jesus' final position has also been legitimated by midrashic interpretation of Isaiah 45.18-25. The words "every knee shall bow" and "every tongue shall confess" are from Isaiah 45.23, where "swear" has been interpreted in terms of early Christian confession of Jesus. The text contains both the name of God, Yahweh, always replaced by "Lord" when it was read, and a word·for God, *Elohim*. Consequently, it can be interpreted of the two figures, Jesus and God. For example, the LXX of Isaiah 45.25 reads, "They shall be justified by the Lord, and in God all the seed of the sons of Israel will be glorified." It is not difficult to interpret that as the Gentile mission, in which Gentiles were justified by faith in the Lord Jesus, and as the ultimate salvation of Israel in accordance with God the Father's overall plan for salvation (cf Rom 9-11).

Two questions remain outstanding. Should we see the incarnation of Jesus in this piece? And does it breach Jewish monotheism? I propose to argue that the answers to these questions are a matter of perception rather than of reality. Whether Jesus is perceived to be incarnate depends partly on how the term "incarnation" is defined. In this book, a relatively strict definition of the term has been used to refer to the process by which a fully divine being is born as a person. This is because this is the most fruitful way of looking at early christological development, not because this definition is "right" and others "wrong".[36] If we use a less strict definition to include the birth of any exalted pre-existent figure, Jesus qualifies in this passage, but incarnation ceases to be a distinguishing characteristic of Christianity, and does not imply deity. On a strict definition of "incarnation", Philippians 2.6-11 does not qualify because Jesus was not fully divine, in the view of the original author. As we have seen, "form" overlaps too much with "image", "equality with God" is too close to "like God", and "highly exalted" throws into relief the final status of Jesus as still below that of God the Father even when he was more exalted than when he was pre-existent. Not only that - monotheism was an identity marker of the Jewish community. Consequently, an author could breach it, in his own view, only deliberately, not by mistake. If an author so imbued with Jewish culture as this one, legitimating his view of Jesus from the Adam story and from Isaiah 45.18-25, does not say that Jesus is God, we must infer that he did not believe that Jesus was God. Only the clarity of the Johannine prologue should convince us that such an author did believe in the deity of Jesus.

None the less, the figure portrayed in this piece is very nearly of divine status. What is required to turn him into a full deity? Nothing more, or less, than sympathetic Gentile perception. Two forms of Gentile perception are relevant. One is the ordinary Gentile perception which was normal when this document was written. "In the form of God" could be read as a description of full deity by a keen Gentile Christian, and "equality with God" could be read equally highly. Anyone familiar with the stories of Heracles and Apollo, and with the deity of Caesar and Augustus, could then take "in the likeness of men" and "in appearance as a man" in a strong sense, and interpret this piece as setting forth a deity who appeared on earth as if he were a man. This perception illustrates the distance christology has come from Jesus of Nazareth, and the short step needed to arrive at the Johannine prologue. At the same time, the lack of conflict about christology in documents from the pre-Johannine church means that it cannot have been common. The disputes extant in Acts and the epistles are about *halakhah* rather than christology, and if there had been a general perception among Jewish members of the communities that other Christians were hailing Jesus as fully God, there would have been disputes severe enough for us to hear of them.[37]

The second relevant form of Gentile perception is ours, informed not by the Greco-Roman pantheon but by later Christian doctrine. This has been profoundly influential in biblical exegesis since the patristic period (e.g. Chrysostom, *Hom VI on Philippians,* ad loc.). The piece can be read against a dogmatic background as portraying the full deity of Jesus both before and after his earthly life. If the arguments used above are correct, however, this is not the view of the original author.

If a piece perceived by its author not to portray Jesus as fully God could and can be perceived by others to so portray him, we have the seeds of stage three of christological development sown in stage two. All we need is a conflict situation, which will make Jews object to Jesus' position, leaving Gentile perception dominant in the churches. Once *only* Gentile perception is exercised, the deity of Jesus is inevitable. Since he is already regarded as pre-existent, incarnation in the strictest sense will come with deity. This is the story which will unfold as we pass through other Christian writers to the Johannine community.[38]

Similar remarks may be made about Colossians 1.15-20.[39] So much of it has static parallels from Jewish speculation about Wisdom[40] that we must infer an author who felt that what had previously been believed of Wisdom was true of Jesus. It begins with Jesus' pre-existence and role in creation: "who is an image of the invisible God, firstborn of all creation, for through him was created everything in heaven and on earth." This description must mean that Jesus, rather than Wisdom, or as Wisdom, was the first created being (cf Prov 8.22f; Philo, *Qu in Gen.,* IV, 97). This was written centuries before Arius, when no-one believed that Jesus was the second person of the Trinity. The assertions that he was created before the world and participated in its creation were a significant advance on previous thought. They could not have been made unless it was supposed that Jesus was pre-existent, as Wisdom was perceived to have existed before the creation of the universe that she was believed to have created.[41] Colossians 1.16-17 expands this midrashically, using Proverbs 8.22-29, and moving back from Proverbs 8.22 to Genesis 1.1.[42]

Colossians 1.18 states the position of Jesus as "the head of the body, the Church", the mixed community of Jews and Gentiles which needed an ever more developed identity factor to enable it to hold together. The resurrection follows, with another series of phrases which have been interpreted as portraying the full deity of Jesus:

> Who is a beginning, firstborn from the dead, so that he might himself be the first among all, for in him all the fullness was pleased to dwell and through him to reconcile everything to him, whether things on earth or things in heaven, making peace through the blood of his cross.

The term "beginning" is again from Proverbs 8.22 and Genesis 1.1, this time reinterpreted with a second use of "firstborn" of Jesus' resurrection. The meaning is that of 1 Corinthians 15.20,23, and his position as first among all both reflects the position of Jesus in the Christian community and emphasises the Christians' hope of their own resurrection. There is a cultural connection, for the firstborn became the head of the family.[43] The next two verses offer some explanation of Jesus' pre-eminent position. The first point is the indwelling of "all the fullness". The term "fullness" is difficult. The indwelling of Wisdom is, however, known from the Wisdom literature (e.g. Wsd 7.27; 9.17), and at Proverbs 8.21 Wisdom says that she will fill the treasuries of those who love her. This may be what led the author to use the expression, perhaps also because some people interpreted the figure of Jesus in Greek terms as someone on whom part of the divine *logos* had dwelt. The further definition, "all the fullness of deity bodily" (Col 2.9), provides the correct sense. This gives a cosmic significance to Jesus' death. The reconciliation achieved by Jesus' death is expounded at Romans 5.10, and extended to the world at 2 Corinthians 5.18-19. "Everything" is almost a keynote of the Colossians piece, perhaps picking up the "everything" of Genesis 1.31; 2.3 (cf Ex 20.11). It was believed that both the creation and various supernal powers were hostile to God, so the scope of Jesus' death has been vigorously broadened. This is expounded with particular reference to the cross, and the piece finishes off with reference to the earth and heaven, probably a midrashic use of Genesis 1.1. and Proverbs 8.26-27.

The christology of this piece is in no way less developed than that of Paul. As at Philippians 2.6-11, Jesus is on the verge of deity. We may not infer that Jesus was perceived as fully God, because monotheism was such a significant identity factor of the Jewish and early Christian communities that any perceived alteration could only be made deliberately. This explains the use of Wisdom speculation grounded in scripture to expound the significance of Jesus, so that the author could feel he had not breached the monotheism revealed to Israel. At the same time, only sympathetic Gentile perception is required to turn Jesus into a deity.[44]

Both pieces, Philippians 2.6-11 and Colossians 1.15-20, belong quite firmly in stage two of christological development. Neither epistle can be dated before about A.D.50, and a date in the early 60s is more probable. The *Sitz im Leben* of both pieces is as important as their date. Both epistles are sent from the ethnically half-Jewish Timothy,[45] together with Paul, and both Paul and Timothy assimilated into the Gentile world in order to preach the Gospel. If these two pieces were not written by the authors of Philippians and Colossians, their authors are unknown to us, as is their self-identification. We must not analyse this with too simple a concept of what it is to be Jewish or Gentile. If the authors of these pieces were ethnically Jewish, they must have been assimilating like St Paul in order to have been so closely associated with his mission for him to take over their work. If they were ethnically Gentile, they were, from a Gentile perspective, judaizers. Their massive intake of Jewish culture included the rejection of Greco-Roman religion, the acceptance of Jewish scriptures and morals, and most fundamental of all, centring life around a Jewish person. Consequently, to understand the high position of Jesus in their compositions we should look primarily to Adam and Wisdom speculation rather than to the deification of people in the Greco-Roman world. The chief importance of the latter is that, as Gentiles took on so much Jewish culture, christological growth would fit naturally into the unconscious pattern already established by the deification of Heracles, Augustus and others. The content of Christianity was such that no inhibiting factor was produced at this point. The assertion that Jesus was, for example, "firstborn of all creation" (Col 1.16), or even "in the form of God" (Phil 2.6), was too remote in content from declaration of the deification of Heracles or Augustus to be perceived as pagan.[46] This is the function of the use of Adam and Wisdom material in these hymns. The early Christian author could be sure of being on firm revelatory ground with such material, for it was so completely grounded in scripture and tradition.

The setting of Philippians 2.6-11 and Colossians 1.15-20 is therefore quite different from that which must be inferred for the early speeches in Acts, *maranatha*, Romans 1.3-4, 1 Corinthians 11.23-25 and 1 Corinthians 15.3ff. Philippians 2.6-11 and Colossians 1.15-20 properly belong where they are now found, in stage two of christological development. The factors involved in their production were thus the same as those which produced the christology of St Paul himself, and for this we can turn to the more extensive evidence of his epistles as a whole.

---

1. For a study of one such group, see I.O.Glick, "The Hebrew Christians: A Marginal Religious Group", in *The Jews. Social Patterns of an American Group,* ed. M.Sklare (1958), 415-31.
2. Supra, 23-40: infra, 156-9.
3. Cf H.Grass, *Ostergeschehen und Osterberichte* (1956. 4th ed., 1970); W.Marxsen, *The Resurrection of Jesus of Nazareth* (1968. ET 1970); C.F.Evans, *Resurrection and the New Testament*, SBT 2.12 (1970); R.H.Fuller, *The Formation of the Resurrection Narratives* (1971); R.Pesch, "Zur Entstehung des Glaubens an die Auferstehung Jesus", *TQ* 153, 1973, 201-28; H.W.Bartsch, "Inhalt und Funktion des urchristlichen Osterglaubens", *ANRW* II.25.1 (1982), 794-890; P.Perkins, *Resurrection: New Testament Witness and Contemporary Reflection* (1984); P.Carnley, *The Structure of Resurrection Belief* (1987); J.I.H.McDonald, *The Resurrection. Narrative and Belief* (1989). For recent defences of the conservative view, W.L.Craig, "The Bodily Resurrection of Jesus", in *Gospel Perspectives,* ed R.T.France and D.Wenham, vol I (1980); "The Empty Tomb of Jesus", ibid., vol II (1981), 173-200; M.Harris, *Raised Immortal: resurrection and immortality in the New Testament* (1983); W.L.Craig,

"The Historicity of the Empty Tomb of Jesus", *NTS* 31, 1985, 39-67. For a remarkable Jewish contribution, P.Lapide, *The Resurrection of Jesus* (1983). Cf further infra, 110, with note 26.

4. Cf infra 104-6.

5. Supra, 41-4; infra, 105-6, 133-4, 149.

6. Cf supra, 44-6.

7. Supra, ch 5, esp 72-5.

8. Cf supra, 18-9.

9. The inaccurate chronology is similar to that of Josephus and other sources. Cf Schürer-Vermes-Millar III.1, 248-9.

10. Supra, 45, 58-9.

11. Cf supra, 90-1.

12. Supra, 51-2, 64-7.

13. Cf J.A.T.Robinson, "The most primitive Christology of all?", *JTh S NS* 7, 1956, 177-89; J.A.T.Robinson, *Twelve New Testament Studies*, SBT 34 (1962), 139-53.

14. Supra, 68, 79.

15. Infra, 110.

16. Supra, 41-4.

17. Cf supra, 42-3, 79, 82.

18. Cf P.G.Müller, *CHRISTOS ARCHEGOS. Die religionsgeschichtliche und theologische Hintergrund einer neutestamentlichen Christusprädikation* (1973); G.Johnston, "Christ as Archegos", *NTS* 27, 1980-81, 381-5.

19. Cf especially L.Hartmann, "'Into the name of Jesus'. A suggestion concerning the earliest meaning of the phrase", *NTS* 20, 1974, 432-40; L.Hartmann, "Baptism 'Into the Name of Jesus' and early Christology", *StTh* 28, 1974, 21-48.

20. Cf supra 64-5, 69, 72-5; D.C.Allison, "Jesus and the Covenant: A Response to E.P.Sanders", *JSNT* 29, 1987, 57-78.

21. Supra, 105-6.

22. M.D.Goulder, "The Two Roots of the Christian Myth", in *The Myth of God Incarnate*, ed J.Hick (1977), 64-86; G.N.Stanton, "Samaritan Incarnational Christology?", in M.D.Goulder (ed), *Incarnation and Myth* (1979), 243-6; M.D.Goulder, "The Samaritan hypothesis", ibid., 247-50. More generally, cf K.Beyschlag, *Simon Magus und die christliche Gnosis*, WUNT 16 (1974); G.Lüdemann, *Untersuchungen zur simonianischen Gnosis*, GTA 1 (1975); R.McL.Wilson, "Simon and Gnostic Origins", in *Les Actes des Apôtres*, ed J.Kremer, BETL 48 (1979), 485-91; D-A.Koch, "Geistbesitz, Geistverleihung und Wundermacht. Erwägungen zur Tradition und zur lukanischen Redaktion in Act 8,5-25", *ZNW* 77, 1986, 64-82; R.Bergmeier, "Die Gestalt des Simon Magus in Act 8 und in der simonianischen Gnosis - Aporien einer Gesamtdeutung", *ZNW* 77, 1986, 267-75; G.Lüdemann, "The Acts of the Apostles and the Beginnings of Simonian Gnosis", *NTS* 33, 1987, 420-26.

23. Cf A.M.Hunter, *Paul and his Predecessors*, Hastie Lectures (1939. 1940); R.Deichgraber, *Gotteshymnus und Christushymnus in der frühe Christenheit*, StUNT 5 (1967); J.T.Sanders, *The New Testament Christological Hymns. Their Historical Religious Background* (1971); Kl.Wengst, *Christologische Formeln und Lieder des Urchristentums*, StNT 7 (1972. 2nd ed., 1974).

24. Cf supra, 79 with note 2.

25. Cf further supra, 68; infra, 113-4, 133; W.Kramer, *Christ, Lord, Son of God* (1963. ET SBT 50, 1966), 65-107.

26. Supra, 98. Cf J.Kloppenborg, "An Analysis of the Pre-Pauline Formula 1 Cor 15.3b-5 in Light of Some Recent Literature", *CBQ* 40, 1978, 351-67; P.J.Kearney, "He

Appeared to 500 Brothers (I Cor XV.6)", *NT* 22, 1980, 264-84; J.Murphy O-Connor, "Tradition and Redaction in 1 Cor 15:3-7", *CBQ* 43, 1981, 582-9.

27. Cf supra, 65. The classic discussion remains J.Jeremias, *The Eucharistic Words of Jesus* (2nd ET. 1964). Cf further, in addition to the commentators, I.H.Marshall, *Last supper and Lord's supper* (1980); H.Merklein, "Erwägungen zur Überlieferungsgeschichte der neutestamentlichen Abendmahlstraditionen", *BZ* 21, 1977, 88-101, 235-44; O.Hofius, "Herrenmahl und Herrenmahlparadosis: Erwägungen zu 1Kor 11,23b-25", *ZThK* 85, 1988, 371-408. On the social background and function of Paul's comments, S.C.Barton, "Paul's Sense of Place: an Anthropological Approach to Community Formation in Corinth", *NTS* 32, 1986, 225-46. Detailed criticism of the secondary literature cannot be attempted here.

28. Cf J.D.G.Dunn, "Jesus - Flesh and Spirit: An Exposition of Romans i.3-4", *JThS NS* 24, 1973, 40-68; C.E.B.Cranfield, *A Commentary on the Epistle to the Romans*, vol I, ICC (1975), ad loc.; V.S.Poythress, "Is Romans i.3-4 a Pauline Confession After All?", *ExpT* 87, 1976, 180-3.

29. Supra, 46.

30. Supra, 106.

31. Infra, 134-5.

32. Cf infra, 149-50.

33. The massive secondary literature is still influenced by Lohmeyer and Käsemann: cf E.Lohmeyer, *Kyrios Jesus: Eine Untersuchung zu Phil. 2,5-11* (SHAW, 1928); E.Käsemann, "A Critical Analysis of Philippians 2:5-11" (1950), ET *JThC* 5, 1969, 45-88; R.P.Martin, *Carmen Christi: Philippians ii, 5-11*, MSSNTS 4 (1967); W.Schenk, "Der Philipperbrief in der neueren Forschung (1945-1985)", *ANRW* II.25.4 (1987), 3299-3313. Further, M.D.Hooker, "Philippians 2,6-11", in *Jesus und Paulus*. Festschrift für W.G.Kummel zum 70 Geburtstag, ed. E.E.Ellis & E.Grasser (1975), 151-64; F.Manns, "Un hymne judeo-chrétienne: Philippiens 2,6-11", *ED* 29, 1976, 259-90; J.Murphy O'Connor, "Christological Anthropology in Phil 2,6-11", *RB* 83, 1976, 23-50; G.Howard, "Phil 2:6-11 and the Human Christ", *CBQ* 40, 1978, 368-87; C.J.Robbins, "Rhetorical Structure of Phil 2.6-11", *CBQ* 42, 1980, 73-82; T.Nagata, "A Neglected Literary Feature of the Christ-Hymn in Phil 2:6-11", *AJBI* 9, 1983, 184-229; N.T.Wright, "*harpagmos* and the meaning of Philippians 2:5-11", *JThS NS* 37, 1986, 321-52; M.Rissi, "Der Christushymnus in Phil 2,6-11", *ANRW* II.25.4 (1987), 3314-26; C.A.Wanamaker, "Philippians 2.6-11: Son of God or Adamic Christology?", *NTS* 33, 1987, 179-93; J.A.Fitzmyer, "The Aramaic Background of Philippians 2:6-11", *CBQ* 50, 1988, 470-83; U.B.Müller, "Der Christushymnus Phil 2.6-11", ZNW 79, 1988, 17-44.

34. For the contrary view, C.H.Talbert, "Pre-existence in Philippians 2.6-11", *JBL* 86, 1967, 141-53: Murphy O'Connor, op. cit.; Dunn, *Making*, 114-21. For criticism, cf especially A.T.Hanson, *The Image of the Invisible God* (1982), ch 3, esp 62-6.

35. Cf infra, 134-5, 147.

36. Cf infra 166-8.

37. Cf infra, 135-8.

38. Cf infra 135-8, 142-3, 144-6, 156-9.

39. Cf H.J.Gabathuler, *Jesus Christus, Haupt der Kirche - Haupt der Welt. Der Christushymnus Colosser 1,15-20 in der theologischen Forschung der letzten 130 Jahre*, AThANT 45 (1965); N.Kehl, *Der Christushymnus im Kolosserbrief. Eine motivgeschichtliche Untersuchung zu Kol 1.12-20*, SBM 1 (1967); W.Pohlmann, "Die hymnischen All-Prädikationen in Kol 1,15-20", *ZNW* 64, 1973, 53-74; P.Benoit, "L'hymn christologique de Col. 1.15-20", in J.Neusner (ed), *Christianity, Judaism*

119

and Other Greco-Roman Cults. Essays in honour of M.Smith, SJLA 12 (1975), vol I, 226-63; F.Manns, "Col. 1,15-20: midrash chrétien de Gen.1,1", *RevSR* 53, 1979, 323-39; J.C.O'Neill, "The Source of Christology in Colossians", *NTS* 26, 1979-80, 87-100; P.Beasley-Murray, "Colossians 1, 15-20: An Early Christian Hymn Celebrating the Lordship of Christ", in *Pauline Studies.* Essays presented to Professor F.F.Bruce on his 70th Birthday, ed D.A.Hagner & M.J.Harris (1980), 169-83; J.N.Aletti, *Colossiens 1,15-20: Genre et exégèse du texte. Fonction de la thématique sapientielle*, AnBib 91 (1981); T.E.Pollard, "Colossians 1.12-20: A Reconsideration", *NTS* 27, 1981, 572-5.

40. Cf supra, 88-90.
41. For a denial of this view, Dunn, *Making,* 187-96, with detailed bibliography.
42. For detailed attempts to reconstruct the midrashic process on these lines, C.F.Burney, "Christ as the *arche* of Creation", *JThS* 27, 1926, 160-77; Manns, op. cit., *RevSR* 53, 1979, 100-10.
43. There are also semantic connections: Manns, op.cit.
44. Cf supra, 114-5.
45. Cf supra, 16.
46. Cf supra 37, 105.

Chapter 8
The Christology of St Paul

1. Identity and Mission

"There is no Jew nor Greek, there is no slave nor free, there is no male and female, for you are all one in Christ Jesus." Galatians 3.28 puts the social function of Pauline theology in a christological nutshell, and with it the key to the success of the Gentile mission. From a Jewish perspective, the differences between Jew and Gentile, slave and free, male and female, were the biggest differences between people in the Greco-Roman world. That between Jew and Greek was at the centre of Paul's mission. Jesus could hold together a mixed community of Jews and Gentiles only if he embodied the community's identity.[1] The acceptance of Gentiles by Jews was not without precedent: but if they obeyed what were later regarded as the Noachic rules and attended the synagogue on the sabbath, they remained in a subordinate position. If they were to approach equality with ethnically Jewish people, they had to become proselytes. That meant circumcision for men, and for everyone it meant undertaking to keep the Law. Even then proselytes, though superior to Gentiles, were not wholly on an equal footing with ethnically Jewish people.[2]

This gives us some measure of the revolution which Paul sought to bring about. What is more, ethnically Jewish people who did not have faith in Jesus were thereby excluded from the covenant community. In Romans 9-11, Paul seeks to explain this with a *midrash* including the supernatural hardening of Israel (11.25ff). He predicts that they will finally be converted and join the community, much as the Qumran community imagined that the congregation of Israel would join them in the last days (1Q Sa I.1ff; cf 4QpNah III, 1-8).

The acceptance of Gentiles led Paul to redefine the term "Jew" itself.

A Jew is not a person who is visibly a Jew, nor is circumcision the circumcision which is visible in the flesh. But a Jew is a person who is a Jew secretly, and circumcision is circumcision of the heart in the spirit not in the letter, for which praise is received not from men but from God (Rom 2.28-9).

This dramatic redefinition shows how seriously assimilated St Paul himself was. It effectively excludes non-Christian Jews from salvation.

Observant Jews were bound to conclude that Paul had abandoned Judaism.

The Pauline epistles were written to communities which included both Jews and Gentiles, and which were predominantly Gentile (cf 1 Cor 12.2; Gal 1.16; 2.9,11ff; 3.2-5; 4.8al; Phil 3.2-4; Col 2.11-13,16; 3.5-7; 1 Thess 1.9; 2.14). It is fruitful to analyse how Jewish the Pauline Christians had to become, using the eight identity factors isolated in chapter 2. They did not have to be ethnically Jewish, and Paul was strongly opposed to the circumcision of Gentiles. He objected to the observance of the sabbath, and of Jewish festivals (cf Rom 14.5-6; Gal 4.10; Col 2.16), and there was no question of the observance of purity laws. Monotheism is the only identity factor of the Jewish community which was maintained, and it was highly functional. If the new community was to be clearly marked off from the Gentile world, it had to be significantly different from it. Monotheism guaranteed the uniqueness of the community's revelation, and it appealed to cultured Gentiles. From the inside, it was the centre of Judaism as a religion. It also involved everything that assimilating Jews felt was right, because God was held to have revealed Jewish morals.

Two identity factors show signs of being problematic. The dietary laws were bound to be troublesome. Some basic prohibitions were deeply ingrained in Jewish feelings, intensified as these were by persecution and Gentile scorn, as well as the lengthy habituation of tradition, commanded in scripture. Moreover, some of the meat eaten by Gentiles was sacrificed to a deity before being sold: eating it could therefore be perceived as idolatry. Paul argued in favour of eating Gentile meat, for this was virtually inevitable in predominantly Gentile communities. He argues strongly against eating in an idol temple, because this put Christians in the wrong community, a point reinforced by the concept of other gods as demons (1 Cor 10.16-22, cf 8.4ff). He argues however that Christians should not enquire about the origin of meat bought in the market or served to them by a non-Christian (1 Cor 10.25-27): only if someone makes a fuss should one refuse to eat it, and that is because of the *other* person's conscience (1 Cor 10.28-29). At Romans 14.2-3, he likewise argues for the acceptance of the "weak" Christian who eats only vegetables, the natural reaction of an observant Jew who does not have access to kosher meat, and at 1 Corinthians 8.13, faced with Christians who insist upon their freedom, he declares he would prefer never to eat meat rather than to scandalize his brother. He himself clearly felt that it was right to eat any meat, but in practice he sought the most sociable compromise, with allowances for "weaker brethren" to hold the community together.

The second problematical identity factor was scripture. Paul believed and taught the divine authority of a collection of sacred books which approximates to our Old Testament. Like monotheism, this helped the community to maintain its identity as it changed. Paul needed the Old Testament for the exposition of salvation in Jesus and for legitimation of the new community. On the other hand, the Old Testament contains injunctions to do the Law, with a large number of detailed regulations which would have prevented most Gentiles from entering the community. Paul was determined to drop them. He therefore produced lengthy arguments from these same scriptures to demonstrate that salvation came from faith in Jesus, without the works of the Law. Two midrashim, in Galatians 3 and Romans 4, use the story of the pre-Mosaic patriarch Abraham for this purpose. Paul argues from Abraham's justification by faith to the justification of Christians by faith, and therefore without the works of the Law. 2 Corinthians 3 tackles the question of which community's use of scripture is right, arguing that the veil which covered Moses' face on Mt Sinai remains over Jews who have not accepted Jesus: "For until the present day the same veil remains unremoved at the reading of the old covenant, for it is done away in Christ. But to this day whenever Moses is read a veil lies over their heart: but whenever one turns to the Lord, the veil is removed" (2 Cor 3.14-16, interpreting Ex 34.34).

At Romans 9-11, Paul again argues that salvation is for those who are children of the Old Testament promises, not those who are ethnically Jewish. His interpretation of Deuteronomy 30.14 is almost programmatic: "But what does it say? 'The word is near you, in your mouth and in your heart' (Deut 30.14). This refers to the word of faith which we preach, for if you confess 'with your mouth' Jesus as Lord, and believe 'in your heart' that God raised him from the dead, you shall be saved" (Rom 10.8-10). Paul concludes by arguing that the ethnic group of Israel will be saved when the Gospel has been preached to the Gentiles. Thus Paul could perceive himself and his converts as accepting scripture. Other Jewish people, however, might conclude that they did not accept scripture, because they had not taken upon themselves the yoke of the Law.

Thus Gentile converts in a Pauline church took on about one and a half of the eight identity factors isolated in chapter 2. Paul might accept them as real Jews as Paul was prepared to redefine that term, but 1.5 out of 8 correctly represents the obvious fact that, from a Jewish perspective, Gentile converts did not become Jews when they became Christians. What has this to do with the development of christology? It is a major factor in explaining the need for it. We are very clearly in stage two of christological development. The churches contained many Jews, including apostles from Jesus' historic ministry. At the same time, Pauline churches contained mostly Gentiles. How were Christians to hold together in one community? Paul met this situation with further development of the figure of Jesus, a commitment for which his conversion on the Damascus road ideally prepared him.[3]

Paul persecuted the church when it was a Jewish sub-group with Jesus as its only specific identity factor, and it is against that group that he is known to have struggled, not against the Law which he was apparently content to observe. The blinding flash brought a vision of Jesus, not of the Gentiles, speaking Aramaic with a purely Greek metaphor, as only the vision of a bilingual person could. "Saul, Saul, why do you persecute me?" (Acts 9.4).

Not, as one might have thought, "Why do you persecute my servants?", or "the righteous who preach the good news". No, Jesus was already central, hence "Why do you persecute *me*? It is hard for you to kick against the goads" (Acts 26.14). Paul did not know what had hit him. "Who are you, Lord?" "I am Jesus whom you are persecuting." Again the centrality of Jesus, the sole identity factor of the earliest church. The longest account of the conversion follows with the call to be a missionary to the Gentiles (Acts 26.17-18). Though this account may have been somewhat written up in transmission, the basic fact of the call to evangelize the Gentiles is central to the witness of St Paul himself (e.g. Gal 1.16; 2.2,9; Rom 15.15-16). It is not however clear that he concluded immediately that the Gentiles need not do the Law, a view which he may have reached during his time in Arabia or even later (cf Gal 1.15-24). It was 17 years before he laid before Peter, Jacob, John and others the Gospel which he preached to the Gentiles (Gal 1.15-2.10), a Gospel which by that stage must have included justification by faith.

None of the extant epistles was written soon after Paul's conversion. All come from a time when stage two of christological development had been in existence for some years. The Christian community had a profound need for the developments which Paul voiced. While the Jewish community was held together by ethnicity and by a whole culture expressed in the Law, the mixed Christian community now proceeded to hold itself together by the generation of more christological belief. The mode of development did not however change. We have seen that the figure of Jesus was developed in the same way as other messianic and intermediary figures.[4] Paul was culturally Jewish, and he too proceeded to develop Jesus in the same way, but with more vigour because of the increased need which his personal experience enabled him to realise. We must consider the developed picture of Jesus in epistles written some 20 or 30 years after Paul's conversion.

2. The Figure of Jesus[5]

Paul believed that Jesus had existed before his earthly life. We have seen this belief taken over from two basic sources, Wisdom christology (Col 1.15f) and comparison with Adam (Phil 2.6ff). Adam speculation also legitimated the claim that Jesus was "in the form of God" when he was pre-existent, so exalted that he had to empty himself to live a human life at all (Phil 2.6-7). The appropriation of static parallels from Wisdom speculation legitimated the view that Jesus was involved in the creation of the world (cf 1 Cor 8.6, Col 1.15ff).[6]

Paul says little about Jesus' earthly life. He does however assume the absolute authority of Jesus' teaching. The classic passage is 1 Corinthians 7.10-17, where Paul knows Jesus' remarkable prohibition of divorce, but has to apply it to a new situation, in which one partner is Christian and the other is not. This led him to distinguish with great clarity between his own judgement and the teaching of "the Lord". This is a significant point of contact with the transmission of the synoptic tradition. Jesus' authority as a teacher was one aspect of the starting-point of christology, and it was not dropped in the Pauline churches as the soteriological and cosmic significance of his death and resurrection were worked out. The fundamental significance of the historical Jesus is implied equally strongly by the preservation of *Abba* (Rom 8.15; Gal 4.6), and by the use of his words at the Last Supper (1 Cor 11.23-5).[7]

Jesus' death and resurrection were extensively developed. I have noted that a sacrificial interpretation of Jesus' death was put forward by him at the Last Supper, and the regular repetition of the words of institution will have facilitated further development of this aspect of it. Jewish sacrifices were frequently used as symbols for the forgiveness of sins, and in the early formula at 1 Corinthians 15.3 Christ is said to have "died for our sins."[8] At Romans 3.21ff, Paul sets forth "the redemption which is in Christ Jesus, whom God set forth as a propitiation, through faith, by means of his blood." This event is placed in the centre of salvation history. Sin entered the world with the sin of Adam, bringing death. Jesus' obedience in going to his death is to be contrasted with Adam's disobedience, and it brought to an end the domination of sin (Rom 5.12-21). God had to punish sin in order to be righteous, but in previous times he had in his forbearance passed over the punishment of sin, storing it up for the Day of Wrath. Now Jesus had taken this upon himself and the righteousness of God had been shown forth, and his people, being justified by faith, would be saved from the Wrath (Rom 3.25-6; 5.9). Thus we have redemption in Christ Jesus (Rom 3.24), or, "being enemies, we were reconciled to God through the death of his Son" (Rom 5.10). In Colossians, the cosmic significance of Jesus' death is further developed by the assertion that on the cross he defeated the evil powers (Col 2.15).

These developments are a fruitful context in which to see Paul's assertion that Jesus was sinless during his earthly life (2 Cor 5.21; cf Rom 8.3). This view first appears in Paul. It is not without static parallels in Jewish traditions.[9] These parallels show that there is nothing unJewish about the elaboration of a concept of a sinless person, and that sinlessness does not imply divinity. The locus of the development was however different. Jewish patriarchs might be perceived as sinless because they obeyed the Law perfectly, a view which the earliest apostles may not have thought of applying to Jesus of Nazareth. Paul, not having known the historical Jesus, puts forward his sinlessness in the context of his death. This is at one level a consequence of the sacrificial interpretation of his death, for sacrifices had to be without blemish.[10]

Jesus' resurrection was just as fundamental as his death: "if Christ has not been raised, your faith is empty - you are still in your sins" (1 Cor 15.17). His resurrection involved the conquest of death itself. It did more than remove the effects of Adam's sin, and it is a foretaste of the general resurrection (1

Cor 15.20-23). Paul took over the earlier belief that Jesus is now in heaven at the right hand of God. He had seen Jesus in glory at least on the occasion of his conversion (cf also Acts 7.55-8.1; 2 Cor 12.1ff). Paul adds that he is interceding for us, and sends grace and peace from him, associated with God, to the recipients of his epistles. Paul took over the earlier belief that Jesus would come soon at the last day (1 Cor 16.22; Phil 3.20-21; 4.6), and he expected that Jesus himself would take part in the eschatological judgment (2 Cor 5.10; 2 Thess 1.7-8). 1 Thessalonians 4.13ff gives a graphic picture of meeting the Lord in the air when the dead are raised, and at 1 Corinthians 15.24ff Paul draws on scripture to give a picture of the final events. This has Christ in a dominant position as ruler of the universe, though at the same time subordinate to God himself.

All these events are properly eschatological, that is, they belong to the last days. Since the death and resurrection of Jesus had already occurred, Paul had to make some adjustments to the standard apocalyptic scheme of the last days. The common hope was that God would establish his kingdom soon. In the conviction that he would do this, some Jews saw the events of their own time as belonging to the last days. For example, the authors of the book of Daniel saw the persecution of Antiochus Epiphanes as a decisive event which belonged to the last three and a half years of normal human history. They portrayed the Seleucid kingdom as the last kingdom, to be destroyed by God after a number of events of their own time recognizable in the activities of the little horn of the fourth beast. The author of 4 Ezra 11-12 altered the identification of the fourth kingdom to the Roman, and created a new set of details to ensure that the events of *his* own day were recognizable as belonging to the last times.

Paul's apocalyptic scheme was formed by means of the same generative pattern of change. He shared the belief of those authors that the End was at hand, but he believed that the decisive salvific act of God in Jesus had already occurred. Thus for the first time the decisive act of salvation is placed before the end of all things, whereas non-Christian Jewish documents place before the End evil events, such as the persecution of Antiochus Epiphanes, and the suffering of the righteous. This new structure must be borne in mind in dealing with apparent inconsistencies in Paul's comments on God's act in Jesus, and its appropriation by the believer. He may use past tenses because Jesus has already lived, died and risen and believers have been saved, but he may use future tenses because these events are in an abstract theological sense proleptic. Christians still sin and die, and in so far as they are saved, they are saved by appropriating now the consequences of God's favourable judgment of them in the future.

3. Christ, the Believer and the Community
In the area of the appropriation of Christ's work by the believer, we find

massive christological development. The role of faith is central to this, and the commonest metaphor used to explain how Christians are saved by faith is justification, essentially a legal metaphor. Paul argued that all men deserved to be condemned by God at the last day, Jews and Gentiles alike (Rom 1-3). From this they were saved by Jesus, whose work ensured that in the final judgment God, who would otherwise have had to bring in a verdict of "guilty", can bring in a verdict of "righteous". This verdict can be anticipated in the present, so that salvation depends not on membership of the Jewish community, manifested in the works of the Law, but on faith in Jesus Christ, the distinctive identity factor of the new Christian community. Paul expounded this contrast with especial vigour in conflict with judaizers who felt that Gentile Christians should become Jews. It was this conflict which caused him to contrast faith with works, for faith in Jesus bound together the Christian community, whereas doing the works of the Law showed people's intention of entering, or remaining, in the Jewish community.[11] Consequently, Paul argued that the Gospel was no good to people who became Jewish.

Look, I Paul tell you that if you are circumcised Christ will be of no help to you. Now I bear witness again to every man who is getting circumcised that he is under obligation to do the whole Law. You who are being justified in the Law, you were removed from Christ, you fell from grace, for we wait for a hope of righteousness by the Spirit on the basis of faith (Gal 5.2-5).

Paul might have been expected to argue that if Gentiles were converted to Christianity, it made no difference if they became like the first apostles, circumcised, observing the sabbath and other Jewish identity factors. This would not, however, have been adequate for the Pauline mission, because the visible movement of Gentile converts into Judaism would have undermined the success of the Gentile mission as a whole. For Paul, conversion to Judaism undermined the basis of salvation by means of Christianity. Hence the centrality of faith, isolated in the programmatic statement of the Gospel at the opening of Romans (Rom 1.16-17, quoting Hab 2.4). The theoretically eschatological nature of this concept, and its dependence on the finished work of Christ, are both brought out at Romans 5.9: "Being justified now by his blood, we shall be saved from the Wrath."

Within this overall structure, Paul related Jesus' saving work to all the main events of the Christian life. He goes far beyond the original interpretation of baptism in the name of Jesus: "Or do you not know that we who were baptised into Christ Jesus were baptized into his death? We were therefore buried with him through baptism into his death ..."(Rom 6.3-4).

Colossians has us rise with him in baptism too (Col 2.12-13), but Paul's argument in Romans 6 is all the more striking for being more circumspect. His teaching should be seen as socially grounded at two levels. Firstly, it functions as legitimation of Pauline ethics. This was important, because of the potential lack of grounding for personal behaviour brought about by the admission to the Christian communities of Gentiles who did not undertake to observe the Jewish Law. If the Law had been completely dropped, the Pauline communities would have been left with no morals at all. This antinomian position was a logical deduction from Paul's view that Gentile Christians did not have to be circumcised and take on the observance of the Law, but it was not Paul's view. He was culturally Jewish, and viewed theft, adultery, idolatry and so on with horror. He had moved from his native Jewish position only to accept Gentiles as Gentiles, knowing that any demand that Gentiles become Jewish would reduce the Gentile mission to a trickle of proselytes. Thus his decisions correspond approximately to the retaining of Jewish Law, minus all those requirements which would have prevented large numbers of Gentiles from joining Christian communities. He allowed the eating of meat which was not kosher, pork necessarily included, even if it might have been offered to an idol (1 Cor 10.25-27). This position was morally and religiously horrifying to many pious Jews, so Paul made allowances for their scruples in the advice which he gave, arguing for the acceptance of Christians who ate only vegetables (Rom 14.2-3, cf 1 Cor 8.13).[12] The logic of all these judgements is that they entail the acceptance of all Christians, without demanding the acceptance of socially impossible conditions.

At the same time, Paul did not alter his Pharisaic attitude to sex. In 1 Corinthians 7, despite giving advice on marriage and divorce, he puts forward an oral law according to which "it is good for a man not to touch a woman" (1 Cor 7.1). He even boasts in his own achievement: "I like everyone to be like me ... but I say to the unmarried and to the widows, it is good for them if they remain like me" (1 Cor 7.7-8). Paul could get away with this boasting in his oral law because, like any Pharisee, he allowed the keeping of the law to a lower standard than that practised by himself (1 Cor 7.28). Provided that marriage is allowed, and sex within it, Paul's judgements are socially functional because their effect is to prevent sex outside marriage, without in practice preventing Christians from marrying and having children.

In terms of Jewish Law, however, Paul's position is completely unpredictable, ranging from rejection of the Law to expansion of the Law with optional *halakhah*. Moreover, the laws rejected include the most basic identity factors of the Jewish community, so that observant Jews were bound to deduce that he was advocating an antinomian position. In these circumstances, theological legitimation of Paul's position was essential, and at one level this is what Romans 6 provides. Here the antinomian position is vigorously rejected, and the general view that Christians should not be sinful is derived in the first place from the community's initiation rite, now interpreted in terms of the central event of salvation history.

This is the second level at which Paul's position is socially grounded: he has made it wholly dependent on the community's distinctive identity factor. This was the most functional path that he could have taken, since it made the grounding of Christian ethics unique, and dependent upon Christian commitment. At the same time, this grounding does not prescribe any particular ethical decisions. That people should not sin, because they have died and risen with Christ, does not tell them whether eating meat sacrificed to idols is sinful or not, still less, whether they should marry. This was an ideal position for the developing community, since it could effectively make ethical decisions on the basis of its own identity. Paul's own position was especially well legitimated like this, since the presence of Jews and Gentiles in the same community necessarily produced conflicts, and these might be resolved by appeal to the community's own identity. Whatever built up the community was necessarily what you would do "in Christ".

Paul also associates Jesus with all kinds of events in the community's life, both the mundane and the theologically significant. For example, Paul's imprisonment became known "in Christ" (Phil 1.13), while at a more theological level believers who have died are described as "those who fell asleep in Christ" (1 Cor 15.18). "In Christ", or more fully, "in Christ Jesus", is the commonest expression used in statements of this kind, and it is tempting to put all the occurrences together and deduce a concept of "being in Christ". We may then go further and deduce a concept of what sort of being "Christ" is, and take in Paul's statements about Jesus which do not use the expression "in Christ". We shall then find that we have a mysteriously corporate being, quite unparalleled in Judaism, and we may conclude that as a result of a striking new development, Paul naturally believed that Jesus was divine.[13]

I shall argue that such a procedure is faulty, but the statements we can use are quite dramatic. In addition to Paul's use of "in Christ" with reference to numerous events, "the free gift of God is eternal life in Christ Jesus our Lord" (Rom 6.23): "if anyone is in Christ, he is a new creation" (2 Cor 5.17): "There is neither Jew nor Greek, there is neither slave nor free, there is no male and female, for you are all one in Christ Jesus" (Gal 3.28). Paul expresses himself differently at Galatians 2.19-20: "I have been crucified with Christ. It is no longer I who live, but Christ lives in me." The title "Lord" is also used in significant theological statements of this kind: "You are the seal of my apostleship in the Lord" (1 Cor 9.2): "So that whoever eats the bread or drinks the cup of the Lord unworthily, is guilty of the body and blood of the Lord ... so many among you are feeble and sick and some have died" (1 Cor 11.27,30). The corporate nature of Christ can then be pushed home with 1 Corinthians 10.16-17 and the elaborate metaphor of 1 Corinthians 12.12ff, where Christ is like a human body with many members, and "You are the body of Christ, and members individually" (1 Cor 12.27, cf Rom 12.4ff).

There are three reasons why we should not use such texts to deduce a corporate concept of Christ, and attribute that concept to Paul. Firstly, Paul does not expound such a corporate concept, not even in Romans, where it should have been important, if he believed in it. Secondly, no satisfactory account of such a concept has ever been given, either in terms of its intellectual consistency or its origins. Thirdly, we can offer an alternative explanation of his statements in terms of their social and theological functions. I have noted the position of Jesus as the central identity factor of a new mixed community which contained both Jews and Gentiles. This is the generative key to this whole set of developments. To put it epigrammatically, Christians are all one in Christ Jesus because otherwise they cannot be one at all.

This does not mean that we should undervalue the very high position of Jesus implied by such statements: it means that a concept of a unique kind of corporate being, and therefore a divine being, is not what should be deduced from them. They rather indicate the fundamental significance of the act of God in Christ Jesus, by means of which the mixed community of Jews and Gentiles had been formed and through which it was to be held together. The term "Christ" is used in the expression "in Christ" because it was established in functional contexts and was distinctive of the Christian community. The Greek preposition "*en*" is used because it has a massive semantic area which includes all sorts of functional uses. The free gift of God is eternal life in Christ Jesus our Lord (Rom 6.23), because it is the redemptive work of Christ Jesus by means of which God has freely given us eternal life. A person in Christ is a new creation (2 Cor 5.17), because the salvation brought by Christ's redemptive work has enabled people to live changed lives. Christians are "all one in Christ Jesus" (Gal 3.28) because his redemptive work enabled his apostles to found a united community containing both Jews and Greeks. Even "Christ lives in me" (Gal 2.20), though it is experiential, does not make a corporate deity of Christ. It interprets Christian experience on the analogy of the indwelling of Wisdom or the Holy Spirit, and it is too rare for us to draw out its implications and attribute them to Paul.

Similar comments may be made about Paul's use of the term "body" (of Christ). Apart from literal references to Jesus' body on the cross (Rom 7.4; Col 1.22), these may be divided into two groups. Paul inherited the eucharistic words of Jesus, according to which the bread at the Last Supper and hence the Lord's Supper was Jesus' body. This is symbolic, and we should not squeeze a literal interpretation from it. The term "body" was also in use to mean "community", and Paul's description of the community as "the body of Christ" is a development of this in the light of Jesus' position as the exalted head of that community (cf Col 1.18). The two uses are combined at 1 Corinthians 10.16-17, which relies on the fundamental importance of eating together in mixed communities of Jews and Gentiles, but the statement "we many are one bread" indicates how metaphorically it is to be taken. Paul's statements about being "in Christ" and the "body of Christ" should therefore be integrated into his christology as a whole. They are further evidence of the very exalted position of Jesus as the central identity factor of the community, the agent of creation and redemption. They are however in large measure functional and in some cases metaphorical. They do not indicate a corporate personality, and they are not assertions of deity.

4. Christology, Experience and Identity

The Christian community could not be held together only by abstract theology. Paul's christological developments can be traced without much reference to experience because they were so closely related to experience that they were confirmed by experience. This experiential grounding was fundamental to holding the community together. It began with conversion. Not everyone saw a blinding light on the Damascus road. Everyone however had to turn afresh towards God to join a Pauline community, and the story of Paul's conversion appealed so much to the author of Acts that he tells it three times. At this stage, conversions into a community centred on Jesus must have been a normal feature of life in it. Conversion was followed by baptism. Paul's theological development of this experience perceived it as participation in the death and resurrection of Christ, and as the cause of Christian behaviour.[14] Pauline Christians were necessarily reminded of their own baptism whenever new members joined the community by means of this dramatic, and dramatically interpreted, ceremony.

The gift of the Spirit was also perceived early in the Christian life, so much so that Paul could remind Galatian Gentiles that they had received it before they began to observe the Law. He was then able to use this fact to legitimate his view that salvation was through faith in Christ crucified (Gal 3.1ff). A list of gifts of the Spirit is given in 1 Corinthians 12, beginning with a basic confession: "No-one can say 'Jesus is Lord', except by the Holy Spirit." The gifts include prophecy, speaking with tongues, healing, words of wisdom and of knowledge. The effects of these gifts on christological development will have been partly direct, as when a passage of scripture was newly interpreted to refer to Jesus' saving work. Indirect effects will have been equally important. Any act of commitment to, or participation in, the Christian community worked towards christological development because it made the community more important, and the community's increased importance was bound to be reflected in the development of its distinctive identity factor. Paul facilitated this process by declaring that events such as his imprisonment became known "in Christ" (Phil 1.12-14).

Another major community event was the Lord's Supper. Eating together was generally very important to the community, because Jewish dietary laws might prevent Jews from eating with Gentiles. Hence the significance of the quarrel at Antioch when Jewish Christians refused to eat with their Gentile brethren (cf Gal 2.11-21). Paul's report of the question which he put to Cephas reveals his standard of judgement: "If you, being a Jew, live like a

Gentile and not like a Jew, how can you compel Gentiles to judaize?" (Gal 2.14). The assumption is that the community must eat together, so if Jewish Christians will not eat with Gentiles, Gentile Christians will have to eat Jewish food. That would be the thin end of the wedge, for if Jewish Christians compelled Gentile Christians to observe one of the basic identity factors of Judaism, the observance of other identity factors was bound to follow.

In this context, the Lord's Supper was the most important meal of all, because it became the symbolic meal of the community. In seeking to regulate behaviour at the Lord's Supper in Corinth, Paul repeats a developed version of Jesus' words at the Last Supper (1 Cor 11.23-5). This reinforced the community's identity. Despite the fact that it consisted largely of Gentiles, the community identified itself as the same community as the disciples gathered round Jesus on the night of his betrayal. The developments include the double command to do this in memory of Jesus,[15] a command which legitimates the existence of the obedient Pauline community. Paul's immediate comment relates this both to Jesus' death and to his second coming (1 Cor 11.26). He goes on to argue that anyone who eats and drinks unworthily is guilty of the body and blood of the Lord, and he attributes sickness and death in the Corinthian community to their misbehaviour at this meal (1 Cor 11.30). This makes the most of the common view that sickness and death were due to sin. The whole passage is a classic example of secondary legitimation.

I have noted two other old traditions, the repetition of which will have helped to maintain the community's identity. One is the tradition of Jesus' resurrection at 1 Corinthians 15.3-7.[16] Paul validates it with the resurrection appearances, beginning with those to Cephas and the twelve. This could not fail to reinforce the community's identity by reminding it of its origins in the saving acts of God. Paul then uses the resurrection of Jesus to demonstrate the correctness of the Pharisaic belief in a general resurrection. This is a perfect example of a Pauline shift. Paul had believed in the general resurrection when he was a Pharisee: he now made that belief dependent on the story of the vindication of the Christian community's central identity factor. He thereby made the community more dependent on its own identity, and divorced his belief in the resurrection from its Pharisaic origins.

Another ancient church tradition was the Aramaic expression of hope for the second coming of Jesus, *maranatha* (1 Cor 16.22).[17] A further example is the Aramaic *abba*: "God sent his Son, born of a woman, born under the law, to redeem those under the law, so that we might receive adoption. Now since you are sons, God sent the spirit of his Son into our hearts, crying 'Abba, Father'" (Gal 4.4-6, cf Rom 8.14-16). As a Jew, Paul had always believed that Jews were sons of God. In this passage we have another Pauline shift. It is now Christians rather than Jews who are sons of God, and their sonship has been made dependent for the first time on the sonship of Jesus. This is made particularly clear with the term *abba*, obviously not a Greek word, and in fact the mode of addressing God typical and distinctive of the historical Jesus.[18] This evidence is very striking. Paul declares that he handed on long ago the authentic traditions of 1 Corinthians 11.23ff and 15.3ff, *abba* was important to Jesus himself and *maranatha* is derived from the very earliest period of the church. We must infer that these ancient traditions were very important in maintaining the identity of the churches.

5. The Titles and Nature of Jesus

Paul used three major christological titles, "Lord", "Christ" and "Son of God".[19] "Lord" occurs over 200 times in the Pauline corpus. We have seen that it originated in the Aramaic-speaking church, and other evidence of its early date.[20] This is consistent with its being the commonest christological title in the relatively early Thessalonian epistles (c. 40 occurrences).

In taking over Philippians 2.9, Paul shows his awareness that "Lord" could function for the name of God. He does not however repeat this, and we must remember that it is speculative *midrash* rather than systematic theology. It is none the less evident that Paul could use "Lord" to express the complete submission and devotion of the Christian to the person who brought about salvation. At 1 Corinthians 12.3, he uses it, in the form of the earlier confession "Jesus (is) Lord", as a decisive indication of whether a person is inspired by the Holy Spirit. His varied use elsewhere includes greetings and exhortations "in the Lord". The beginning of the Christian life may be described as being called "in the Lord" (1 Cor 7.22), an expression which may function effectively as a description of Christian being (cf e.g. 1 Cor 9.1-2; 15.58; Phil 2.19).

"Christ" is the commonest christological term in Paul's works, being used some 250 times in the major authentic epistles (Rom, 1 Cor, 2 Cor, Gal, Phil). Paul sometimes uses it virtually as a personal name, though he knew that it means "anointed". He seems to have regarded it as the most appropriate term for expressing certain aspects of the believer's appropriation of salvation history. We can only conjecture the reasons for this. "Jesus" was the everyday name of the Jesus of history, and might therefore not appear suitable on its own in descriptions of the present Christian life. "Lord" and "Son" both point to Jesus' status rather than his function, and "Son" was not yet a common term. "Christ" had however originated as a functional term.[21] Jesus had been anointed to carry out the most fundamental task in salvation history. This had led to the salvation of the Gentiles in a unique community of Jews and Gentiles, and his task would shortly be consummated at his second coming. As well as being functional, the term was also distinctive, so much so that it gave rise to the term "Christian" (Acts 11.26). "Lord" had also originated as a description of the exalted Jesus, so "Christ" may have become the normal term in the context of the main events of salvation history before "Lord" was conventionally used for the Jesus of history. These may be the reasons why the term "Christ" is so dominant in functional contexts. It is extensively used in the expression "in Christ", or "in Christ Jesus", a common expression in descriptions of the Christian life as a whole and of the major events in it.[22]

The third major christological title is "son", or more fully, "son of God". In contrast to their frequent use of "Lord" and "Christ", however, the Pauline epistles have this title only 15 times. The term was already in use with reference to any faithful Jew, and we have seen that Paul transferred this usage from Jews to Christians.[23] We should deduce that its use of Jesus in particular was a recent development, preceded only by the use in the pre-Pauline piece at Romans 1.3-4, where Jesus' position as "son of God in power" is dated from the resurrection.[24] We are not in a position to know whether Paul was himself responsible for the next development, by means of which "son" became a distinctive term for Jesus without reference to any particular moment. Paul tends to use it in passages of especial theological importance, as for example at Romans 5.10: "For if, being enemies, we were reconciled to God through the death of his Son...." Here, as elsewhere, the term "son" was useful to Paul because it both indicates a close and direct relationship to God and yet allows for the prime initiative, uniqueness and superiority of God himself. Paul, however, makes no attempt to define this in metaphysical terms. I have noted one other significant development towards the ultimate marking out of Jesus' sonship as unique: at Galatians 4.4-5, Paul makes the sonship of all believers dependent on the sonship of Jesus.[25]

We should not go further than this, especially not by associating "son" with particular features of the few contexts in which it occurs, or by regarding any more or less formulaic statements as pre-Pauline.[26] Galatians 4.4 may have been assumed, by a person who wrote or took over 1 Corinthians 8.6 and Philippians 2.6-7, to imply the pre-existence of Jesus. The sentence itself, however, does not necessarily mean this, so it cannot have been a significant point in Paul's exposition, still less, in a "concept" of Jesus' sonship. The term "son" is used because it gives Jesus a pre-eminent place close to deity, at the same time as it attributes the action to God himself. Galatians 1.16 uses the term "son" for the same reason, and it should not be associated with Acts 9.20. The report of Acts is propositional in form, having Paul preach that Jesus "is the Son of God". This propositional statement has neither Pauline parallel nor a satisfactory *Sitz im Leben* as early as Luke places it, for it could not yet have had sufficient meaning to be so important. We must therefore conclude that it is a Lukan summary of the true historical fact that Paul preached the centrality of Jesus for salvation soon after his conversion. The sending of the Son in passages such as John 3.17 and 1 John 4.9 cannot turn Pauline sentences into pre-Pauline formulae because the Johannine literature is later in date, and the recurrence of the sending of the Son has a firm background in God's sending of prophets and the increasing function of the term "son" as christology rose. The term "son" is used at

Romans 8.3 and Galatians 4.4 because it is so functional. The beginning of Christ's earthly life was both an action of God and the beginning of the most important life in salvation history, the life of a person who has reached the verge of deity in Pauline theology. It is that combination which made the term "son" functional enough to be used at climactic points before it became common. It became central only in the Johannine community, when the deity of Jesus was declared.[27]

"Christ", "Lord" and "Son": pre-existent in the form of God, the central figure in salvation history, whose death and resurrection brought salvation to mankind, Jew and Gentile alike. Was this figure in Paul's view actually God? There is one controversial text which appears to say so. Romans 9.3-5 may reasonably be translated: "I might pray that I personally be anathema from Christ for the sake of my brothers and relations according to the flesh, who are Israelites, whose is adoption, the glory, the covenants, the Law, the Service and the promises, whose are the patriarchs, and from whom is the Christ according to the flesh, who is over all, God blessed for ever, Amen." This is not the only possible way to read this text. Paul may have assumed that when he had enumerated the great benefits of the historic Israel, ending with "of whom is the Christ according to the flesh", it was appropriate to pause with a doxology: "May he who is over all, God, be blessed for ever, Amen." The first of these two views is perhaps to be regarded as the more probable. The grammatical structure of the sentence favours it, and it is intelligible that a figure with all the functions of Paul's Jesus, and the three major titles, should be termed "God" by him in one passage. This description does not however recur, and this must be seen in the light of similarly occasional descriptions of other Jewish figures, as well as in the context of Pauline theology. It was when Melchizedek was presented as the final redeemer of Israel that he had scriptural passages containing two of the Old Testament words for "God" interpreted as him (11Q Melch). Likewise, it is at a climactic point of his *Life of Moses* that Philo calls Moses "God and king of the whole nation", an expression which he nowhere repeats. Again, Philo refers to the *logos* as "the second God", but he does so no more than twice.[28] This is one context in which Paul's possible description of Jesus as God should be seen. Romans 9.5 is a climactic point, and if Paul called Jesus "God" here, it is also important that he did not repeat this description in the extant epistles.

The author of Colossians produced another striking expression, "in him dwells all the fullness of the Godhead bodily" (Col 2.9). This takes up Colossians 1.19, and this underlines the fact that, Romans 9.5 apart, it is the non-Pauline pieces of Philippians 2.6-11 and Colossians 1.15-20 which make the greatest claims for Jesus' status. We must put this in its overall context. We have seen that both these pieces have the same *Sitz im Leben* as the epistles in which they are embedded, firmly in stage two of christological development. Of equal importance is their background in Adam and Wisdom material respectively, for this is a legitimating mode.[29] This is the factor which resolved any tension between christological development on the one hand, and Jewish monotheism on the other. This tension was not liable to occur most threateningly in occasional comments like 1 Corinthians 8.6, nor in expositions of Jesus' salvific function such as Romans 3.21-26, for these have God's control of the universe or his salvific purpose very clearly in mind. It was more likely to happen in christological pieces which concentrated on Jesus himself. Hence the need for legitimation is greatest in these pieces.

6. Christology and Monotheism in Changing Communities

We must consider finally the nature of Jewish monotheism as part of the community's identity, and as a restraining factor in christological development. It is the only restraining factor detectable in the rise of other Jewish figures.[30] There were no other rules, such as that a person could not be seen as pre-existent and involved in the creation of the world. No human being provides a static parallel to Jesus' pre-existent involvement in the creation of the world because no non-Christian Jewish community had a single human identity factor which they needed to develop in this way. Theoretically, Jesus' pre-existence and involvement in creation might have been added in stage one of christological development, but it is probably not due to lack of documents that it is not attested until stage two. There was insufficient need for such development in stage one, whereas the community's need to develop its central identity factor increased as Gentiles were admitted into the churches without becoming Jewish. The development of Jesus was highly functional, because he might hold the community together. He could perform this function because of the position which he already held during stage one. In the historic ministry he had from the disciples' perspective embodied Judaism, and throughout stage one he was the community's only unique identity factor. From the perspective of Gentile converts, Jesus had by his saving work enabled them to be admitted to salvation without becoming Jews. He thus embodied all that was right, all that was religious and salvific, in Judaism, without ethnic customs such as circumcision and dietary laws. These factors drove christology upwards, and drove it more vigorously than comparable figures because of the uniqueness of the community.

The influence of Jewish religion and culture none the less remained extensive, so the pattern of development remained available. With Wisdom legitimating the high christology of Colossians 1.15-20, the author of Colossians could sail ahead with Colossians 2.9. We must distinguish between dramatic comments of this kind and the determined effort of the final redactor of the fourth Gospel to declare the deity of Jesus, against the known opposition of "the Jews". In the view of people like Paul and Timothy, we are still within the bounds of Jewish monotheism, and there are no accusations of blasphemy in sight.

What distinguishes the Christian community from the Jewish is that all such christological developments were functional for it. Even someone as observant as Jesus' brother Jacob might be impressed by hymnic utterances such as Philippians 2.6-11 because he already felt that Jesus had been the embodiment of Judaism, and he belonged to a culture in which the mode of development was a standard feature. It was however the Gentile mission which was the additional driving force behind the christological growth of stage two, the Gentile mission which was always most likely to produce hymnic passages like Philippians 2.6-11 and Colossians 1.15-20, the Gentile mission alone which could produce functional developments such as the grounding of morals in Christ in Romans 6, and the Gentile mission which needed developments such as the presentation of the mixed community as the body of Christ. Consequently, the christological developments found in stage two would appeal most strongly to assimilating rather than observant Jews, for it was they who needed the figure of Christ to be so powerful that he would hold together the mixed community of Jews and Gentiles.

We can now see the seeds of stage three of christological development firmly rooted in stage two. A successful Gentile mission needed Jews like St Paul, who were not observant when they were with Gentiles. The situation is most graphically illustrated by St Peter's behaviour at Antioch (cf Gal 2.11ff).[31] Peter had been behaving like a Gentile among Gentile Christians, but when the men from Jacob arrived he ate with them, and consequently he no longer ate with Gentile Christians. He could hardly have done otherwise. The men from Jacob the Lord's brother were emissaries of the Jerusalem church, and are likely to have included people from the historic ministry whom Peter knew well. In refusing to eat with Gentiles, they were observing the Law, as Jesus had always done and had expected them to do. It was therefore natural that Peter should eat with them. From his point of view, Christians were refusing to eat with each other whatever he did. He chose to eat with his natural companions. Since they were not usually there, he may well have taken the view that the Christian community would not suffer from temporary feeding arrangements. The important thing for him was that the Gospel was spread to the Gentiles, a mission which was part of God's plan but the task of Paul rather than himself (Gal 2.8).

From a Pauline perspective, however, the Christian community had to be held together over against pressures of that kind. This could not be done with people like the men from Jacob, for however much they thought that Jesus' teaching embodied the nature of Judaism, they could not give up their observance of the identity factors of Judaism. Indeed, the fact that it was *Judaism* which they saw embodied in Christianity was the very fact which ensured that they could not drop the sabbath, circumcision and so on. For these their forbears had died, and Jesus had observed them throughout his ministry. Thus the Gentile mission necessarily went ahead, with assimilating

Jews like St Paul leading the way, with vigorous support from ethnically half-Jewish people like Timothy and flexible people like Peter, who was prepared to drop Jewish observances in the context of the Gentile mission. The consequent decline in the observance of the Jewish Law in the Christian community drastically increased the requirement for a higher christology. At the same time, the most strictly observant Jews were by and large removed from the environment in which christological developments took place. Those people who were most liable to object to developments such as Philippians 2.6-11 and Colossians 1.15-20 were not there at the time.

All this explains why objections to the Pauline mission were concentrated on *halakhah* rather than christology. Christological developments went ahead to a point far beyond the development of any other Jewish figure because of the internal drive produced by Jesus' embodiment of Judaism followed by the Gentile mission, with only perceived monotheism to restrain them. Non-Christian Jewish communities were however gradually likely to find the results of this process unacceptable, since the churches increasingly did not obey the Law and did generate christological developments which observant Jews might find unconvincing. It could only be a matter of time before the conflicts of the early period reached the stage when Judaism would reject Gentile Christianity, and Gentile Christianity, already objecting to Jews "after the flesh" (cf Rom 2.28-29, Phil 3.2-3), would reject "the Jews" as Gentiles had always done. We shall see that the non-Pauline documents of the New Testament show us independent developments on these same lines. When we have taken them into account, we shall be able to trace the point at which the conflicts intensified by war between Israel and Rome drove christological development up to the deity of Jesus, and expelled the Johannine community from the synagogue.

---

1. Cf supra, 72-5, 110-1.
2. Cf supra, 15-6.
3. Cf especially J.Dupont, "The Conversion of Paul, and its Influence on his Understanding of Salvation by Faith", in W.W.Gasque and R.P.Martin (eds), *Apostolic History and the Gospel*. Biblical and Historical essays presented to F.F.Bruce on his 60th Birthday (1970), 176-94; J.G.Gager, "Some Notes on Paul's Conversion", *NTS* 27, 1981, 697-704; P.Frederiksen, "Paul and Augustine: Conversion Narratives, Orthodox Traditions, and the Retrospective Self", *JThS NS* 37, 1986, 3-34; H.Räisänen, "Paul's Conversion and the Development of his View of the Law", *NTS* 33, 1987, 404-19; T.L.Donaldson, "Zealot and Convert: The Origin of Paul's Christ-Torah Antithesis", *CBQ* 51, 1989, 655-82.
4. Supra, chs 6-7.
5. Cf L.Cerfaux, *Christ in the Theology of St.Paul* (1951. ET 1959); N.A.Dahl, "The Messiahship of Jesus in Paul" (1953), rev ET in N.A.Dahl, *The crucified Messiah and other Essays* (1974), 37-47; C.K.Barrett, *From First Adam to Last* (1962); W.Kramer,

Christ, Lord, Son of God (1963. ET SBT 50, 1966); M.E.Thrall, "The Origin of Pauline Christology", in W.W.Gasque and R.P.Martin, op.cit., 304-16; M.D.Hooker, "Interchange in Christ", *JThS NS* 22, 1971, 349-61; M.D.Hooker, "Interchange and Atonement", *BJRLM* 60, 1977-8, 462-81; F.Froitzheim, *Christologie und Eschatologie bei Paulus* (ForB 35, 1979); P.Grech, "Christological Motives in Pauline Ethics", in *Paul de Tarse: Apôtre de notre temps.* La Communauté Monastique de S.Paul en memoire de Pape Paul VI. Ed L.de Lorenzi (1979), 541-8; M.D.Hooker, "Interchange and Suffering", in *Suffering and Martyrdom in the New Testament.* Studies presented to G.M.Styler by the Cambridge New Testament Seminar, ed. W.Horbury and B.McNeil (1981), 70-83; H.H.Schade, *Apokalyptische Christologie bei Paulus. Studien zum Zusammenhang von Christologie und Eschatologie in den Paulusbriefen,* GTA 18 (1981. 2nd ed., 1984); S.C.Barton, "Paul and the Cross: A Sociological Approach", *Theol.* 85, 1982, 13-19; M.Hengel, "'Christos' in Paul", (1982), ET in *Between Jesus and Paul* (1983), 65-77; S.C.Barton, "Paul and the Resurrection: A Sociological Approach", *Rel* 14, 1984, 67-75; M.D.Hooker, "Interchange in Christ and Ethics", *JSNT* 25, 1985, 3-17; C.Wanamaker, "Christ as Divine Agent in Paul", *SJTh* 39, 1986, 517-28.

6. For more detailed discussion, supra 112-7. Cf A.Feuillet, *Le Christ Sagesse de Dieu d'après les épîtres Paulinniennes,* EtB (1966); R.A.Horsley, "The Background of the Confessional Formula in 1 Kor 8,6", *ZNW* 69, 1978, 130-35; J.Murphy O'Connor, "1 Cor 8,6: Cosmology or Soteriology?", *RB* 23, 1978, 253-67.

7. Cf supra, 60,111; infra, 132-3.

8. Supra, 65, 111.

9. Supra 80, 82.

10. Cf infra 145, 147.

11. I cannot discuss here the vigorous debate of these issues, especially as sparked off by E.P.Sanders. Cf E.P.Sanders, *Paul and Palestinian Judaism.* A Comparison of Patterns of Religion (1977); K.Stendahl, *Paul Among Jews and Gentiles* (1977); M.Barth, "St. Paul - A Good Jew", *HBT* 1, 1979, 7-45; J.D.G.Dunn, "The New Perspective on Paul", *BJRLM* 65, 1983, 95-122; J.D.G.Dunn, "The Incident at Antioch (Gal 2.11-18)", *JSNT* 18, 1983, 3-57; H.Räisänen, *Paul and the Law,* WUNT 29 (1983); E.P.Sanders, *Paul, the Law and the Jewish People* (1983); R.Heiligenthal, "Soziologische Implikationen der paulinischen Rechtfertigungslehre im Galaterbrief am Beispiel der 'Werke des Gesetzes'. Beobachtungen zur Identitätsfindung einer frühchristlichen Gemeinde", *Kairos* 26, 1984, 38-53; J.D.G.Dunn, "Works of the Law and the Curse of the Law (Galatians 3.10-14)", *NTS* 31, 1985, 523-42; H.Räisänen, "Galatians 2.16 and Paul's Break with Judaism", *NTS* 31, 1985, 543-53; T.Holtz, "Der antiochenische Zwischenfall (Galater 2.11-14)", *NTS* 32, 1986, 344-61; F.Watson, *Paul, Judaism and the Gentiles. A Sociological Approach,* MSSNTS 56 (1986); H.Räisänen, op. cit., *NTS* 33, 1987, 404-19; T.L.Donaldson, op. cit..

12. Cf supra, 122.

13. The extensive and varied scholarship so briefly summarized cannot be documented here. It has recently been taken up by Moule, *Origin,* esp ch 2. Cf further E.Best, *One Body in Christ* (1955); A.J.M.Wedderburn, "The Body of Christ and Related Concepts in 1 Corinthians", *SJTh* 24, 1971, 74-96; R.H.Gundry, *Soma in Biblical Theology,* MSSNTS 29 (1976), ch 17; A.J.M.Wedderburn, "Some Observations on Paul's Use of the Phrases 'in Christ' and 'with Christ'", *JSNT* 25, 1985, 83-97.

14. Supra, 127-9.

15. Cf supra, 111.

16. Supra 98, 110-1.

17. Supra, 110
18. Supra, 60.
19. For general discussion of these titles, v. supra, 41-6, 68, 79, 105-6, 109-12, 129-31.
20. Supra 105-6, 109-11, 113-4.
21. Supra, 106.
22. Supra, 129-31.
23. Supra, 132-3.
24. Cf supra, 111-2.
25. Supra, 132-3.
26. Both tendencies are widespread in scholarship, but a full critical discussion of the secondary literature cannot be given here. Cf e.g. the pre-Pauline "sending formula" (Rom 8.3, Gal 4.4f) found e.g. by Kramer, op. cit., 111-5; E.Schweizer, "Zum religionsgeschichtlichen Hintergrund der "Sendungsformel", Gal 4.4f., Ro 8.3f., Joh 3.16f., 1 Joh 4.9", *ZNW* 57, 1966, 199-210, = E.Schweizer, *Beiträge zur Theologie des Neuen Testaments* (1970), 83-95. Both scholars argue that Jesus is pre-existent in this pre-Pauline formula: against this, e.g. Dunn, *Making* (1980), 38-46. For the suggestion that Paul already presupposed the centrality of Son of God at the time of his conversion, cf Cerfaux, op. cit., 6-7; M.Hengel, *Son of God* (ET 1976), 10; S.Kim, *The Origin of Paul's Gospel* (1981), 64, 100-36, 225-6, 251-2.
27. Supra, 23-7. Infra, 156-9.
28. Cf supra 79, 83-5, 92-3.
29. Supra, 112-7.
30. Supra ch 6, esp 93-4.
31. Cf supra 131-2, 139, note 11.

Chapter 9
From Paul to John

1. The Revelation of St John the Divine

And I saw, standing in between the throne and the four creatures and the elders, a lamb as it were slaughtered. He had seven heads and seven eyes, which are the spirits of God sent forth to the whole earth. And he came and took from the right hand of Him who sat on the throne. And when he took the scroll, the four creatures and the 24 elders fell down before the lamb. Each of them had a harp and golden bowls full of incense, which are the prayers of the saints. And they sang a new song; 'You are worthy to take the scroll and to open its seals, because you were slaughtered, and with your blood you bought for God people of every tribe and language and people and nation, and you made them a kingdom and priests for our God, and they shall reign upon the earth.'(Rev 5.6-10).

This dramatic picture was written by an Aramaic-speaking Jew somewhat later than the epistles of St Paul. The slaughtered lamb is his central christological image,[1] and 5.9-10 presents his death as the vital factor enabling Gentiles to enter the churches. John himself was an Aramaic-speaking Jew, profoundly absorbed in Jewish culture. He regarded eating meat offered to idols as quite wrong (2.20), and chapter 7 makes clear that he was prepared to visualise 144,000 of the people of Israel sealed. The messages to Smyrna and Philadelphia both speak of Jews who are not real Jews (Rev 2.9; 3.9), which should probably be interpreted as John's rejection of ethnically Jewish people opposed to Christianity.[2] In chapter 7, the sealing of the 144,000 is followed immediately by a multitude of Gentiles whom no-one can number (7.9). We must infer John's acceptance of the successful large-scale mission to the Gentiles.

Circumstances of severe persecution must also be inferred, and it is this which explains the centrality of Jesus' death both in John's theology and in his imagery. It also aligns his work with other major Jewish apocalypses. The need for this form of revelation was produced by suffering to the point of extinction: it developed from the dreams and visions which were normal in less troubled times.

John uses three major christological titles, "Lord" (about four times), "Christ" (seven times), and "Son of God" (at 2.18 only), but, apart from the Lamb (29 times), he preferred to express Jesus' lordship by means of a riotous profusion of assertions and images. Jesus is "the Word of God" (Rev 19.13), "the beginning of the creation of God" (3.14), "the lion from the tribe of Judah, the root of David" (5.5, cf. Gen 49.9-10), "the alpha and the omega, the first and the last, the beginning and the end" (22.13). He is enthroned in heaven (3.21), and, apparently identical with the Spirit, he encourages and admonishes the churches. He is "the Amen" (3.14), "king of kings and Lord of Lords" (19.16), he has the keys of death and of Hades (1.18). His second coming was to be expected shortly (e.g. 22.12,20, cf. 19.11ff). This was perceived at Daniel 7.13 (Rev 1.7), but there is no sign of the Gospel title "Son of man", the expression "one like a son of man" being used once of Jesus (Rev 1.13, cf. Dan 10.16) and once of an angel (Rev 14.14).[3]

The humanity of Jesus is clearly retained in circumstances which owe much to the position of John as representative of martyred churches. The description of Jesus as "the faithful witness" (Rev 1.5, cf. Ps 88.38 LXX), "the faithful and true witness" (Rev 3.14), was significant because Christians facing persecution needed his example of witness unto death (cf. Rev 2.13; 17.6; also 1 Tim 6.13; Rev 20.4). Hence also the direct reference to his crucifixion outside Jerusalem (Rev 11.8). At 1.5, the reference to him as "the faithful witness" is immediately followed by the description of him as "the firstborn from the dead" (cf. Ps 89.28), for his resurrection guarantees the Christian's resurrection after martyrdom: from the strictly christological point of view, this is very similar to Paul's argument in 1 Corinthians 15 (cf. Col 1.18). It is the picture of him in heaven which almost approaches deity. In chapter 5, the slaughtered lamb is praised by angels and all other creatures, and John ends this episode of praise:

> And I heard every created thing in heaven and on earth and under the earth and on the sea, and everything in them, saying, 'To him who sits on the throne and to the lamb be blessing and honour and glory and power for ever and ever!' And the four creatures said 'Amen'. And the elders fell down and did obeisance (Rev 5.13-14).

This is almost heavenly worship, but it does not have to be perceived as such. Here, as always, the lamb is carefully distinguished from God, and he is not said to be divine. He does have other exalted functions. It is as a lamb that Jesus is victorious over the kings of the earth (17.14), and he shepherds the victorious martyrs (7.17). The eschatological vengeance is described as "the wrath of the lamb" (6.16), while those who are saved have their names written "in the book of life of the lamb who was slaughtered" (13.8). The wrath of God and the book of life were already well-known features of Jewish culture: like Paul, John has shifted known features of Judaism directly onto the community's central identity factor. The lamb is also the temple, lamp and bridegroom of the heavenly city (21.9,22-23), and he sits on the throne of God (3.21; 22.1).

Yet God is precisely what this figure is not, and this illustrates the social nature of the restraining factor of monotheism. John belonged to a mixed community of Jews and Gentiles under great pressure from persecuting Romans and from two "synagogues of Satan" (2.9, at Smyrna, 3.9 at Philadelphia), so the christology has gone upwards and forwards with the greatest vigour to a point where Jesus as the slaughtered lamb would be perceived as a god by non-Christian gentiles. Monotheism has none the less remained a characteristic of the community, for otherwise it would lose its Jewish members, including the author of this document. Therefore, there is no real worship of this being on this earth here and now, and he is not actually hailed as divine even in the pictures of him being praised in heaven. The change required for John's slaughtered lamb to be perceived as divine was the exercise of sympathetic Gentile perception.[4] Consequently we have to wait for stage three until we find it, in a community whose Jewish members had been thrown out of the synagogue.

2. The Epistle to the Hebrews

The epistle to the Hebrews was also written by a person whose self-identification was Jewish. Its audience was diaspora Judaism, people who spoke Greek, were generally familiar with Greek culture, and had ceased to observe most of the enactments of the Jewish Law. This follows from the argument as a whole, rather than from specific statements, for the author gives us little direct information about himself or his recipients. He regarded himself as belonging to the same community as the Fathers and the Exodus generation, "the people" (cf. 1.1-2; 4.1ff; 5.3). The point at which Jews need no longer observe the Law is defined chronologically and causally as the death of Jesus (cf. 2.10ff; 5.7-10; 9.11ff; 12.24). As a result, Jesus is the mediator of a new and better covenant (8.6ff), and the first one is growing old and ageing near to the point of extinction (8.13, cf. 10.9), so that the word of the oath announcing Jesus' highpriesthood is *after* the Law (7.28), and we now belong to Christ's house rather than that of Moses (3.6). The whole trend of such arguments is to legitimate non-observance of the Law. Jewish people who did observe the Law might remain in such a Christian community, and Gentiles might join it (cf. 5.9), but neither group is discussed. This is especially striking because of the prominent role of Jesus' death, which was elsewhere seen as important chiefly because it permitted the entry of Gentiles to the Christian communities.[5]

If we try to measure the identity of this author and his recipients on my eight-point scale, they get a lot of ethnicity (the exact degree cannot be measured), monotheism, and some scripture, but as in Paul scripture is so interpreted as to remove the enactments of the Law. We must infer from the arguments just noted that this author believed it was no longer necessary to perform circumcision, to observe sabbath, festivals, purity and dietary laws. This means that many Jews will have perceived him and his recipients as apostate - whether this has any connection with the persecution of 10.32-4 we do not know. These points place the epistle in stage two of christological development, for Jesus is the sole distinctive identity factor who could keep together a community which was no longer observing the Law. Although the word "Christian" is not used, it is evident that the author identified himself and his followers over against the rest of mankind by their attitude to Jesus.

This involved vigorous christological development.[6] The author uses the major titles "Christ" (12 times) and "Lord" (about four times), and the most fundamental for him was "Son (of God)", (nine times, three in OT quotations). The expression "son of man" occurs in a quotation of Psalm 8.5 at Hebrews 2.6, but it is not taken up in the subsequent discussion nor elsewhere in the epistle, so a "son of man" christology should not be attributed to this author.

The first use of the term "son" occurs in the opening of the work, where it is the "more excellent name" which the angels do not possess. As in Paul, Jesus is portrayed in the highest possible position, in a context where God is in overall control of events.[7] Just as the Son is superior to the prophets as a mode of revelation, none the less it is God who has spoken through him. Even as the Son is the agent of creation and redemption, it is God whose image and effulgence he is, and on whose right hand he sits. The need for the category of sonship arises precisely in contexts of this kind, where Jesus is so close to God that other christological terms are not sufficiently elevated and clear, and yet something that indicates his subordination to the Father is essential. Only two examples are propositional, but these are significant, because they are legitimating quotations of Psalm 2.7 (Heb 1.5; 5.5).

The first quotation from Psalm 2.7 (Heb 1.5) begins a scriptural argument showing that Jesus was superior to the angels. The prologue has already made clear that he was pre-existent and instrumental in creating and sustaining the universe, and that he in some sense possesses and reveals the nature of the Father. For this purpose, Jewish speculation about Wisdom and perhaps the Word of God has been used, and as in the pre-Pauline hymns of Philippians 2.6ff and Colossians 1.15ff, this use of tradition found in scripture has an important legitimating effect.[8] The argument that Jesus was superior to the angels was necessary because the identification of such an exalted being as angelic rather than human was a live option. Such a view could cope with most existing beliefs about him and with the church's activities. It could not however cope with the reality of his death, and the soteriological interpretation of Jesus' death had been part of the community's identity since the days of the historic ministry. His atoning death was also highly functional for a community which did not observe the Law. Thus the author held fast to Jesus' humanity. None the less, in the process of arguing that Jesus is superior to the angels, he interprets of him Psalm 45.6, "Your throne, O God, is for ever." One must not exaggerate: 11Q Melchizedek applied two similar passages to Melchizedek (Pss 7.7-8; 82.1).[9] As in Paul and Revelation, we are very close to the deity of Jesus, but the restraining factor of monotheism prevented this author from consistent exposition of the divinity of Jesus. As with the use of Wisdom christology, the application to Jesus of a passage of scripture functions as a legitimating mode.

At the conclusion of his argument for the superiority of Jesus over the angels, the author defends the humanity of Jesus with a new formulation which was much quoted in patristic debates: "Consequently, he had to be like his brothers in every respect, so that he might become a merciful and faithful high priest in divine matters, so that he could expiate the sins of the people" (Heb 2.17). The circumstances of Jesus' death are almost the only aspect of the Jesus of history to be mentioned. There is an allegorical interpretation of his suffering outside Jerusalem in chapter 13, and a vigorous portrayal of his prayers to be delivered from the need to die (5.7-8, cf. 2.9). The author's awareness of the conventional belief that supernatural beings could not suffer, a significant bar to the interpretation of Jesus as an angel, lies behind his declaration that, "Although he was the Son, he learnt obedience from what he suffered" (5.8). This is immediately followed by one of the many statements of the fundamental effects of Jesus' suffering and death: "And being perfected, he became the cause of eternal salvation for all those who obey him" (5.9). It is however typical of this stage of christological development that the very high estimation of the pre-existent Son, in the same document as his learning by suffering, has not led the author to explore the ontological nature of God's Son or the process by which he began his life on earth. There is no mention of the virgin birth, though this has been thought to be implied in the comparison with Melchizedek at 7.3.

The comparison with Melchizedek is part of this author's most striking and original contribution to christology, the highpriesthood of Christ. The category comes straight from a central aspect of Jewish culture, one to which his recipients were no longer to give literal adherence: the extensive theological use of it enabled the author to retain at an intellectual level something which had in practice been dropped, thereby reducing the loss of identity inherent in no longer observing the Law. Like the use of Adam and Wisdom christologies, the concept of the highpriesthood of Christ legitimates christological development, for the traditions known in life and found in scripture were so basic to the community's identity that re-use of them could be perceived as profound.

The highpriesthood of Christ may also be seen as a further development of the sacrificial interpretation of Jesus' death.[10] The earthly high priest sacrificed for the whole people: the understanding of Jesus' death as the supreme atoning sacrifice now enabled him to be seen as a greater high priest because he made that sacrifice. The author also asserts that he is in heaven making intercession for us now. "But he, since he remains 'for ever' (Ps 110.4), has the unchangeable priesthood: consequently, he can save completely those who approach God through him, for he is always alive to intercede on their behalf"(7.24-5). His sinlessness is similarly derived. We have seen this quality occasionally ascribed to a Jewish person in terms of doing the Law, and ascribed to Jesus as a sacrifice by St Paul:[11] now we find him sinless as a high priest, "holy, innocent, undefiled, separated from sinners" (7.26). Philo was also able to generate the sinlessness of the high priest *(Spec Leg* I, 230; cf. *Fug* 108; *De Somn* II, 185). Christ's position as high priest for ever in heaven also justifies the earlier Christian belief that Jesus had ascended to heaven and is now there at the right hand of God.

The author further argues that Jesus was high priest after the order of Melchizedek, not the order of Levi, and that the priesthood after the order of Melchizedek is superior to that after the order of Levi. This enabled him to produce a perfectly christocentric argument for believing that Christianity is the true form of Judaism, and the new dispensation has replaced the old (7.15-22). The midrashic argument from Melchizedek is amplified in subsequent chapters with another argument which treats the earlier covenant with Israel as a foreshadowing of the superior covenant which has come with Jesus. Hebrews 9.11-15 is a typical piece:

But Christ has come, the high priest of the good things which are, through the greater and more perfect tent which is not made with hands, that is, does not belong to this creation; he entered the sanctuary once for all, not through the blood of goats and calves but through his own blood, securing eternal redemption. For if the blood of goats and bulls and the sprinkling of the ashes of a heifer sanctify defiled people with regard to the cleansing of the flesh, how much more does the blood of Christ, who through the eternal Spirit offered himself as an unblemished offering to God, cleanse our conscience from dead works for the service of the living God. And therefore he is the mediator of a new covenant, so that in view of his death for the expiation of transgressions committed under the first covenant, those who have been called might receive the promise of the eternal inheritance.

These arguments show that the decisive act of salvation history has been the Jesus event: it marks a new covenant, as a result of which most of the Law no longer has to be observed. The point is further amplified by the argument in chapter 3 that Jesus is superior to Moses. Jewish Christians could easily take the opposite view. They could value Christianity as the true form of Judaism, but remain observant and regard the revelation to Moses on Mt Sinai as more fundamental than its renewal through Jesus. Hence the argument to the contrary, with scriptural legitimation of the position of both Moses (Num 12.7 at Heb 3.5) and Jesus (especially sonship from Ps 2.7 and 2 Sam 7.14/1 Chron 17.13 at Heb 1.5, taken up at Heb 3.6). Jesus' fundamental function at the centre of salvation history is also the reason for the development of the relatively "low" christological terms, "founder" (2.10; 12.2, cf. Acts 3.15; 5.31),[12] "forerunner" (6.20) and even "apostle" (3.1). These illuminate one way in which the believer follows Jesus.

All these arguments are striking for their originality and for their independence of Paul, and this further clarifies their nature as secondary legitimation. The fact to be legitimated, that the Law is no longer to be observed, is sufficient to take this community most of the way out of the Jewish people into the Gentile world. The replacement of the sacrificial system with the death of Jesus is especially remarkable, for it is expounded in language which implies a date before A.D.70, and it is the same kind of development as led to the replacement symbolism of the fourth Gospel.[13] A community like this needed only the situation after A.D.70 to remove it from the Jewish people, and the christology, with the almost divine Son, needs only removal from Judaism to alter perception of him and make him God. In this document we see again that removal of the restraining factor of Jewish monotheism is all we need to take the christology into stage three.[14]

3. The First Epistle of Peter

This epistle also belongs to stage two of christological development. The author regarded "the Gentiles" as an outside group (cf. 1 Pet 2.12; 4.3-4), and his own self-identification is explicitly "Christian" (4.16). He writes to the elect of the diaspora in Pontus, Galatia, Cappadocia, Asia and Bithynia (1 Pet 1.1.). This is an area where we know from Paul and Acts that Gentile converts had been made, and it goes well beyond the known confines of the specifically Pauline mission. The Gentile origin of some of the recipients is indicated at 1 Peter 2.10; 4.3.

Consistently with his self-identification as "Christian", the author's favourite christological term is "Christ" (22 times), and he uses the expression "in Christ" three times (3.16; 5.10,14). He also calls Jesus "Lord" at least three times (1.3; 2.3; 3.15), two examples being Old Testament quotations applied to Jesus rather than to God the Father (Ps 34.8 at 1 Pet 2.3; Is 8.12-13 at 1 Pet 3.14-15). The term "son of God" is not used. At 1.3, the description of God as "the Father of our Lord Jesus Christ" functions to distinguish the two persons.[15] The author apparently assumes that Jesus was pre-existent (1.11, cf. 1.20). Old Testament passages applied to Jesus include Isaiah 53 (2.21-25), on the basis of which he is perceived to have been sinless,[16] and the redemptive significance of Jesus' death is clearly brought out (cf 1.18-19; 2.21-24; 3.18). This is what enabled the recipients to turn to God (2.24-25).

After his death, Jesus is said to have preached to the dead (1 Pet 3.19, 4.6). This speculation is in some respects unique to this author, and it is further evidence of the vigour of christological development during this period. The resurrection is the source of the Christian's hope (1.3), and through it Jesus went into heaven, where he is at the right hand of God, with angels, authorities and powers subject to him (3.21-2). The author shared the common Christian hope that Jesus would come again soon (e.g. 1.7; 4.13). Christians appropriate Christ's saving work in the present. They are initiated by saving baptism (3.21), and by the death and resurrection of Jesus they have been enabled to live new lives (2.24, cf. e.g. 4.1). The importance of faith is stressed (e.g. 1.5; 5.9), and Christians are described as "those in Christ" (5.14).

It may be concluded that the christology of 1 Peter is generally similar to that of St Paul.

4. Matthew, Mark and Luke

The synoptic Gospels also belong to stage two of christological development, as does Acts. The form of the Gospel significantly affected the exposition of christology. In principle, it was possible for Matthew, Mark and Luke to put all their christology into sayings and discourses attributed to Jesus, as John did.[17] These authors, however, knew a largely accurate tradition of the sayings and deeds of Jesus, and one of their purposes was to transmit this tradition to the faithful and the interested.

All three Gospels give Jesus an elevated status and a unique revelatory function,[18] surrounding him with Peter and other apostles who were important during the historic ministry and, in some cases, during the spread of the Gospel. When a Gospel was read at a church meeting, Christians will have perceived themselves as members of a community which was in all fundamental respects the same as it always had been. Their central identity factor appears as the Son of God, revealing the truth, healing the sick, and confuting the orthodox Jews who opposed the church, and who especially opposed its mission to the Gentiles.

These are also the reasons why Gospel traditions were handed down and expanded throughout stages one and two of christological development. We must infer that stories and teachings of Jesus, and important facts about his life, helped to maintain the identity of Christian communities throughout this period, and some evidence shows that this was true of Pauline churches as well as others (cf *Abba* at Rom 8.15 and Gal 4.6; 1 Cor 7.10-17; 11.23-25; 15.3-7).[19] There is also sufficient evidence that some parts of the tradition were written down in Aramaic. These include Marcan narratives, as well as sayings in Q.[20] We must deduce that Aramaic-speaking people handed on these pieces at a time when eye-witnesses were available to tell of their experiences. The access of the evangelists to these traditions explains the large proportion of authentic material in Mark and Q. None the less, received traditions were often rewritten, and it was normal to attribute new ideas to the perceived fountainheads of traditions. We have seen that the major christological titles in the synoptics are secondary as titles, although they have their roots in old traditions.[21] We must now look at secondary development in the synoptic Gospels as a whole.

The most immediately striking development is the production of three major titles, son of God, Christ and son of man. Mark inherited a parable in which Jesus symbolised himself as the "beloved son" (Mk 12.6), and a little material in which Jesus was hailed as "son of God" by demoniacs (Mk 5.7; cf 3.11). He interpreted this as supernatural knowledge of Jesus' exalted status as "the Son of God", and he has similar revelation from a heavenly voice at Jesus' baptism and transfiguration (1.11; 9.7). At a third climactic point, Jesus accepts all three of Mark's major titles (14.61-62). At Jesus' death, the centurion confesses that he was "son of God" (15.39). These secondary examples are propositional in form. We must infer that Mark is supplying legitimation of a proposition which was very important to him. None the less, Mark has Jesus use the term "the Son" only once (13.32). This saying is not propositional in form, for it tries to come to terms with a quite different matter, the delay in the parousia.

Both Q passages illustrate the churches' concerns. In the midrashically developed account of the temptation of Jesus (Mt 4.3,6/Lk 4.3,9), the devil uses "son of God" propositionally. His suggestion that Jesus perform miracles presupposes that "son of God" is a christological title rather than a description of a faithful Jew (cf Mk 1.11/Mt 3.17/Lk 3.22). The narrative rejects any accusation that Jesus was in league with the devil (cf Mk 3.22-30; Mt 12.24-32; Lk 11.15-22). At Mt 11.27/Lk 10.22, Jesus declares himself to be the sole channel of revelation. This makes the Christian community essential, and excludes non-Christian Jews from salvation. The Fatherhood of God comes straight from Jesus' use of an ancient Jewish symbol, and the category of sonship is especially suitable for describing the close relationship to God which was essential for excluding outsiders from the community. We have seen that sonship was coming into use in the Pauline epistles, and functional precisely at points where God himself is in overall charge, yet the fundamental role in salvation history is played by Jesus. In this sense too, the saying looks forward to the Johannine community.[22] There are further examples in both Matthew and Luke. Matthew in particular can be seen adding the term in.[23]Matthew also ended his Gospel with a ringing declaration of authorization for the Gentile mission, baptism, and the sonship of Jesus in an almost trinitarian formula which he attributes to the risen Jesus (Mt 28.19).

The development of "messiah", or "Christ", was generally similar.[24] Mark opens his Gospel with it (Mk 1.1). The centre of the Gospel pivots on Peter's confession, "You are the Christ" (Mk 8.29), and Jesus accepts it at his trial (14.61-2). Both these examples are propositional uses of the term, a usage not found in earlier sources. Mark has however only seven examples, none of them clear references by Jesus to himself. He inherited traditions in which the term "Christ" was absent, and "son of God" rarely attested. He also inherited some evidence that Jesus silenced demons. From this Mark, or the tradition before him, deduced that Jesus did not make his real identity generally known during his historic ministry (cf 3.11-12;.8.30; 9.9).

Matthew and Luke repeat this, with some editorial expansion. Luke has propositional examples of both son of God and messiah where his immediate Marcan source has neither: "But he cast out demons from many people. They cried out and said, 'You are the Son of God.' And he rebuked them and did not allow them to speak, because they knew that he was the Christ" (Lk 4.41, cf Mk 1.34, also 3.11-12). Thus the theory of the messianic secret enabled the synoptic evangelists to incorporate some christological development, especially the propositional use of two major titles, without having to produce new material on a large scale. Some of the 25 or so examples in Acts are also propositional, the point being to establish that Jesus is "the Christ", on the assumption that "the Christ" was expected to redeem Israel (so e.g. Apollos refuting "the Jews" at Acts 18.28). Jewish expectation of a triumphant figure who would deliver Israel could be used by non-Christian Jews to show that Jesus was not the Christ. Acts deals explicitly with this problem: Paul is said to have "held discussions with them on the basis of the scriptures, explaining and demonstrating that the Christ must suffer, and that 'he is the Christ, Jesus whom I proclaim to you'" (Acts 17.2-3).

Christian reinterpretation of Jewish expectation of a future king of David's line has traditionally been associated with the term "Christ", though this is not very common in the NT (cf Mt 1.1,17,18,20; 2.2,4; Mk 15.32; Lk 2.4,11; 23.2, 35-9; Jn 7.42; Rom 1.3-4; 2 Tim 2.8).[25] There is not much sign of Jesus' Davidic kingship in Mark (cf Mk 10.47-8; 11.1-10; 12.35-7; 15.2ff, esp 15.26,32), but it is developed in both Matthew and Luke. Matthew has the term "son of David" eight times of Jesus. Matthew and Luke both have genealogies which run back through David (Mt 1.1-17; Lk 3.23-38): their secondary nature is revealed by their comprehensive lack of agreement about Jesus' immediate ancestry. The category of kingship is also significant. Matthew's magi search for "he who was born king of the Jews" (Mt 2.2), and Luke has Gabriel use this category even more vigorously (Lk 1.32-3, cf 1.69; 2.11). Matthew and Luke also edited kingship into their accounts of the entry into Jerusalem (Mt 21.5; Mt 21.9/Mk 11.9/Lk 19.38).

This illustrates the flexibility of categories and exegesis in Second Temple Judaism. The early Christians needed categories to express the centrality of Jesus, and this is the basic reason why some of them fastened on the expectation of a Davidic king. Mockery at the Passion may have been a stimulus, but it was not a sufficient cause. Ancient exegesis was also sufficiently flexible to accommodate the community's needs,[26] and it is this which led to the further reinterpretation of the category of Davidic kingship in early Christianity.

"Son of man" had a different origin.[27]The underlying Aramaic *bar nash(a)* was a normal term for "man". It was used in a number of genuine sayings, all of which were examples of an Aramaic idiom, in which a speaker used a general statement to refer to himself, or himself and a group of associates. When these sayings were translated into Greek, it was natural for translators to use definite articles with both "son" and "man". The resulting expression is the nearest literal equivalent to the underlying Aramaic and, like the definite state of the Aramaic noun, Greek articles could be used generically. When bilingual translators had completed a saying, they could therefore read it as an example of the Aramaic idiom, though a purely Greek-speaking Christian might not know this.[28] The origin of this term also explains why it does not occur outside the Gospels until after the New Testament period (except for Acts 7.56, written by Luke).

In the synoptic Gospels, the use of "son of man" was extended for reasons not directly due to the term itself. Jesus' death was a major fact for the earliest Christians to cope with, and they responded with vigorous development of its significance. Genuine "son of man" predictions were a natural resource, since what might be perceived as a process of clarification could meet the church's need to know that Jesus predicted both his fate and his vindication by God. The central group of Marcan predictions are based on authentic predictions, expanded with details from the actual events and perhaps from scripture. The process of expansion and clarification was continued by Matthew and Luke.

The major group of inauthentic "son of man" sayings incorporate likewise a belief central to the early church, the expectation of Jesus' second coming.[29] Outside the Gospels, this expectation is not associated with the term "son of man", and this difference is to be explained by the Gospels' use of Daniel 7.13. Eight sayings make sufficiently clear their use of Daniel 7.13 by speaking of the "son of man" coming, including three in Mark and one in Q (Mk 8.38, 13.26, 14.62, Mt 24.44/Lk 12.40). There are further sayings in which the influence of Daniel 7.13 is detectable but indirect (e.g. Mt 13.41, drawing on Dan 7.13 only via Mk 13.26-7/ Mt 24.30-31). The traditions used by the synoptic writers produced a handful of other "son of man" sayings too. Most of these also deal with the events of the End (e.g. Lk 21.36), and they include further use of scripture (e.g. Mt 24.38-9/Lk 17.26-7, drawing on Gen 7.7). The picture of the production of secondary "son of man" sayings is thus perfectly coherent. The term was distinctive of genuine traditions and confirmed in scripture. It was therefore used secondarily to expand and clarify the teaching of Jesus on points which were fundamental for the early church.

"Lord" is used much more in Matthew and Luke than it was at the time of Jesus.[30] Matthew has it used of Jesus about 27 times, including several examples where it is not in his Marcan source (e.g. Mt 8.25; 17.4). Luke's Gospel has some

35 examples, including 16 uses of "the Lord" in narrative, and Acts has 67 occurrences. These figures reveal the influence of the early Christian use of "Lord" as a christological title.

Significant non-titular developments include Wisdom christology. The high position of Wisdom in Second Temple Judaism[31] made her a natural resource for christological growth, since this could be carried forward by appropriation of static parallels. The traditional nature of beliefs about Wisdom also meant that new developments in Wisdom christology could be legitimated by scripture and tradition. We have seen this at Colossians 1.15-20 and in the epistle to the Hebrews. Wisdom material was also important in the creation of the Johannine prologue, which carried Jesus clearly up to deity in stage three.[32]

Both Q and Matthew have sayings with such close parallels in the Wisdom tradition that a similar process must be inferred in the creation of some sayings in the synoptic tradition. I have noted this in the central revelatory saying, Matthew 11.27/Luke 10.22. At one level this is a development of the confession that "there is no salvation in anyone else" (Acts 4.12). The content of the new development is approximately paralleled by what is said in different passages about Wisdom (cf Job 28.21,23; Wsd 9.13,14,17; 1 Cor 2.6ff).[33] This has been brought together into a sharp reciprocal saying because of the perceived centrality of Jesus in salvation.

The Matthean context of this saying has further use of Wisdom material. Matthew 11.28-30 again portrays the centrality of Jesus, in terms closely paralleled by what is said of Wisdom at Sirach 51.23-27. Other evidence of the replacement of Wisdom with Jesus is found at Matthew 23.34-6/Luke 11.49-51 (cf also Mt 23.37-9/Lk 13.34-5). The Lukan introduction should be regarded as the older: "Therefore the Wisdom of God said, 'I will send them prophets and apostles, and they will kill and persecute some of them....' " Matthew has this saying spoken by Jesus himself, on his own authority and without reference to Wisdom. He is just the slightest step away from the pre-existence which he was not interested enough to state.

The virgin birth remains a source of controversy.[34] It is mentioned clearly only in Matthew and Luke (cf also Mk 6.3; Jn 1.13; 8.41). Their birth narratives are of a legendary kind and inconsistent with each other. The announcements of the birth are not so much inconsistent as unconnected. In Luke, the angel Gabriel is sent to Mary and tells her that she will give birth to Jesus by the power of the Holy Spirit (Lk 1.26-38). At this stage Mary is betrothed but not married, and certainly not pregnant, for she objects that she does not know a man (Lk 1.34). In Matthew, an angel of the Lord appears in a dream to Joseph, who is apparently unaware of this event *after* Mary has become pregnant, so much so that he considers separating from her quietly (Mt 1.19). The angel tells Joseph to proceed from betrothal to marriage, for Mary's child has been begotten by the Holy Spirit (1.20). The birth in Bethlehem produces equally dissociated features of a dramatic kind. Luke explains it with an inaccurate report of a Roman census (Lk 2.1-7). This is naturally unmentioned by Matthew, who appears to believe that Joseph and Mary lived in Bethlehem (cf Mt 2.21-23).

Matthew, however, has Herod kill all children under two in the area around Bethlehem (Mt 2.16-18, using Jer 31.15), an atrocity not mentioned by Luke or by Jewish sources. This involves Matthew in an account of the flight into Egypt (Mt 2.13-15), which is also unmentioned by Luke, and legitimated with Hosea 11.1 (Mt 2.15). This enables Matthew to get the family to Nazareth (Mt 2.19-23), where Luke correctly believed that they had previously been living (Lk 2.4).

The background culture was perfectly capable of producing such stories. Stories of angels appearing were widespread. Sometimes, as in the book of Daniel, they foretold important events. Other announcements are more personal, as at Josephus A.J.I, 197-8, where three angels announce the forthcoming birth of Isaac to the 90 year-old Sarah (cf Gen 18.1-15). This is hardly less miraculous than virgin birth, and it was caused by direct divine intervention. There are several stories of remarkable births from the Mediterranean world. They are less frequent in Judaism, but Matthew and Luke belong to stage two of christological development, when many Gentiles had joined the Christian communities.

There are two particularly relevant stories in our meagre Jewish sources. The miraculous birth of Melchizedek (2 En 71) is not a virgin birth because Melchizedek's mother had already had other children, but it is a birth without a human father, produced by direct divine intervention. The second story concerns the birth of Noah (1Q Gen Ap II, cf I En 106). As the story turns out, his conception was partly due to normal human intercourse between his parents, but his birth was so unusual that Lamech suspected that conception was by one of the Watchers and the Holy Ones. His wife Bitenosh reminded him of how they had sexual intercourse, and declared that the father was no stranger or Watcher or Son of Heaven (1Q Gen Ap II, 16). Both stories treat these miraculous births as Matthew and Luke treat the virgin birth, as a great sign rather than as something to be kept a modest secret. Before the event is known to be a great sign, however, they express feelings of shame and modesty, and concern that the mother has been immoral.

The birth of Moses was also remarkable. His sister Mary saw an angel in a dream, who said that he would save the people through Moses (Ps-Philo, Ant. Bib. IX, 10). Moses was born circumcised (IX, 13), another miracle due to divine intervention. He survived Pharaoh's orders to kill all male Hebrew children (Ex 1.15-2.10).

These stories show that once a human being was sufficiently highly thought of, secondary stories of his birth might arise within Judaism. Against this cultural background, the absence of the virgin birth from most New Testament documents, combined with the inconsistent and legendary nature of the two major sources in which it is found, shows that the virgin birth of Jesus is a secondary development rather than an historical fact. Stories about Jesus' birth arose because Jesus was the central identity factor of the Christian community, a man already associated with miracles performed by God through him and upon him. Finally, we should note that the virgin birth occurs clearly in two documents neither of which suggests that Jesus was pre-existent. Jesus' pre-existence is found only in documents which cannot be shown to be aware of the virgin birth, and which at least do not regard it as important enough to mention. Not one New Testament document puts forward a view of Jesus as incarnate and born of a virgin.

The resurrection was central to the early church. At the earliest stage, belief that Jesus was exalted to heaven flowed naturally from the death of the embodiment of prophetic Judaism. We have seen that some Jews believed in the resurrection of the body, and that this form of belief in Jesus' survival and exaltation to heaven became dominant because it was functional.[35]There was an early tradition of resurrection appearances (1 Cor 15.3-7, cf Acts 2.32; 3.15), but when Mark wrote his Gospel the early tradition had already been overridden by the need for legitimating the community's existence, and the outworking of this need is very prominent in the dissociated narratives of Matthew and Luke.[36] The Marcan narrative makes the first points, such as that Jesus was certified dead by Pilate, the two Marys went to the right tomb, and they were shown by an angel that Jesus' body had gone because he was risen (Mk 15.44-5; 15.47-16.4; 16.5-6). Matthew and Luke add explanatory details, such as that the tomb was new (Mt 27.60), or that no-one had yet been laid in it (Lk 23.53). It was guarded, so that the body could not have been stolen (Mt 28.11-15), but Jesus rose with a spiritual body (Lk 24.13-35) which was not a mere spirit (Lk 24.36-43).

As church tradition and the editorial work of the evangelists created unambiguous evidence that Jesus had truly and uniquely risen, they also attributed to him the legitimation of the church's other main needs. Matthew portrays the risen Jesus legitimating his sonship, baptism and the Gentile mission (Mt 28.16-20), while Luke similarly legitimates the Gentile mission and the specifically Christian interpretation of scripture (e.g. Lk 24.44-7). We must conclude that secondary material has been produced most extensively at those points where the community needed it most.

The evangelists also followed the Jewish tradition of legitimating their existence and developments from scripture. Mark used an existing testimonium at Mark 1.2-3, for he attributes a mixture of Exodus 23.20, Malachi 3.1 and Isaiah 40.3 to Isaiah. A significant position is given to Jesus with Psalm 118.22-3 (Mk 12.10-11), and his exaltation and second coming were found in Psalm 110.1, Daniel 7.13 and other texts (Mk 13.26-7; 14.62). Matthew and Luke developed this mode of secondary legitimation on a massive scale. Matthew found the title "Son" at Hosea 11.1 (Mt 2.15), "Son of man" at Daniel 7.13 (Mt 24.30; 26.64), and Jesus' kingly entry to Jerusalem at Zechariah 9.9 (Mt 21.5). His birth narratives are virtually centred round scriptural texts, including the virgin birth from Isaiah 7.14 (Mt 1.23). Jesus' healing ministry is found at Isaiah 53.4 (Mt 8.17). Matthew's Gospel almost pivots on another Servant passage, Isaiah 42.1-4 at Matthew 12.18-21, a quotation which looks forward to the successful Gentile mission. In Luke's Gospel, Jesus' ministry is found at Isaiah 58.6; 61.1-2 (Lk 4.17ff), his passion at Isaiah 53.12 (Lk 22.37) and his parousia at Daniel 7.13 (Lk 21.27/Mk 13.26). Development in Luke's Gospel was however limited by his conviction that the disciples did not understand scriptural proofs during the historic ministry (cf e.g. Lk 18.34), so his massive scriptural legitimation of Jesus' ministry is spread over Acts. This includes Jesus' prophetic ministry from Deuteronomy 18.15,19 (Acts 3.22-3), his passion from Isaiah 53.7-8 (Acts 8.30-35), his death and resurrection from Psalm 16 (Acts 2.25-32), the rejection of the Gospel by many Jews from Isaiah 6.9-10 (Acts 28.23-28), and the Gentile mission from Isaiah 49.6 (Acts 13.45-48).

The self-identification of these three authors must also be considered. Evidence of Mark's Gentile self-identification is found in the editorial comments of chapter 7. The tradition related a dispute originating in a complaint that some of the disciples ate bread without first washing their hands. Mark felt it necessary to explain this:

> for the Pharisees and all the Jews do not eat unless they wash their hands 'with a fist', adhering to the tradition of the elders. And when they come from the market-place they do not eat without immersing themselves. And there are many other things which they have received to keep, washing of cups and pitchers and kettles and beds (Mk 7.3-4).

This description shows Gentile self-identification. "The Jews" are mentioned as an outside group, and "all the Jews" did not follow the strict *halakhah* which Mark describes. Mark's comment is due to ignorant acceptance of the public identity of Judaism. Further evidence comes from the hopeful editorial comment "cleansing all foods" (7.19). This is not a necessary interpretation of Jesus' words, and Matthew duly edited it out.

Mark is also distanced from the orthodox wing of Judaism by the other disputes which he reports between Jesus and the scribes and Pharisees. Sabbath disputes with "the Pharisees" (2.23-3.6) are especially important, for they lead to a plot to put Jesus to death. From the point of view of Gentiles and assimilating Jews in mixed churches, Jesus was on the same side as they were, for he was in conflict with the same sort of people as opposed the law-free Gentile mission. Two general references to this mission have also been inserted (13.10; 14.9).

Matthew had Jewish self-identification, but with pronounced tendencies towards assimilation. Of the basic identity factors of Judaism, ethnicity is dropped: "Therefore I tell you that the kingdom of God will be taken away from you (i.e. chief priests and the Pharisees) and will be given to a people who do its fruits" (Mt 21.43, cf 45; 3.7-9; 8.11-12). The rejection of the Gospel by some Jews is portrayed (cf 10.14-15,17). Matthew 23 collects criticisms of "scribes and Pharisees, hypocrites", and the Sadducees have been deliberately edited into the polemic of John the Baptist and Jesus (Mt 3.7; 16.1,6,11,12: not in Lk 3.7 or Mk 8.11-21). Matthew 11.27 makes Jesus essential for knowledge of the Father, and the position of the disciples as those who "know the mysteries of the kingdom of heaven" over against the majority of Israel is found in scripture (Mt 13.10-15, quoting Is 6.9-10). The Gentile mission is vigorously commanded (28.19, cf 12.18-21; 24.14).

Matthew believed that other identity factors should ideally be maintained. We have seen that scripture is extensively quoted,[37] and since the Law should also be kept (Mt 5.17-18; 13.52), the authority of scripture is wholly maintained. As in the teaching of Jesus, monotheism is intensified by teaching on the father-hood of God. Circumcision is assumed, but does not come up for discussion, and the same is largely true of the major festivals, with Jesus' final Passover important as in Mark. The sabbath is also to be kept (cf e.g. Mt 8.16; 24.20), from a conventional rather than an orthodox standpoint. Observance of purity and dietary law is also assumed, from a biblical rather than an orthodox standpoint. The Gentile editing of Mark 7 is removed. Matthew presents a vigorous attack on the hypocrisy of the scribes and Pharisees, and asserts over against the orthodox that "eating with unwashed hands does not defile a man" (Mt 15.20).

Adherence to seven of the eight identity factors and the religious motivation of the criticisms of the orthodox show that Matthew considered himself a faithful Jew. His position in stage two of christological development and his assimilating tendencies are shown by his attitude to the Gentile mission. Matthew knew that it was Law-free, so the vigour of Matthew 24.14 and 28.19 implies the acceptance of assimilation. Matthew 5.17-20 is programmatic. We must infer from 5.17-18 that the Law is still in force. 5.19 has those who abrogate any commandment, and teach others likewise, "called least in the kingdom of heaven". The mildness of the rejection is a significant index of assimilation. Unlike scribes and Pharisees (5.20, and Mt 15, 23 etc), these people do get into the kingdom! This is therefore the law-free Gentile mission, accepting people into the new covenant community which scribes and Phari-sees, and Sadducees, had not entered. The ideal of the scribe who becomes a disciple of the kingdom of heaven (13.52) is further emphasised by the stress on perfection and good works (cf e.g. 5.16,48; 7.24-7; 19.21). These ideals were however for those who would keep them (cf 19.11-12). The crucial facts are that many Jews were not entering the kingdom, and even Gentile missionaries who taught people not to do the Law were accepted into it. With assimilation accepted, even with disapproval, Matthew belongs very firmly to stage two of christological development.

Luke had Gentile self-identification. He portrays Jesus, his family and his disciples as observing the Law during the historic ministry (e.g. 2.21; 5.14). At the same time, he correctly portrays Jesus as on the opposite wing of Judaism from Pharisees and lawyers, for he retails some of his vigorous attacks on them (cf e.g. Lk 11.37-53). Some shifts in the people criticized by Jesus are of a generalizing kind. For example, the accusation that Jesus cast out demons by Beelzebub is made by "some of them" (11.15), that is, "the crowds" (11.14), rather than by "the scribes who came down from Jerusalem" (Mk 3.22). Jesus' reply is thus addressed also to Jewish crowds in general. This presages the rejection of the Gospel by many Jews in Acts. The mission to the Gentiles is commanded by the risen Christ (Lk 24.47), being foretold in Simeon's prophecy (Lk 2.31-2) and at Isaiah 40.3 (Lk 3.6; cf also 4.25ff; 13.29).

The Gentile mission is the central theme of Acts. Here it is argued that Gentiles should not take on observance of the Jewish Law when they become Christians. At Acts 10.13-16 the dietary laws are removed in a vision granted to Peter. The Law-free Gentile mission is further legitimated with the portrayal of Gentile Christians receiving the gift of the Holy Spirit just like Jewish Christians (Acts 10.44-48; 11.15-18). In Acts 15, Pharisees are brought forward to argue that "it is necessary to circumcise them, and to instruct them to keep the Law of Moses" (15.5). The discussion attributes to Peter the highly critical remark, "Now, therefore, why do you test God, to lay on the neck of the disciples a yoke which neither our fathers nor we were able to bear?" (15.10). The decision of the community is that Gentiles should not keep the Law, except that they should refrain from sex outside marriage, from blood in meat and from meat offered to idols. Luke believed this was also Paul's position (Acts 16.4). The author's Gentile self-identification is further seen in his view that Paul preached to the Gentiles because the Gospel was not accepted by "the Jews" (Acts 18.5-6, cf 13.45ff; 28.25-28).

In Acts, the word "Jew(s)" occurs about 80 times. Luke's Gospel, however, has only five examples. Unlike John,[38]Luke was not biased enough to edit a hostile use of this term into his Gospel, and many examples in Acts merely report events in which the differences between Jews and Gentiles were important (e.g. 10.22,28; 14.1). Luke does however have several external and hostile examples which show that he identified against "the Jews" (cf Acts 13.50; 14.4; 20.3; 23.12; 24.9, and the remarkably external use by Peter at 12.11). It follows that Luke had Gentile self-identification.

When we consider all three synoptic evangelists, we see that their christology is determined by the self-identification of the community, rather than the author. Matthew, Mark and Luke all portray Jesus as a person of the highest status and of fundamental function in salvation history: none of them portrays him as fully divine. It made no difference that Mark and Luke had Gentile self-identification, whereas Matthew identified as a Jew. The controlling influence was that of the Christian community as a whole, which still had both Jewish and Gentile members. It needed much christological development to hold together, but the restraining factor of Jewish monotheism could not be removed from a mixed community. It was not removed until members of the Johannine community were thrown out of the synagogue, thereby creating a Gentile community who were in conflict with "the Jews", and who therefore exercised purely Gentile perception when they contemplated the figure of Jesus.

5. Deity, Incarnation and the Johannine Community

This is the situation reflected in the fourth Gospel, and a generally similar christology is found in the Johannine epistles.[39] Two major titles, "Son" (of God) (Jn 27 times, 1 Jn 22) and "Christ" (Jn 19 times, 1 Jn 8), are common and have become distinctive identity markers which may be used in propositional form. "Whoever confesses that Jesus is the Son of God, God remains in him and he in God" (1 Jn 4.15): "Who is the deceiver except he who denies that Jesus is the Christ?" (1 Jn 2.22; cf e.g. Jn 20.31). In John and 1 John, the term "son" is more common than in earlier New Testament documents because it is more functional. Here Jesus is raised up to deity, so a term is needed which both asserts his deity and avoids confusion with God the Father. This is a natural development of the usage of Paul and Hebrews.[40]At the same time, a term was needed which stated the faith briefly in a conflict situation. This need is satisfied by the propositional use.

"Son of man" occurs in the fourth Gospel (13 times) because it was so important in the Gospel traditions. Some sayings predict Jesus' death (e.g. 3.14; 6.62), and some have been developed from Old Testament texts (cf 1.51; 3.14). Even these are however rather remote from synoptic usage. The term has lost its earlier associations, and has become an alternative description of Jesus. It is even used confessionally (9.35), and in a question from the crowd (12.34). It is absent from the Johannine epistles, as from others, probably because it is not natural Greek. "Lord" is common enough in the Gospel, mostly as a form of addressing Jesus (about 28 times), but also as a description (about 13 times) accepted by Jesus himself (13.13-14). Its absence from the epistles may be due to their brevity, but a more probable cause of its absence from 1 John is that it became less functional in concentrated theological exposition, as Jesus rose nearer to deity.

Major theological points which the Johannine literature shares with other New Testament documents include Jesus' atoning death. The Gospel interpreted this as taking away the sins of the world (1.29) and enabling the Gentile mission to take place.[41]The first epistle likewise comments that "he is a propitiation for our sins, though not for ours alone but also for those of the whole world" (1 Jn 2.2, cf 1.7; 3.5; 4.10). The second coming of Jesus is expected (1 Jn 2.28), and had been expected sooner (Jn 21.22-3). Baptism is expounded theologically in John 3, and the concept of being born again is taken up again in 1 John (cf e.g. 2.29; 3.9; 5.18). I have noted the theological exposition of the eucharist in John 6.[42] Thus the Johannine community had most of its basic christology in common with other New Testament documents. In the Gospel, even the push for deity in the prologue further developed the Wisdom christology which is found in Q and Matthew, and which stops short of deity in Colossians 1.15-20 and the opening of Hebrews.[43]

Most of the distinctive christological beliefs which the Johannine epistles share with the fourth Gospel are associated with the final push for deity. Jesus' pre-existence and sonship are associated in 1 John with the term "word of life" (1 Jn 1.1-4, cf Jn 1.1,18). We have noted that "Son" is the most characteristic christological title in both the Gospel and the epistles. It became functional when Jesus had risen almost to deity, and in the final redaction of the Gospel, it is the term usually used when Jesus deity is indicated.[44] The description of Jesus as "only-begotten Son" is even clearer (Jn 3.16,18; 1 Jn 4.9, cf Jn 1.14). Given this cultural background, we should recognize Jesus' pre-existence at 1 John 1.1ff; 4.9; 5.20.

The term "paraclete" is also distinctive of this literature. It probably means "envoy",[45]and it is usually used in the Gospel of the Holy Spirit, who will be sent to the community after Jesus' death (Jn 14.16-17; 15.26; 16.7-15). John 14.16 however calls the Holy Spirit "another paraclete", and 1 John 2.1 explains this: "we have a paraclete with the Father, Jesus Christ the righteous." The expression thus picks up the sending terminology characteristic of the Gospel (cf e.g.

Jn 5.23-4; 7.33; 14.24-6; 17.25; 1 Jn 4.9-10). Finally, the declaration of deity should probably be found in 1 John as well as in the Gospel. This is the most natural interpretation of 1 John 5.20: "and we are in the true one, in his Son Jesus Christ. He is the true God and eternal life." The Greek word *houtos*, "He", normally refers to what has just been mentioned, in this case "Jesus Christ". This author's christology is so high that he can hardly have been unaware of what he can so easily be taken to mean, and after 5.11-13 the description of Jesus Christ as "eternal life" is particularly appropriate (cf 1.2).

In the fourth Gospel, this final step of confessing the deity of Jesus is verifiable at the point where members of the Johannine community were thrown out of the synagogue.[46] The situation behind the Johannine epistles is more difficult to fathom. The term "Jew" does not occur, but some of the author's opponents seem very Jewish. For example, at 1 John 2.22 the "deceiver" is "he who denies that Jesus is the Christ". The author finds it necessary to add, "Everyone who denies the Son does not have the Father either. He who confesses the Son has the Father too" (1 Jn 2.23). This kind of comment was necessary in conflict with Jewish people who did not accept Johannine Christianity. They believed that they had the Father, and they did not accept Jesus as the Christ and the Son. It was, therefore, necessary to state explicitly that they were excluded from salvation, even though they continued in the covenant community which was partly defined by its allegiance to God the Father.

Why are these opponents not identified as Jews? We must infer that the author knew Christians who continued to call themselves "Jews" because they were ethnically Jewish. The elder, who wrote 2 and 3 John, uses the description "Gentiles" as a reference to an outside group (3 Jn 7): however assimilated he was, he must have retained his Jewish self-identification. What the elder thought of the deity of Jesus we do not know - it is not mentioned in two documents too short for the absence of anything to be significant. We can however see him embracing the sonship of Jesus, and the second occurrence is in a context which entails the rejection of anyone who does not do so, and which consequently entails the rejection of most Jewish people (2 Jn 9-11). It must be inferred that the elder and his followers no longer belonged to the Jewish community, even though the Jewish background of some of them caused them to retain Jewish self-identification. As for 1 John, we cannot deduce the self-identification of the author(s) with certainty. It is, however, a very probable hypothesis that he belonged to a community which had effectively Gentile identity in that it did not observe the Law, but that, as in 2 and 3 John, there were enough assimilated Jews who retained Jewish self-identification for him never to use "the Jews" in a hostile sense.

This further illuminates the relationship between identity and christological development. Jewish people who remained in the Jewish community could not hail Jesus as God because this would infringe Jewish monotheism. Gentiles who did not belong to the Jewish community, and who identified against "the Jews", could do so. Only these clear definitions, referring to large and clearly identifiable social groups, can be regarded as firm. Single individuals might do anything, and the precise position of Jews who assimilated out of the Jewish community into a largely Gentile community can be determined only in the light of sufficient data. The fourth Gospel provides sufficient data. The deity and incarnation of Jesus first occur there, and this is dependent on the Gentile self-identification of the Johannine community observable in it.

This is where we find incarnation in the full sense. Jesus had been hailed as pre-existent when he was not regarded as fully divine, Adam and Wisdom christologies being particularly used to legitimate this perception. Incarnation in the strict sense comes with his full deity, and in the Johannine prologue, another author used Wisdom christology, together with the concept of the Word of God, to raise Jesus to carefully expressed deity. In a slightly weaker sense, incarnation may be found in passages such as Philippians 2.6ff. It is particularly important to recall at this point that a weaker definition makes it a less unusual thought.[47] Whatever our definitions, incarnation is clearly declared as the entry of a fully divine being into the world in the Johannine prologue, alone of all New Testament documents.

Jesus was now a figure so elevated that observant Jews such as Jesus of Nazareth and the first apostles could not believe in him. The consequences of this for Christian belief are more serious than they are usually taken to be. They will be considered in the final chapter.

1. Cf T.Holtz, *Die Christologie der Apokalypse des Johannes*, TU 85 (1962. 2nd ed., 1971); J.Comblin, *Le Christ dans l'Apocalypse* (1965); M.de Jonge, "The Use of the Expression *ho Christos* in the Apocalypse of John", in J.Lambrecht (ed), *L'Apocalypse* (1980), 267-81; C.Wolff, "Die Gemeinde des Christus in der Apokalypse des Johannes", *NTS* 27, 1981, 186-97; D.E.Lohse, "Wie Christlich ist die Offenbarung des Johannes?", *NTS* 34, 1988, 321-38; M.G.Reddish, "Martyr Christology in the Apocalypse", *JSNT* 33, 1988, 85-95.
2. Cf A.Y.Collins, "Vilification and Self-Definition in the Book of Revelation", *HThR* 79, 1986, 308-20.
3. Cf M.Kiddle, *The Revelation of St.John*, Moffat NT Commentary (1940), ad loc.; Casey, *Son of Man*, 142-50.
4. Cf supra 114-7; infra, 146, 156-9.
5. On the background of the epistle, W.Horbury, "The Aaronic Priesthood in the Epistle to the Hebrews", *JSNT* 19, 1983, 43-71 (with bibliography). On the function of Jesus' death, supra 28, 29, 30, 65, 111, 125, 127ff: infra 147, 150, 157.
6. Cf J.C.Campbell, "In a Son. The Doctrine of Incarnation in the Epistle to the Hebrews", *Interp* 10, 1956, 24-38; T.F.Glasson, "'Plurality of Divine Persons' and the Quotations in Hebrews 1.6ff", *NTS* 12, 1965-6, 270-2; R.A.Stewart, "The Sinless High-Priest", *NTS* 14, 1967-8, 126-35; E.Grasser, "Zur Christologie des Hebräerbriefes", in *Neues Testament und Christliche Existenz. Festschrift für H.Braun zum 70 Geburtstag*, ed H.D.Betz and L.L.Schottroff (1973), 195-206; Horton, op. cit.; F.Laub, *Bekenntnis und Auslegung. Die paränetische Funktion der Christologie im Hebräerbrief*, BU 15 (1980); Kobelski, op. cit.; W.R.G.Loader, *Sohn und Hohepriester. Eine traditions-geschichtliche Untersuchung zur Christologie des Hebräerbriefs*, WMANT 53 (1981); R.Williamson, "The Incarnation of the Logos in Hebrews", *ExpT* 95, 1983, 4-8; P.Giles, *Jesus the High Priest* (1984); H.Feld, "Der Hebräerbrief: Literarische Form, religionsgeschichtliche Hintergrund, theologische Fragen",

ANRW II.25.4 (1987), 3522-3601, esp 3564-81; J.Swetnam, "Christology and the Eucharist in the Epistle to the Hebrews", *Bib* 70, 1989, 74-95.

7. Cf supra, 134-5.
8. Cf supra, 112-7.
9. Cf supra, 79.
10. Cf supra 65, 111, 125, 127ff, 141-2; infra 147, 150, 157.
11. Supra 80, 125.
12. Cf supra, 107.
13. Supra, 29-31.
14. Cf supra, 114-7, 142-3; infra, 156-9.
15. Cf supra, 113-4.
16. Cf supra 80, 125, 145.
17. Supra, 24-7.
18. Cf F.Christ, *Jesus Sophia. Die Sophia-Christologie bei den Synoptikern*, AThANT 57 (1970); A.Polag, *Die Christologie der Logienquelle*, WMANT 45 (1977); M.Horstmann, *Studien zur Markinischen Christologie. Mk 8,27-9,13 als Zugang zum Christusbild des zweiten Evangeliums*, NTA 6 (1969); N.Perrin, "The Christology of Mark: A Study in Methodology", *JR* 51, 1971, 173-87, also N.Perrin, *A Modern Pilgrimage in New Testament Christology* (1974), 104-21; O.Betz, "The Concept of the so-called 'Divine Man' in Mark's Christology", in *Studies in New Testament and Early Christian Literature. Essays in honor of Allen Wikgren*, ed D.Aune, NT.S 33 (1972), 229-40; U.B.Müller, "Die christologische Absicht des Markusevangeliums und die Verklärungsgeschichte", *ZNW* 64, 1973, 159-93; E.Trocmé, "Is there a Markan Christology?", in *Christ and the Spirit in the New Testament*, ed B.Lindars and S.S.Smalley in honour of C.F.D.Moule (1973), 3-14; E.Schweizer, "Towards a Christology of Mark?", in *God's Christ and his People*. Studies in Honour of N.A.Dahl, ed J.Jervell and W.A.Meeks (1977), 29-42; P.J.Achtemeier, "'He Taught Them Many Things': Reflections on Marcan Christology", *CBQ* 42, 1980, 465-81; J.D.Kingsbury, *The Christology of Mark's Gospel* (1983); M.E.Boring, "The Christology of Mark: Hermeneutical Issues for Systematic Theology", *Semeia* 30, 1984, 125-53; P.Pokorny, "Das Markusevangelium. Literarische und theologische Einleitung mit Forschungsbericht. VI. Die Christologie des Markusevangeliums", *ANRW* II.25.3 (1984), 2006-17; J.Zmijewski, "Die Sohn-Gottes-Prädikation im Markusevangelium. Zür Frage einer eigenstandigen markinischen Titelchristologie", *Stud NT Umwelt* 12, 1987, 5-34; P.G.Davis, "Mark's Christological Paradox", *JSNT* 35, 1989, 3-18; M.J.Suggs, *Wisdom, Christology and Law in Matthew's Gospel* (1970); M.D.Johnson, "Reflections on a Wisdom Approach to Matthew's Christology", *CBQ* 36, 1974, 44-64; L.Gaston, "The Messiah of Israel as Teacher of the Gentiles. The Setting of Matthew's Christology", *Interp* 29, 1975, 24-40; J.D.Kingsbury, *Matthew: Structure, Christology, Kingdom* (1976); D.Hill, "Son and Servant: An Essay on Matthean Christology", *JSNT* 6, 1980, 2-16; G.N.Stanton, "The Origin and Purpose of Matthew's Gospel. Matthean Scholarship from 1945 to 1980. IV.1. Christology", *ANRW* II.25.3 (1984), 1922-5; D.J.Verseput, "The Role and Meaning of the 'Son of God' Title in Matthew's Gospel", *NTS* 38, 1987, 532-56; G.W.H.Lampe, "The Lucan Portrait of Christ", *NTS* 2, 1955-6, 160-75; A.George, "Jésus fils de Dieu dans l'évangile selon Saint Luc", *RB* 72, 1965, 185-209; G.Voss, *Die Christologie der lukanischen Schriften in Grundzugen*, SN II (1965); M.Rese, *Alttestamentliche Motive in der Christologie des Lukas*, SNT 1 (1969); D.L.Jones, "The Title *Christos* in Luke-Acts", *CBQ* 32, 1970, 69-76; I.de la Potterie, "Le titre *kyrios* appliqué à Jésus dans l'évangile de Luc", in *Mélanges*

Bibliques en hommage au R.P.Béda Rigaux, ed A.Descamps and A.de Halleux (1970), 117-46; A.George, "Le sens de la mort de Jésus pour Luc", *RB* 80, 1973, 186-217; E.Franklin, *Christ the Lord* (1975), esp ch 2.

19. Supra, 111, 124-5, 131-3.
20. This cannot be demonstrated here. Cf supra, 75 note 3.
21. Supra, ch 4.
22. Cf supra 45-6, 134-5, 143-5; infra, 156-9.
23. Supra, 44.
24. Cf supra, 41-4.
25. Cf supra 43-4, 82, 106, 112, 141-2.
26. Supra, 82.
27. Supra, 46-54.
28. For detailed technical discussion, P.M.Casey, *JSNT* 29, 1987, 31-4.
29. Supra 52-4, 107, 109, 110, 126, 132, 142.
30. Cf supra 68, 105, 110-1, 113-4, 133.
31. Supra, 88-90.
32. Cf supra 23, 115-7, 144. Infra 157.
33. Supra 45-6, cf 148-9.
34. For a recent defence of its historicity, C.E.B.Cranfield, "Some Reflections on the Subject of the Virgin Birth", *SJTh* 41, 1988, 177-89. For thorough discussion of the birth narratives, cf in addition to the commentators, R.E.Brown, *The Birth of the Messiah* (1977).
35. Supra 65-7, 98-105.
36. Supra 98-105, esp 99-100, 103-5.
37. Supra, 153.
38. Cf supra, 27-38, with note 9.
39. On John's Gospel, supra, ch 3. In addition to the literature cited there, and the commentators, cf. M. de Jonge, "The Use of the Word *Christos* in the Johannine Epistles", in *Studies in John Presented to Professor J.N.Sevenster*, NT.S 24 (1970), 66-74; P.Minear, "The Idea of Incarnation in First John", *Interp.* 24, 1970, 291-302; J.Painter, "The 'Opponents' in 1 John", *NTS* 32, 1986, 48-71; M.C. de Boer, "Jesus the Baptizer: 1 John 5:5-8 and the Gospel of John", *JBL* 107, 1988, 87-106. More generally, K.Wengst, "Probleme der Johannesbriefe", *ANRW* II.25.5 (1988), 3751-72; J.Beutler, "Die Johannesbriefe in der neuesten Literatur (1978-1985), ibid., 3773-90.
40. Cf supra 23-7, 44-6, 79, 111-2, 134-5, 143-5.
41. Supra 25-6, 28-30.
42. Supra 24-6, 29-30.
43. Cf supra 115-7, 144, 151; J.Ashton, "The Transformation of Wisdom. A Study of the Prologue of John's Gospel", *NTS* 32, 1986, 161-86.
44. Supra 23-5, 156-7 with note 40.
45. This cannot be discussed here. For cognate words, cf H.D.Betz, *2 Corinthians 8 and 9* (Hermeneia. 1985) 54, 70-71.
46. Supra ch. 3.
47. Cf infra, 166-7.

Chapter 10
History, Culture and Truth

1. Introduction

Chapters 1-9 have described the origins and development of New Testament christology, and suggested a theory to explain this development. The purpose of this chapter is to outline the consequences of this for our culture. In particular, we must consider how far the proposed results affect the truth or falsity of Christian belief.

The analysis of identity poses a central problem. Jesus belonged to Jewish culture. Christians as a whole do not. Moreover, the relationship between identity and christological development is to some extent one of cause and effect. While christology could rise high enough in stage one to make Jesus into a unique being, the Gentile mission caused developments some of which were alien to Jewish identity. For example, Paul grounded Christian morals in baptism into the death and, as it were, resurrection of Jesus (cf. Rom 6.1-14; Col 2.12-13). In this way, Jesus functionally replaced the Law, for he legitimated the ethical decisions of a community which needed this legitimation because it consisted largely of people who did not observe the Law.[1] The development of stage three is even more serious, because the deity of Jesus was first stated by Christians in conflict with Jews, and those Jews found this declaration blasphemous.

What should be the effect of this on our perception of the Christian faith? To help us answer this question, we may begin with a standard statement of christological belief. After much debate, the Church laid down its official christology in the Definition of Faith agreed at the Council of Chalcedon, in A.D. 451. This was for centuries the faith of the Church, and officially it remains the faith of most Christians. We may therefore turn next to the last part of this Definition.

2. A Definition of Faith

...Following therefore the holy Fathers, we confess one and the same Son, our Lord Jesus Christ, and we all teach in harmony that he is perfect in deity and perfect in humanity, really God and really man, with a rational soul and a body, of the same nature as the Father with respect to his deity and of the same nature as us with respect to his humanity, like us in every way except for sin, begotten from the Father before the ages with respect to his deity, but in the last days the same for us and for our salvation from

162

the virgin Mary mother of God with respect to his humanity: one and the same Christ, Son, Lord, only-begotten, made known in two natures, without confusion, unchangeably, with no division, inseparably, the difference between the natures being in no way removed by their union, but rather the property of each nature being preserved and coming together into one *prosopon* and one *hypostasis*, not being divided or split into two *prosopa*, but one and the same Son and only-begotten God, Word, Lord, Jesus Christ, as the prophets of old and Jesus Christ himself instructed us concerning him, and the symbol of the Fathers handed down to us...

This is quite remote from Jesus of Nazareth. The definition is full of abstract Greek philosophy, an approach to christology which eventually saw the condemnation of the Aramaic-speaking churches. The world-view of even the Gentile part of the church which spoke the same language as Jesus and the apostles was too semitic to think like this.

The rewriting of history is most obvious towards the end of the definition: "Jesus Christ himself instructed us". He did nothing of the kind. To be fair to the Fathers of the Council, they knew the Gospel of John as an account of Jesus' ministry, and some of them took it literally. Yet we should not bend over backwards in defence of them. Patristic exegesis was extraordinarily free in distorting the meaning of texts in the interests of dogma, and there is more at stake than being fair to the Fathers of the Council. Social function is at its most devastating when we fail to observe the fallibility of the work of people whom we consider to be members of our own social group, and so it was in this case. John attributed to Jesus much that he did not say or do.[2]All the subsequent generation had to do was to accept his work uncritically. By such simple means do large groups of people have their history rewritten.

The second way it was done in this formula is in the assertion, "as the prophets of old instructed us concerning him." This conceals considerable differences between the Fathers. Antiochene and other Syrian Fathers, having inherited a strong tradition of Jewish exegesis which believed that most of the words of the prophets had been fulfilled in the deeds of Jewish heroes such as Hezekiah and Judas Maccabaeus, regarded relatively few prophecies as referring to Jesus, at least directly.[3] Others, not having inherited such a tradition, carried on the New Testament habit of applying large numbers of passages to Jesus. Flexibility of method was at its height in the Alexandrian school, though it did not need an Alexandrian exegete to see the deity of Jesus at Genesis 1.26 and, together with the virgin birth, at Isaiah 7.14. It is here that modern critical study of the Old Testament is fundamental in showing us that the Council's claim is substantially false. The Old Testament passages which were interpreted of Jesus do not refer to him, and the Council's doctrine of the two natures does not occur anywhere in the Old Testament.

Both these points involve the infringement of Jewish identity. That Jesus was "perfect in deity" and "really God" could not be found either in the teaching of Jesus or in the prophets of old because all of them unswervingly adhered to Jewish monotheism. Consequently, the cultural tradition of the Fathers exemplified what Rosemary Ruether has called "the left hand of christology": it was very anti-Jewish.[4] The mere existence of Jews was a standing refutation of the Christian claim that with the coming of Jesus the Jewish people had been superseded by the Christians. The Gentile church, no longer content with the Pauline view that Gentiles should not observe the whole of the Jewish law, eventually claimed that Jews should not observe it either. This was an open rejection of Jewish identity. Moreover, Jews did not accept the christological exegesis of the Old Testament. They were therefore vigorously criticized. At Daniel 7.13, for example, "one like a son of man" comes on the clouds of heaven. This figure was intended to be a symbol of the Saints of the Most High, the Maccabean Jews who hoped for deliverance from the persecution of Antiochus Epiphanes. Theodoret knew this interpretation, because it was followed both by Jews and by some of his fellow Christians in Antioch and the surrounding area. Theodoret himself, however, followed the New Testament interpretation of it as a prophecy of the second coming of Jesus.[5] He comments, "This is really a suitable point for saying to Jews what the prophet said to them of old, 'You had the face of a prostitute, behaving shamelessly in front of everyone' (Jer 3.3). For what is clearer than these words? The prophet has in fact announced this like an evangelist and apostle rather than in a prophetic and hidden manner!" Proof follows from Matthew 24.30 and 1 Thessalonians 4.16-17, texts sacred to Christians and not to Jews.

This kind of comment is a vicious development of the view, found in Paul, and inherent in christological exegesis of the Old Testament, that "whenever Moses is read, a veil lies over their heart" (2 Cor 3.15).[6] Its patent falsity is nowhere better illustrated than in Justin Martyr, who interpreted of Jesus an extended version of Psalm 96.10, "Declare among the Gentiles, the Lord reigned from the tree." Finding that Jews did not have the words "from the tree" in their texts of Psalm 96, Justin accused them of leaving them out. Concluding discussion of further examples with an accusation of mutilating the scriptures, he declares it a more dreadful act than making the golden calf, sacrificing their children to demons and killing the prophets (Dial 73-4). Yet it is a false accusation from beginning to end, and its equation with their supposed crime of sacrificing their children to demons shows the lack of proportion and contempt for truth characteristic of anti-Jewish propaganda everywhere. The Chalcedonian Fathers depended on a long tradition of the rewriting of history. It involved pulling Old Testament passages out of their own cultural tradition, pouring scorn on that tradition to which Jesus and the apostles belonged, and appropriating them in the interests of a dogmatic structure correspondingly alien to Jesus and to the first apostles. This dogmatic tradition rejected Jewish identity, even when it was not concerned with inherently unJewish views such as the deity of Jesus.

3. Chalcedon, Truth and Tradition

But, it may be argued, most Christians do not believe in the Definition of Faith promulgated by the Council of Chalcedon. It may be alleged that it should not be taken as authoritative in a literal sense: like all human achievements, it is culturally conditioned, and what is authoritative is the reality to which it witnesses, not the precise meaning of its formulae.

There is substance in these views. Certainly most Christians have never heard of a *prosopon* or a *hypostasis*, and all too few seem to have heard of the Council of Chalcedon. Moreover, it is at least internally consistent to maintain that the revelation of God is continually mediated by culturally conditioned human beings, who cannot do anything but transmit divine revelation in the terms given them by their own culture.[7] As Morgan put it,

> Theologies come and go; the dogma remains. The relevant question to ask of any new theology is whether it witnesses to the same Lord, the same faith, the same baptism, the same God and Father of all; whether it can claim legitimate continuity with past theologies which the Church has accepted as not incorrectly expressing its faith.[8]

This approach is not sufficient to meet the difficulties presented by traditional christology. Christians generally have believed and still do believe that Jesus is divine. Christians who do not know the Chalcedonian Definition of Faith believe this at least as strongly as those who do, so that the official view of many bishops and theologians that it represents the faith is a perfectly reasonable one. Indeed, popular piety has often stressed the divinity of Jesus at the expense of his humanity, so it has supported the major point that is achieved by the most careful and learned analysis of the Chalcedonian Definition. For all scholars have agreed that if the Definition is accepted, the Jesus of history cannot have made any mistakes, and that corresponds to the general Christian view of him. Any other view encounters difficulty in claiming continuity with past theologies. Moreover, the deity of Jesus is one belief that Jews cannot hold while remaining in the Jewish community, for they perceive it as a breach of the monotheistic faith revealed to them by God in the course of their own history. Finally, Christians have generally supposed that the deity and incarnation of Jesus are written in the New Testament, and were revealed by Jesus himself.

We have, however, seen that the christology of the New Testament is quite varied, and bears witness to a rapid process of change during the New Testament period itself. This variety is not confined to imagery and modes of expression, though we have found that as well. The slaughtered lamb of Revelation is quite unique, as is the exposition of the highpriesthood of Jesus after the order of Melchizedek in the Epistle to the Hebrews. No-one suggests that these approaches are present in the teaching of the historical Jesus, nor is that perceived to be a serious problem. New Testament christology, however, varies in real substance, not only in imagery, and a serious problem should be perceived in this variety. There are two significant points.

Firstly, it has been noted that some christological developments became possible only in stage two, when the churches contained a large number of Gentiles. For example, Paul grounds Christian ethics in the appropriation at baptism of the death and resurrection of Christ (Rom 6). In Judaism, ethics were grounded in the Law, so Paul's exposition would not be found in stage one. Then again, Paul's exegesis of the Old Testament included a number of passages interpreted of Jesus, and at 2 Corinthians 3 he argues that a veil lies over the heart of the sons of Israel when Moses is read. Earlier Christians did not hold all these views, because Christianity had not been a partly Gentile organization.[9] Changes could take place, with ethics partly dependent on the teaching of Jesus and some scribes and Pharisees excluded from salvation. While Christianity was Jewish, however, ethics could not become independent of the Law, nor could the sons of Israel be so criticized as a complete group.

Developments of this kind became more harmful in stage three, when Christianity became an essentially Gentile religion. In John 5, Jesus addresses a whole discourse to "the Jews", concluding, "Do not think that *I* shall accuse you to the Father - your accuser is *Moses*, on whom you have set your hope, for if you had believed Moses, you would have believed me, for he wrote about me. But if you do not believe his writings, how will you believe my words?" (Jn 5.45-7). Here we have the transition to the treatment of opponents of Christianity as an ethnic group, "the Jews", who are blamed for not accepting Jesus. Christological exegesis has become a ground for the charge that "the Jews" do not believe Moses, a charge which is patently false. It is at this point that both the variety of the New Testament witness and the false attribution of these words to Jesus become crucially damaging. It is not just that Jesus *did* not say this, but that he *would* not have said it. We have passed from internal prophetic criticism of other Jews to wholesale condemnation of a rejected ethnic group.

Nor is the charge only *historically* false. It is also *morally* unsatisfactory, though we must be careful not to lay too much blame for this in the wrong place. It should not be argued that the author of the fourth Gospel was wicked. His comments are only too comprehensible as a product of the conflict situation in which he found himself, and his comments are those of the oppressed, not of oppressors. Rather, the elevation of inaccurate condemnation of an ethnic group into scripture so sacred that it is known to be true is morally unsatisfactory. The assertion that Moses accuses the Jews, the declaration that the Jews do not believe in their own sacred scriptures, these accusations must be morally wrong if they are empirically false. The history of Christian measures against Jews shows that it is morally unsafe to have false accusations in a sacred text. They fuel prejudice, they are liable to be acted upon, and they have been acted upon abundantly.

There is a second aspect of New Testament christology where variety is difficult to reconcile with truth, and that is the deity and incarnation of Jesus. We have found these beliefs only in the Johannine literature, and we must take seriously the obverse of this fact - most New Testament writers did not believe that Jesus was incarnate and divine. Neither did Jesus of Nazareth, nor did the first apostles. We should not get round this problem by playing with definitions, but the possibility of doing so is serious enough to demand that we explore briefly the results of using different definitions of the term "incarnation".[10] By "incarnation", I mean the process by which a fully divine figure is born as a person. It would be possible not to insist on the figure being fully divine, and this might seem to have the advantage of taking in passages like Philippians 2.6ff, or even Galatians 4.4. We then have Paul as a witness to the incarnation of Jesus. The epistle to the Hebrews obviously follows. If we read pre-existence into the stories of the virgin birth, we have Matthew and Luke as well. We now have most of the New Testament, and everything in the garden is lovely.

Unfortunately, we have a nasty crop of weeds as well. The most poisonous is Simon Magus, carefully cultured by Michael Goulder and popping up his ugly head from Acts 8.9-10, "saying he was someone great. And everyone paid attention to him, from small to great, saying 'This is the power of God called Great'." Samaritan studies may be a difficult field, but there is no doubt that this description has its *Sitz im Leben* in Samaria rather than in the theology of Luke.[11] It is quite clear that Simon is God Incarnate in the most general sense, possibly in a tighter one, and the Samaritan *Sitz im Leben* takes us back at least some years before the writing of Luke. Moreover, if we do not define incarnation too tightly, we certainly have the incarnation of Melchizedek in 2 Enoch, the incarnation of Jacob in the Prayer of Joseph, and surely also the incarnation of Enoch in the Similitudes of Enoch.[12] In the Greco-Roman world, it was frequently held that the soul was a pre-existent divine spark, which could give us the incarnation of quite a lot of people. If we read pre-existence into virgin birth, it becomes difficult to see why we should insist on an actual birth. Then perhaps we should count Raphael as incarnate in the book of Tobit, and consider seriously Wisdom in 1 Enoch 42: suppose she had found somewhere to dwell among men, would she have been incarnate too?

The results of using different definitions illuminate the central point. If our definition of incarnation is not reasonably tight, incarnation loses its importance as a feature of New Testament christology. Hence the steam generated by exegetical arguments concerning Philippians 2.6ff and Romans 9.5. It is frequently argued that Romans 9.5 testifies to the deity of Jesus. If Philippians 2.6 is interpreted in the light of subsequent theology, if the "form" of God can be interpreted as his "essence", if we interpret the Greek word *harpagmon* to mean that Jesus already possessed equality with God and was entitled to keep it, then Paul joins John as a witness of the deity and incarnation of Jesus in the fullest sense. Recent work has however demonstrated the desperate fragility of arguments of this kind. Single words are usually flexible enough to be used in more than one way. The *morphe theou* was not God's essence in the culture of St Paul, and *harpagmon* cannot tell us whether equality with God was already possessed by Jesus, still less, what *isa theo* really meant.[13] Hence the importance of studying the original cultural background.

This underlines the importance of recent work on the figure of Adam and the use of this figure in Pauline christology. The position of Adam in Judaism, and the use of comparison with him in Pauline christology, show that the language of Philippians 2.6-11 could be used of someone who was not God in the Johannine, let alone the Chalcedonian sense. That is to say, in the opinion of the original author, the bounds of Judaism have not quite been passed, and the figure has not yet been perceived as God incarnate.[14] Similar remarks apply to Romans 9.5. It is possible that Jesus is called God here, and if it be true it is comprehensible. But again, occasional terminology of this kind does occur in the Judaism of this period. One uncertain use of the term "God" does not take us up to the ontology of the Johannine community. Still less should we take one possible interpretation of Romans 9.5 and read the deity of Jesus from it into the christological hymn of Philippians 2.6ff.

We can now see how carefully the evidence was selected by some of those scholars who sought to defend the faith from the onslaughts of *The Myth of God Incarnate*. Hebblethwaite put the matter in a nutshell:

But do the doctrines of the Incarnation and the Trinity belong, in the same way, to the essence of Christianity? I am persuaded that they do. It is these doctrines, expressed in all the creeds and confessions of the historic churches, that have given Christian belief its characteristic shape down the centuries.

One of the reasons which Hebblethwaite gives is his membership of the church.

I find myself considering these matters as a participant in what I think of as the body of Christ, the community of those who by adoption and grace are united with God through the risen Christ and drawn consciously within the sphere of the operations of the Spirit. It is a direct consequence of this that I cannot suppose the church's credal faith to have been mistaken over so central a matter as the divinity of Christ.[15]

The selection of creeds rather than, say, the opinion of Jesus or Paul, ensures that major aspects of the church's beliefs are unaffected precisely because history had already been sufficiently rewritten to satisfy the needs of a Gentile church. Furthermore, the New Testament does have equivalents of the later creeds in the relatively short statements of belief found in the early speeches of Acts and in kerygmatic formulae such as Romans 1.3-4. None of these asserts the deity and incarnation of Jesus. We should not cast aside the evidence of Jesus of Nazareth in this way, nor that of the New Testament, with its limited support for Christian belief. Above all, we should note that most of its writers do not declare the full deity of Jesus, for this is contrary to Jewish identity.

4. Deity, Reality and Perception

Two points are especially important in undermining belief in the deity of Jesus. One is Jesus' expectation of the kingdom: he predicted that it would come very soon, and his predictions were mistaken.[16] Moreover, Jesus' mistake is easy to understand if we perceive it as the mistaken prophecy of a fallible Jew. It is in no way the mistake of a madman. It is a mistake repeated by numerous Jews at crisis points in Jewish history, because it arises naturally from the dynamic of normative Jewish expectation. At times of persecution, Jews have interpreted their covenant relationship with God their Father to mean that he must shortly deliver them. Jesus' teaching shows particular appreciation of the fatherhood of God at a time of severe Roman oppression, when Jewish society was dominated by people whose religion he regarded as inadequate. These factors will have made him more likely to produce predictions of this kind. They are not precise because his knowledge was not based immediately on the predictions of Daniel or on evidence of that kind, but on the profundity of his religious convictions, a dimension of life which may produce certainty rather than precision.

Jesus' inaccurate predictions are not consistent with the portrayal of his two natures in the Chalcedonian Definition. All interpreters of it have agreed that, whatever its precise nuances, the Definition entails that the Jesus of history could not have made any mistakes. In this respect, the Chalcedonian Definition represents the broad run of popular Christian piety. The normal Christian portrayal of Jesus, heavily influenced by the inaccurate developments found in the Gospel attributed to St John, is that of a divine being who made no mistakes. Accordingly, the problem affects any christology which may reasonably claim continuity with centuries of Christian tradition. It should follow that, whatever Jesus was, he was not God. But then, he did not claim to be. That takes us to the second point: the deity of Jesus is a belief which could have developed only in a predominantly Gentile church.

The basic reason for this is historical, social and religious. Monotheism was an identity marker of the Jewish community. You could not both generate belief in the deity of Jesus and remain within the Jewish community.[17] We have seen this restraining factor operate in stage two of christological development, when the church consisted of both Jews and Gentiles. If Paul had hailed Jesus as fully God in the Johannine sense, he would have offended his own Jewish culture, caused a major split with the first apostles and driven faithful Jews and even many assimilating Jews out of his churches. Paul was himself too Jewish, and too aware of the Jewish faith of many Christians, to behave like this. Nor could others effectively hail Jesus as God in stage two of christological development. Once such an idea became serious and in any sense pervasive, there would necessarily be a clash which would produce stage three, in which the church lost its committed Jewish members and took on Gentile self-identification.

We have seen this happen in the Johannine community.[18] The efforts of Judaism to renew itself after the Roman war of A.D.66-70 involved, at least in some places, the exclusion of Jewish Christians. In this cultural context, the Johannine community identified "the Jews" as the people who had thrown them out. They took on Gentile self-identification, a negative form of identity which essentially meant that they were not Jews. They were, therefore, free to develop the deity of Jesus, for that made the centre of their life and the sole identity factor of their community all the more important, and it was highly functional in conflict with "the Jews", who were now condemned because they rejected God himself. "Jesus said to them, 'If God were your Father, you would have loved me'" (Jn 8.42, cf. e.g. 1 Jn 2.22).

Some Jewish Christians, however, did not leave the synagogue (cf. Jn 12.42-3). They will have remained in the Jewish community because their self-identification was irretrievably Jewish. Jesus and the first apostles were uniformly Jewish, and early Christianity could be perceived as a form of Judaism. Some Jewish Christians therefore knew with all their being that neither God the Father nor the teaching of Jesus could possibly require them to leave the covenant community, the chosen people. It is at this point that the second serious historical and theological problem arises that casts doubt on the truth of Christian belief in the deity and incarnation of Jesus. If anything like an orthodox Christian view of the Old Testament period is right, Jewish identity in general, and monotheism in particular, was formed in the course of their divinely controlled salvation history. Thus most Jews have ultimately been prevented from accepting the Gospel by God's revelation of himself to them.

Monotheism in quite a strict sense is not a late development. For clear statements of it we do not need to turn to the Talmud or the *Shulhan Aruch*, but to the *Shema* in the Pentateuch: "Hear, Israel, YHWH is our God, YHWH is one: and you shall love YHWH your God with your whole heart, your whole being and all your strength" (Deut 6.4). The first commandment (Ex 20.2-3/Deut 5.6-7) is equally straightforward. The monotheism of our Jewish sources is absolutely clear, and it was rammed home well before the time of Jesus in the persecution of Antiochus Epiphanes. Many Jews were tortured and killed because they refused to disobey the Law of the one God, not least by refusing to sacrifice to any other God. This could only strengthen the identity factors of the community, among which monotheism was already fundamental.[19] Thus the basic reason why the deity and incarnation of Jesus have been unacceptable to Johannine Jews and to the Jewish community ever since is the oneness of God, revealed to them by God himself in the course of their salvation history, and reinforced by exile and persecution. This is not consistent with the general Christian view that the deity and incarnation of Jesus were revealed in the New Testament period to Jews as well as to Gentiles, and should have been accepted by them.

5. Tradition, Scholarship and Truth

These two major problems, Jesus' prediction of the coming of the kingdom, and the inconsistency between the deity of Jesus and Jewish identity, have traditionally been concealed by inaccurate transmission of early Christian history and by attacks on "the Jews". It has frequently been supposed by Christians, learned scholars and ignorant faithful alike, that Jesus did not predict the imminent coming of the kingdom, and the commonest approach has been to deny that the relevant sayings really mean what they say. There have been two versions of this. Either it is supposed that Jesus did not really mean that the coming of the kingdom would be in the near future, or it is argued that the sayings were fulfilled in the coming of something else.[20]

For centuries, a common argument of the latter kind has been that these sayings were fulfilled in the church. For example, Gregory the Great interpreted Luke 9.27 as meaning the contemporary church (*Hom in Ev* XXXII, 6). Bede followed suit, interpreting Mark 9.1 (*In Marci Ev. Expositio,* ad loc.). Bucer did the same, interpreting Matthew 3.2; 4.17; 10.7; Mark 1.15 and Luke 10.9 as instructions for Christians in the contemporary kingdom of Christ (*De Regno* I,4).[21] Some modern scholars have argued on similar lines. H.B.Swete saw the primary fulfilment of Mark 9.1 in "the coming of the Spirit and the power manifested in the triumphant march of the Gospel throughout the Empire which was already assured before the death of at least some of the original apostolate". A partial fulfilment of Mark 14.25 was similarly seen "in the Eucharists of the universal Church", its ultimate accomplishment in the risen life not being related to any time content in the original prediction. At Matthew 13.24-30 "the church comes clearly into view", so much so that "it is very wonderful to see exactly how our Lord has foreseen the course which Church history would take...."[22]

As a description of what Jesus meant, this view has not the remotest degree of plausibility. The most basic reason for this is a straightforward cultural one. Statements generally like those attributed to Jesus occur in other Jewish sources. They refer to the end of the present era of human history in the very near future, and they were falsified.[23] Consequently, Jesus must have known that if he said "the kingdom of God is at hand", his hearers would suppose that he meant that the end of normal human history would occur reasonably soon, with the final establishment of the kingdom of God. If Jesus said "The kingdom of God is at hand" and meant "I am founding the church", he grievously misled those whom he claimed by divine authority to teach. Secondly, if Jesus intended to predict and describe the church, he could easily have said so. There was no need for him to talk about the kingdom instead. Thirdly, if Jesus meant to predict and describe the church, some of his disciples should have had some inkling of what he meant. Peter and Paul, who played such an outstanding and obvious role in the early church, should have said this in Acts and the Pauline epistles.

Conservative scholarship has produced a number of alternative explanations which achieve the same result of removing the scandal of Jesus' inaccuracy. Some of these are based on careful linguistic study. For example, C.H.Dodd argued that some of Jesus' most obviously eschatological sayings did not mean what they say, a view achieved by the assertion of an extraordinary Aramaic underlay for one word of Mark 1.15, and a hair-raising analysis of the Greek grammar of one word of Mark 9.1.[24] Almost everything is wrong with this view. The meaning of Jesus' sentences should not be divorced from their culture in this way. The Aramaic versions of Jesus' sayings do require reconstruction, but they cannot be understood by means of the Greek text with the substitution of one Aramaic word when convenient. No sane bilingual translator would have used Mark's *engikken*, "has come near" (Mk 1.15), to render the Aramaic *meta*, "is here". We must therefore suppose that the original Aramaic was *qrab*, "has come near". Mark 9.1 was discussed as a Greek text, despite the use made of Aramaic at 1.15, and Dodd's interpretation was based on the force of the perfect participle in *Greek*. Greek grammar is not a feasible basis for the interpretation of Aramaic sayings. The only use made of Aramaic was a reference to the old Syriac and Peshitta translations of the saying *into* Syriac, a hopelessly inadequate approach to the problem of what the original Aramaic might have been.[25] Yet this theory was taken seriously for years.

Why? Surely because of its function. A significant function of scholarship has been to ward off anything too uncomfortable, and if Schweitzer, Weiss and others made it clear that Jesus had made a serious mistake, at least Dodd and others enabled people to believe that serious scholars did not agree with them. As in all cases of social function, this is not to cast doubt on the integrity of C.H.Dodd, nor of those who believed in his hypothesis even though they did not understand it. It is merely to observe that the most learned scholarship does have a function among less learned people, and that function operates to support the community to which they belong.

A more theological approach to the same problem occurs in conventional New Testament scholarship in the work of C.E.B.Cranfield. Taking up the problem under the form of the nearness of the end in Mark 13, Cranfield declares,

> If we realize that the Incarnation-Crucifixion-Resurrection-Ascension, on the one hand, and the Parousia, on the other, belong essentially together and are in a real sense one Event, one divine Act, being held apart only by the mercy of God who desires to give men opportunity for faith and repentance, then we can see that in a very real sense the latter is always imminent now that the former has happened. It was, and still is true to say that the Parousia is at hand - and indeed this, so far from being an embarrassing mistake on the part either of Jesus or of the early Church, is an essential part of the Church's faith. Ever since the Incarnation men have been living in the last days.[26]

This view replaces historical research with theological convictions. Statements generally like those in the most eschatological parts of Mark 13 are found in our Jewish sources: they do refer to the end of normal human history in the very near future, and they were falsified.[27] Anyone who said sayings such as Mark 13.30 would know that they would be taken to be referring to the end of normal human history. If therefore Jesus knew what Cranfield says he knew, he misled his hearers most grievously. But there is nothing like Cranfield's theory in the teaching of Jesus. The incarnation and ascension do not occur there and, if the arguments put forward in chapter 4 are right, neither did the parousia.[28] Cranfield's comments form a modern construction remote from the teaching of Jesus and from the theology put forward by New Testament writers, yet this is supposed to have been what Jesus meant.

Problems of this kind are increased when a person's field of expertise is dogmatic theology rather than New Testament studies. The relatively radical work of Pannenberg may serve as an example. Unlike many dogmatic theologians, Pannenberg admits that Jesus was mistaken in making his predictions, but he none the less argues that his prediction of the imminent coming of the kingdom was fulfilled in his resurrection. He comments:

> It was fulfilled in the only way it is possible to speak of the fulfilment of prophetic proclamations and promises, namely, in such a way that the original sense of the prophecy is revised by an event that corresponds to it but none the less has a more or less different character than could be known from the prophecy alone.

With methods like that, much false prophecy can be seen to be fulfilled somewhere, somehow.

> The Christian Easter message speaks of the mode of fulfilment of Jesus' imminent expectation. It was fulfilled by himself, insofar as the eschatological reality of the resurrection of the dead appeared in Jesus himself. It is not yet universally fulfilled in the way in which Jesus and

his contemporaries had expected. In spite of this, Jesus' resurrection justifies the imminent expectation that had moved him and established anew the eschatological expectation fulfilled in him for the rest of humanity.[29]

This approach also replaces history with theology, and it is vulnerable to some of the objections already made. Firstly, there is no proper relationship between prediction and fulfilment. Resurrection was a well known belief, and had Jesus wanted to foretell it, he could have done so. In fact, as Pannenberg recognizes, he did predict it in the form of predictions of the general resurrection, but these are quite separate from the predictions of the coming of the kingdom. Secondly, no-one noticed at the time. When God vindicated Jesus by his mighty saving act, he did not reveal that this was the fulfilment of Jesus' prophecies - he let the early church go on expecting the End soon, with consequent troubles in Thessalonica, behind 2 Peter, John 21 (cf. Mk 9.1) and surely elsewhere. None of the earliest apostles understood Jesus' teaching well enough to realize that his predictions were being fulfilled in the dramatic events of their own ministries.

Thirdly, there is a serious historical problem about the reality of the supposed event. That the resurrection occurred at all is a statement of faith rather than history, and Pannenberg's reliance on the early Christian witness points up the rejection of Judaism characteristic of his culture. For example, Pannenberg declares that Jesus' claim to authority was "blasphemous for Jewish ears. Because of this, Jesus was then also slandered by the Jews before the Roman governor as a rebel." This is untrue. All Jesus' disciples and all the earliest Christians were Jewish. They did not regard Jesus' claims as blasphemous, neither did they slander him before the Roman governor, as this Johannine use of "the Jews" implies. Pannenberg continues,

> If Jesus really has been raised, this claim has been visibly and unambiguously confirmed by the God of Israel, who was allegedly blasphemed by Jesus. This was done by Israel's God. A Jew - and for the moment we are speaking only of Jews - could certainly not take an event of this kind as one that came to be apart from the will of his God.[30]

Here, as so often in his discussion of the early church, Pannenberg has ignored the witness of most Jews, who did not believe that this event took place. If we look at the whole of contemporary reaction t · this supposed event, the terms "visibly and unambiguously" are as inappropriate as any terms could be.

This takes us to the final and crucial point. Pannenberg's comments are remote from the original situation because they belong to a different and very positive tradition. Pannenberg began from within a tradition which *knows* that something like orthodox christology is right before it examines the evidence. As Hebblethwaite put it, "I find myself considering these matters as a participant in what I think of as the body of Christ, the community of those who by adoption and grace are united with God through the risen Christ...."[31] This is the point where all christologies "from above", and many "from below", go wrong. The whole approach "from above", and any effort like that of Pannenberg "from below", are unsatisfactory because sooner or later they collide disastrously with primary evidence, and they do so because theologians are controlled by the communities to which they belong. It is here that the work of Schweitzer remains fundamental, however much further investigation has required us to modify the details of his findings. Jesus made a verifiable mistake - not the mistake of a madman, but the mistake of a profoundly religious Jew. This disproves a central tenet of orthodox christology, and of christologies which are sufficiently orthodox to be in continuity with Christian tradition.

6. Monotheism, Judaism and Gentile Perception

It has been argued above that the deity of Jesus is a Gentile perception, and that Jews have consequently not been able to accept it without ceasing to be Jewish. From the patristic period onwards, this has been met with vilification of "the Jews". We have seen this begin in John's Gospel.[32] It was taken up repeatedly in the patristic period. For example, St John Chrysostom was confronted with the possibility that people might worship God in the synagogue. He comments,

But they (i.e. the Jews) will assuredly say that they, too, worship God. But that should certainly not be said. No Jew worships God! Who says this? The Son of God. 'If you were to know my Father', he says, 'you would also know me. But you neither know me nor do you know my Father' [Jn 8.19, in a variant text]. What more trustworthy witness than this could I produce? If, then, they do not know the Father, they crucified the Son, they reject the help of the Spirit, who should not boldly and plainly declare that the place is a dwelling of demons? God is not worshipped there. Certainly not! But it is, furthermore, a place of idolatry *(Discourses against the Jews* I, 3).[33]

A Homily for Palm Sunday is one of many pieces which take up the fall of Jerusalem:

Where is the beauty of your youth and the riches of your betrothal?... Where is the house that Solomon the king built to your glory? Where is the priest and the ephod which stood for your ministry.... Where is the ark, and the tablets of stone that were in it?... Your rejoicing has come to an end, and the sound of the exultation of your chanting.... And look! Lamentations are chanted among you, by the mouths of you and your children. What is your wickedness, daughter of Jacob, that your punishment is so severe? You have abused the king and the king's Son, you shameless prostitute. The king was abused in the wilderness, and the king's Son moreover in Jerusalem. The Father was exchanged for the calf and different images, and the Son also was exchanged for a robber and murderer: and you provoked the Spirit of the Lord among foreign nations. You despised and blackly hated the Trinity who is from eternity, and you loved vain gods, demons, gods of fortune and images. (Ps-Ephraem, *Homily for the Holy Feast of Palm Sunday.*[34])

A number of passages focus on the identity factors of Judaism. For example, Chrysostom comments on John 12.35,

How many things, indeed, the Jews do now, and do not know what they are doing, but as it were walk in darkness. They think they are going the right way, but they are walking in the opposite direction - keeping the Sabbath, and maintaining the Law, and observing the dietary laws. And they do not know where they are walking. *(Homilies on St John* LXVIII, ad loc.).[35]

As Christians became more powerful, anti-Jewish writing was accompanied by specific practical measures against the Jewish community, and especially against Jews who sought to maintain their identity. In the Reformation period, Luther drew on centuries of Christian persecution of Jews in a work of baleful influence. Unable to convert them, he compared his efforts with preaching the Gospel to a pig, referring to the veil over Moses' face which still prevented them from understanding God's commandment (cf 2 Cor 3). He referred to John 8.39,44 to characterize them as children of the devil: John 5.23; 15.23 for the rejection of those who reject the Son: and Matthew 27.42; John 7.31,41; 11.47 for his appearance as the expected Messiah during his ministry being obvious. This was buttressed with traditional christological exegesis of the Old Testament. One of the "lies" of which he accused the Jews is that they claimed that Christians believe in more than one God. Thus the Jewish perception that the doctrine of the Trinity is not monotheistic was put forward as a reason for condemning the Jewish people. Luther's recommendations included burning down the synagogues or schools of "the Jews", destroying their houses, confiscating all copies of their prayer books and Talmud, and forbidding their rabbis to teach on pain of death.[36] With these recommendations, the architect of the Reformation erected a signpost to the holocaust. He is often thought to have provided the key to understanding St Paul: but in Paul the cross is to be borne, not inflicted.

Anti-Jewish polemic is not in accordance with the teaching of Jesus. Consistent elements in it include the transference of internal prophetic criticisms to all Jews of a later period, a use of Jewish identity which is at the heart of anti-semitism, and the use of Jewish misfortune as a proof of God's anger.[37] The central point for this discussion is monotheism, and Gentile Christians have normally sought to meet the perceived threat to monotheism by pointing to the doctrine of the Trinity. This is not, however, satisfactory because it wards off the threat only from a Gentile perspective. It was an answer in terms of Greek philosophical theology to intellectual aspects of the problem which arose from the profound convictions already present in the Johannine community, that Jesus is God and God is one. Jews have not, however, perceived this result as monotheistic. There is limited point in trying to debate whether it is or is not. What is so misleading about a philosophical approach to a problem of this kind is the assumption that there is a really true answer to it, when there are only perceptions of it. Two such perceptions are central. The Gentile Christian perception is that the Trinity is monotheistic: the Jewish perception, rooted in Jewish identity as it was at the time of Jesus and the first apostles, is that it is not monotheistic. Jewish perception of the doctrine of the Trinity, with Jewish rejection of the deity of Jesus, is conditioned by the supposed revelation of God's oneness to the chosen people. It cannot, therefore, reasonably be put down to the blindness of the Jewish people.

This is the second point at which orthodox christology is difficult to reconcile with truth. Not only does it rewrite history to avoid the implications of Jesus' preaching of the imminence of the kingdom, it also obscures the Gentile nature of the deity and incarnation of Jesus. The deity of Jesus is, therefore, in a different category from his messiahship. The messiahship of Jesus is already fundamental in the Jewish-Christian dispute portrayed in Justin's *Dialogue with Trypho*. It has remained so, and the beginning of this process can be seen at John 9.22. As a threat to Jewish identity, however, the messiahship of Jesus is a *result* of the split between Judaism and Christianity. Though Jesus did not reveal himself as "the Messiah", it was a perfectly Jewish term which he could have used in combination with other terms to describe his role. It was used by the earliest disciples when the church was still largely Jewish, and it was very common in stage two.[38] Since then, other figures have been hailed as messiah, notably Simeon son of Kosiba and Shabbatai Zevi.[39] The expectation of a future messiah has also been vigorously held by many Jews. In short, messiahship is part of Jewish identity, not a threat to it. When the earliest Christians produced the messiahship of Jesus, that was part of their Jewish identity. Only in stage three, when the Christian community took on Gentile self-identification, do we find the messiahship of Jesus a reason for being thrown out of the synagogue, and only subsequent history has caused the messiahship of Jesus to be perceived by Jewish people as an index of Gentile identity.

The deity of Jesus is, however, *inherently* unJewish. The witness of Jewish texts is unvarying: belief that a second being is God involves departure from the Jewish community.[40] Hence the deity of Jesus was deliberately expounded in the Johannine community at the point where it took on Gentile self-identification, and it occurs together with accusations of blasphemy on the part of "the Jews". It follows that the development of New Testament christology cannot be an example of the Holy Spirit guiding the church into all truth. The Holy Spirit could hardly lead the church into an evaluation of the Jesus of history which Jesus in his revelatory ministry could not hold, and which leads directly to the condemnation of the chosen people because they have cherished the revelation of God's oneness to them.

As a human process, however, the development of christology is basically comprehensible. It was, and has remained, a means of holding together a large social group. As Christianity spread to the Gentiles, the bonding forces had to be altered. Judaism is held together by a whole culture expressed in the Law, so much so that we can measure assimilation by whether people observe its major points. In stage two, this had to change, because Gentiles did not do most of the Law. As Paul saw so clearly, if Gentiles had had to do the Law in order to become Christians, the Gentile mission would not have been the resounding success which he did so much to make it. This basic change from Judaism involved a significant shift from activity to belief. The sheer amount of belief required to hold together the mixed community of Jews and Gentiles was necessarily greater than that of a subgroup within Judaism.

Throughout stage two and even more in stage three of christological development, the increasing role of belief was attached primarily to the central identity factor of the community itself, thereby increasing the pressures which led to the deity of Jesus. The social function of this belief in holding the community together also meant that it became increasingly desirable that all Christians should hold the same beliefs. To some extent this occurred naturally, as Christians defined themselves over against other people. A deliberate attempt to set a limit to the variability of belief is found in 1 Corinthians 15. Some Jewish people believed in the resurrection of the dead, while others did not. In 1 Corinthians 15, Paul is confronted with Christians who did not hold this belief. He argues vigorously that all Christians must believe in the resurrection of the dead because of a central fact about the community's central identity factor, Jesus' resurrection from the dead. We can see the argument passing the point where Paul no longer regards disagreement as legitimate: "But if there is no resurrection of the dead, Christ has not been raised either: but if Christ has not been raised, then our preaching is vain and your faith is vain. Moreover, we are found to have borne false witness about God...." (1 Cor 15.13-15). There are however no instructions to remove anyone who does not accept Paul's arguments.

We can see the tendency to insist on right belief becoming more serious at the point where members of the Johannine community were thrown out of the synagogue.[41] At this point, failure to agree about Jesus meant schism. The schism involved activity, but belief was also a major factor: "For this reason the Jews sought rather to kill him, because he not only abrogated the Sabbath but also called God his own Father, making himself equal to God" (Jn 5.18). This portrays an actual split between Christianity and Judaism, with the development of a belief that violated one of the identity factors of Judaism. There is also evidence in this Gospel which indicates that some Jews left the Christian community at a rather earlier stage of its development. So after the eucharistic discourse of chapter 6, "From this point many of his disciples withdrew completely and no longer walked with him" (Jn 6.66).[42] Once beliefs of this kind were seen as reasons for schism, a fateful pattern was established. We can see this happening in the Johannine epistles, though it is not always possible to locate the schismatic groups. The split with Judaism left the community without all those people who opted to remain with "the Jews", so that the Greek wing necessarily became more prominent. We find people who believed that Jesus had come, but apparently not "in the flesh" (cf 1 Jn 4.1-3; 2 Jn 7-8). Whatever the precise nature of this group, the significant fact is the occurrence of schism. We have the pattern set for the patristic and mediaeval periods.

As time went on, disagreement about the intellectual formulae of the faith was more and more considered sufficient to exclude whole groups of people from the Christian community, including eventually most Jewish Christians and virtually the whole Aramaic-speaking church, that is, those people who most nearly shared the culture and thought-world of Jesus and the first apostles. There are those who see this as the work of the Holy Spirit: if this be right, his left hand[43] is the condemnation of many thousands of people who have professed and called themselves Christians. That was not John's fault: indeed, the schism with Judaism itself cannot be shown to have been John's fault. None the less, we can see in the Johannine community a shift of perception towards the fundamental importance of belief sufficient to render schism inevitable, and the deity of Jesus at the centre of that belief system. Together with it goes the removal of all sayings which declare the imminence of the kingdom, and thereby any evidence that Jesus made any mistakes. The result is held to be holy scripture, divinely inspired and wholly true.

9. Scripture, Culture and Truth

Scripture is the Rhinegold of Truth. It offers us the whole truth, and exclusive salvation, but it leads us into the usual human muddle of truth and falsity, grasping greedily to make it true just at those points where it is false. John's misleading picture of Jesus is at the centre of this. It makes him divine and infallible and has him condemn the Jews, to whom the historical Jesus preached, and from whom he selected his apostles and accepted his disciples and supporters. We cannot reasonably believe in all the results of that developmental process. If Christianity is to remain a viable option for honest and well-informed people, it should surely undo that process of development, and emerge as something nearer to the religion of Jesus of Nazareth.

This would not remove the whole of Christianity. Despite movement from activity to belief in stages two and three, Christianity has never consisted solely of its beliefs. Active heretics have included Albert Schweitzer, retiring to do good in Lambaréné, following his clear demonstration of Jesus' outstanding mistake. Official Christian activity includes the Church of England's recent report on our inner cities.[44] Its obvious concern for the welfare of the poor is a direct line to the teaching of the Jesus of history, and one which does not have to be made dependent on the Gentile perception of him as incarnate and divine.

If the standard picture of Jesus as incarnate and divine is too much a part of the churches' identity to be shifted, official Christianity will become increasingly a matter of belief in the impossible, as its evangelical and catholic wings may already be thought to be. Even then, people need not be dishonest to follow the teaching of Jesus. Jesus did not found the church, St Paul did not accept the authority of the first apostles, and the Reformation wrecked the authority and damaged the social structure of the corrupt church in which it began. We should not regard the institutional structure of churches as sacrosanct. If churches as organizations must insist on false belief we can always leave them, and follow from outside their orbit those aspects of the teaching of Jesus which we judge relevant to our lives 2,000 years later.

1. Supra, 127-9.
2. Supra, 24-7.
3. The nature of Antiochene and Syrian exegesis is well documented, but the background in Jewish exegesis and the social function of this form of Christian exegesis both require further work. Cf e.g. D.Gerson "Die Commentarien des Ephraem Syrus im Verhältnis zur jüdischen Exegese", *MGWJ* 17, 1868, 15-33, 64-72, 98-109, 141-9;

L.Pirot *L'Oeuvre Exégètique de Théodore de Mopsuestia* (1913); F.Gavin, "Aphraates and the Jews. A study of the controversial homilies of the Persian sage in their relation to Jewish thought", *JSOR* 7, 1923, 95-166; R.Devréesse, *Essai sur Théodore de Mopsueste*, StT 141 (1948); M.F.Wiles, "Theodore of Mopsuestia as representative of the Antiochene School", *The Cambridge History of the Bible* I (1970), 489-510; S.P.Brock, "Jewish Traditions in Syriac Sources", *JJS* 30, 1979, 212-32; Casey, *Son of Man* ch 3; B.de Margerie, *Introduction à l'histoire de l'exégèse. 1. Les Pères grecs et orientaux* (1980); J.G.Snaith, "Aphrahat and the Jews", in J.A.Emerton and S.C.Reif (eds), *Interpreting the Hebrew Bible. Essays in Honour of E.I.J.Rosenthal* (1982), 235-50; R.Macina, "L'énigme des prophéties et oracles à portée 'Machabéenne' et leur application *ek prosopou* selon l'exégèse antiochienne", *OrChr* 70, 1986, 86-109; P.M.Casey, "The Fourth Kingdom in Cosmas Indicopleustes and the Syrian Tradition", *RSLR* XXV, 1989, 485-403.

4. R.Ruether, *Faith and Fratricide. The Theological Roots of Anti-Semitism (1977);* R.Ruether, *To change the world. Christology and cultural criticism* (1981), ch III. Cf T.A.Indinopoulos and R.B.Ward, "Is Christology Inherently anti-Semitic? A Critical Review of Rosemary Ruether's *Faith and Fratricide*", *JAAR* 45, 1977, 193-214; A.T.Davies (ed), *Antisemitism and the Foundations of Christianity* (1979); infra, 181 note 37.

5. For detailed discussion of this text, and ancient exegesis of it, Casey, *Son of Man*. For the text of Theodoret's commentary on Daniel, PG 81, cols 1257-1545.

6. Cf supra, 122-3.

7. Full documentation of a whole field of study cannot be given here. For a brief general survey, K.Runia, *The Present-day Christological Debate* (1984). The following works display different approaches to the numerous problems involved in expounding a modern christology: K.Rahner, "Current Problems in Christology", *Theological Investigations,* vol I (ET 1961), 149-200; H.W.Montefiore, "Towards a Christology for To-day", in *Soundings,* ed A.R.Vidler (1962), 147-72; W.Pannenberg, *Jesus - God and Man* (1964. ET 1968); J.McIntyre, *The Shape of Christology* (1966); K.Rahner, "On the Theology of the Incarnation", op.cit. vol IV (ET 1966), 105-20; K.Rahner, "Dogmatic Reflections on the Knowledge and Self-Consciousness of Christ", op.cit., vol V (ET 1966), 193-215; J.Knox, *The Humanity and Divinity of Christ* (1967); N.Pittenger (ed), *Christ for Us To-Day* (1968); N.Pittenger, *Christology Reconsidered* (1970); P.Schoonenberg, *The Christ* (ET 1971); J.Moltmann, *The Crucified God* (1972. ET 1974); K.Rahner and W.Thusing, *A New Christology* (1972. ET 1980); W.Kasper, *Jesus the Christ* (1974. ET 1976); E.Schillebeeckx, *Jesus. An Experiment in Christology* (1974. ET 1979); K.Rahner, "Remarks on the Importance of the History of Jesus for Catholic Dogmatics", op.cit. vol XIII (ET 1975), 201-12; K.Rahner, "The Two Basic Types of Christology", ibid., 213-23; J.N.D.Anderson, *The Mystery of the Incarnation* (1978); D.Cupitt, *The Debate about Christ* (1979); C.Tuckett, "Christology and the New Testament", *SJTh* 33, 1980, 401-16; H.D.Lewis, *Jesus in the Faith of Christians* (1981); K.Rahner, "Christology To-day?", op.cit., vol XVII (1981), 24-38; S.M.Ogden, *The Point of Christology* (1982); A.T.Hanson, *The Image of the Invisible God* (1982); D.G.A.Calvert, *From Christ to God* (1983); C.Gunton, *Yesterday and To-day: A Study of Continuities in Christology* (1983); J.P.Mackey, *The Christian Experience of God as Trinity* (1983); B.Hebblethwaite, *The Incarnation. Collected Essays in Christology* (1987); L.D.Lefebure, *Toward a Contemporary Wisdom Christology. A Study of Karl Rahner and Norman Pittenger* (1988). On the background to some recent discussion, A.E.McGrath, *The Making of Modern German Christology. From the Enlightenment to Pannenberg* (1986). More

generally, cf G.A.Lindbeck, *The nature of doctrine* (1984).

8. R.Morgan, "Non Angli sed Angeli: Some Anglican Reactions to German Gospel Criticism", in S.W.Sykes and J.D.Holmes (eds), *New Studies in Theology* 1 (1980), 1-30, at p.22.

9. Cf supra 122-3, 127-9.

10. Cf e.g. the six definitions supplied, in their proper context of nineteenth-century christology, by S.Coakley, *Christ without Absolutes. A Study of the Christology of Ernst Troeltsch* (1988), 104-6.

11. Cf supra, 109-110.

12. Cf supra 87-8, 91-2, 152.

13. Cf supra, 112-5.

14. Supra 114-5.

15. B.Hebblethwaite, in M.D.Goulder (ed), *Incarnation and Myth* (1982), pp.15-6, 19.

16. Supra, 58-9.

17. Cf supra 114-5, 136-8, 156-9.

18. Supra 27-38, 156-9.

19. Cf supra, 18-19.

20. Cf T.W.Manson, *The Teaching of Jesus* (1945), 279-82; G.E.Ladd, *Jesus and the Kingdom* (1966), 2nd ed *The Presence of the Future* (1974), 262-77: H.M.Kunzi, *Das Näherwartungslogion Matthaus 10,23. Geschichte seiner Auslegung*, BGBE 9 (1970): H.M.Kunzi, *Das Näherwartungslogion Markus 9,1 par. Geschichte seiner Auslegung mit einem Nachwort zur Auslegungsgeschichte von Markus 13,30 par*, BGBE 21 (1977).

21. For the texts, PL 76, 1075-1312; *Bedae Venerabilis Opera*, Pars II.3... *In Marci Evangelium Expositio*, ed D.Hurst, CChr.SL CXX (1960); *Martini Buceri Opera Latina*, vol XV, *De Regno Christi* (1550), ed F.Wendel, PUF (1955), ET in *Melanchthon and Bucer*, ed W.Pauck, LCC XIX (1969), 155-394.

22. H.B.Swete, *The Gospel According To St.Mark* (1905), ad loc.: H.B.Swete, *The Parables of the Kingdom* (1920), 32.

23. Cf supra 58-9, 100-2.

24. C.H.Dodd, *The Parables of the Kingdom* (1935) 36-7, 43-4.

25. For recent work on the methodology of the Aramaic level of sayings of Jesus, Schwarz, op.cit.; L.D.Hurst, "The Neglected Role of Semantics in the Search for the Aramaic Words of Jesus", *JSNT* 28, 1986, 63-80; Casey, op.cit., *JThS NS* 41, 1990, 11-12.

26. C.E.B.Cranfield, *The Gospel according to St.Mark,* (1959), 408.

27. Cf supra 58-9, 100-2, 170-1.

28. Supra 46-54, esp 52-4: and on the imminence of the kingdom rather than the parousia, 58-9, 100-2, 170-1.

29. W.Pannenberg, op.cit., 226. Cf W.Pannenberg, *The Apostles' Creed. In the Light of To-day's Questions* (ET 1972), 52-4: W.Pannenberg, in J.M.Robinson and J.B.Cobb, jr (eds), *New Frontiers in Theology*, vol III *Theology as History* (1967), 114-7. For criticisms, cf W.R.Clark, "The Relation of Present Experience of Eschatological and Christological uniqueness in Schleiermacher, Tillich and Pannenberg", Ph.D thesis, Univ of Iowa, 1973 (1979), 243ff.

30. W.Pannenberg, *Jesus - God and Man,* 67.

31. Hebblethwaite, as quoted supra, 168 and note 15.

32. Supra, 27-38.

33. For the text, PG 48, 839-942; ET *Saint John Chrysostom. Discourses against Judaizing Christians* (sic!). Tr P.W.Harkins, FaCh 68 (1977).

34. *Des Heiligen Ephraem des Syrers Sermones II,* ed E.Beck, CSCO 311-2, S 134-5 (1970), Sermo III, 388-9, 392-5, 406-7, 412-30. ET *Select Works of S.Ephrem the Syrian.* Tr J.B.Morris (1847), 61-83.

35. For the text, PG 59, 5-482; ET *The Homilies of Saint John Chrysostom ... on the Gospel of St. John,* LoF 36 (1852); *Saint John Chrysostom. Commentary on Saint John the Apostle and Evangelist. Homilies 48-88.* Tr Sr. T.A.Goggin, S.C.H., FaCh 41 (1959).

36. M.Luther, "Von den Juden und ihren Lügen" (1543), in *D.Martin Luther's Werke. Kritische Gesamtausgabe* (1883-), vol 53, 417-552; ET "On the Jews and Their Lies", tr M.H.Bertram, ed F.Sherman, in *Luther's Works,* ed J.Pelikan and H.T.Lehman, vol 47 (1971), 123-306.

37. In recent years, this has become a matter of profound concern to Christians as well as Jews, and a feature of Jewish-Christian dialogue. The bibliography is again massive. Cf e.g. G.Baum, *Is the New Testament Anti-Semitic?* (1965); M.B.McGarry, *Christology after Auschwitz* (1977); Ruether, op.cit.; S.Sandmel, *Anti-Semitism in the New Testament?* (1978); Davies, op.cit.; P.Lapide and J.Moltmann, *Jewish Monotheism and Christian Trinitarian Doctrine* (1979. ET, with forewords by L.Swidler and J.B.Agus, 1981); L.Swidler, "The Jewishness of Jesus: Some Religious Implications for Christians", *JES* 18, 1982, 327-36; N.A.Beck, *Mature Christianity. The Recognition and Repudiation of the Anti-Jewish Polemic of the New Testament* (1985).

38. Cf supra 41-4, 79, 82, 105-6, 129-31, 133-4, 141, 143, 146-7, 149.

39. Cf supra,82: G.Scholem, *Sabbatai Sevi, the mystical Messiah, 1626-1676* (1973).

40. Cf supra 37-8, 91-4, 114-5, 136-8, 142-6, 156-9.

41. Cf supra 23-4, 31-8, 156-9.

42. Cf supra, 35-6.

43. I use this phrase in Ruether's sense: supra, 164, and note 4.

44. *Faith in the City: a call for action by church and nation.* The report of the Archbishop of Canterbury's Commission on Urban Priority Areas (1985). When this lecture was originally delivered, this was a recent publication, being condemned by government ministers as "marxist" (where "marxist" effectively meant "evil and subversive").

General Bibliography

This bibliography contains general works on New Testament christology. More detailed treatments of individual New Testament books, christological titles, and such matters, are given in the footnotes. For a comprehensive, annotated bibliography, see now the work of Hultgren listed below. Text editions, tools of study, dictionary articles and commentaries are not normally listed.

R.E.Berkey, and S.A.Edwards (eds), *Christological Perspectives*. Essays in Honor of Harvey K.McArthur (1982).

R.E.Brown, *Jesus, God and Man* (1968).

F.B.Craddock, *The Pre-existence of Christ in the New Testament* (1968).

O.Cullmann, *The Christology of the New Testament* (1957. ET 2nd ed., 1963).

J.D.G.Dunn, *Christology in the Making: A New Testament Inquiry into the Origins of the Doctrine of the Incarnation* (1980).

J.D.G.Dunn, "Was Christianity a Monotheistic Faith from the Beginning?", *SJTh* 35, 1982, 303-36.

P.Fredriksen, *From Jesus to Christ. The Origins of the New Testament Images of Jesus* (1988).

R.H.Fuller, *The Foundations of New Testament Christology* (1965).

F.Hahn, *The Titles of Jesus in Christology: Their History in Early Christianity* (1963. ET 1969).

R.G.Hamerton-Kelly, *Pre-Existence, Wisdom and the Son of Man. A Study of the Idea of Pre-Existence in the New Testament*, MSSNTS 21 (1973).

A.J.Hultgren, *Christ and His Benefits. Christology and Redemption in the New Testament* (1987).

A.J.Hultgren, *New Testament Christology*, Bibliographies and indexes on religious studies, no.12 (1988).

L.W.Hurtado, *One God, One Lord. Early Christian Devotion and Ancient Jewish Monotheism* (1988).

R.Jewett, with L.W.Hurtado and P.R.Keifert (eds), *Christology and Exegesis: New Approaches*, Sem 30 (1985).

L.E.Keck, "Toward the Renewal of New Testament Christology", *NTS* 32, 1986, 362-77.

I.H.Marshall, *The Origins of New Testament Christology* (1976).

C.F.D.Moule, *The Origin of Christology* (1977).

P.Pokorny, *The Genesis of Christology. Foundations for a Theology of the New Testament* (1985. ET 1987).

E.Schillebeeckx, *Christ. The Christian Experience in the Modern World* (1977. ET 1980).

V.Taylor, *The Names of Jesus* (1953).

V.Taylor, *The Person of Christ in New Testament Teaching* (1958).

Index of References

Other Jewish Sources

Index

Select Index of Names and Subjects

Index